James Abram · Steve Williams

English in Context
Student's Book

Language and Skills Practice

LEHRPLAN 2017

6

VER1TAS

Gemeinsam besser lernen

Dieses Werk wurde auf Grundlage eines zielorientierten Lehrplans verfasst. Konkretisierung, Gewichtung und Umsetzung der Inhalte erfolgen durch die Lehrerinnen und Lehrer.

Liebe Schülerin, lieber Schüler,
du bekommst dieses Schulbuch von der Republik Österreich für deine Ausbildung. Bücher helfen nicht nur beim Lernen, sondern sind auch Freunde fürs Leben.

Content Key – Wie nutzen?
In diesem Buch finden sich auf einigen Seiten **Content Keys**: Sie verweisen auf zusätzliche Inhalte im Internet. Dazu auf dem PC die Webadresse mit dem jeweiligen Content Key eingeben, z. B. *http://english-in-context6.veritas.at/key/735*
Ausführlichere Informationen unter *http://www.veritas.at/key*

Mit Bescheid des Bundesministeriums für Bildung vom 19.04.2017, GZ 5.050/0029-IT/3/2016, gemäß den Lehrplänen 2017 als für den Unterrichtsgebrauch an allgemein bildenden höheren Schulen für die 6. Klasse im Unterrichtsgegenstand Englisch (1. Lebende Fremdsprache) geeignet erklärt.

Schulbuchnummer: **165.366** und Schulbuchnummer: **176.238** (Set Buch + E-Book)

Basiert auf Context 21 Starter (erarbeitet von Ingrid Becker-Ross, Barbara Derkow Disselbeck, Birgit Ohmsieder, Gunthild Porteous-Schwier, Angela Ringel-Eichinger, Allen J. Woppert sowie Mervyn Whittaker)

© Cornelsen Schulverlage GmbH, Berlin 2009/2010

Für Österreich bearbeitet von James Abram und Steve Williams
Beratende Mitwirkung: Ronald Kemsies, Sieghild Oberwinkler, Birgit Öllerer-Einböck, Martina Spielauer, Renate Wurm-Smole

© VERITAS-VERLAG, Linz
Alle Rechte vorbehalten, insbesondere das Recht der Verbreitung (auch durch Film, Fernsehen, Internet, fotomechanische Wiedergabe, Bild-, Ton- und Datenträger jeder Art) oder der auszugsweise Nachdruck.

5. Auflage (2020) – Entspricht der Rechtschreibreform 2006.
Die 4. und 5. Auflage sind nebeneinander verwendbar.
Auf umweltfreundlichem Papier gedruckt bei: siehe https://produkt.veritas.at/31239#additional
Projektleitung: Iris Santa
Korrektorat: Sonja Jäkel, Berlin
Herstellung: Alois Kandler, Verena Maxwald
Bildredaktion: Susanne Suk
Umschlaggestaltung und Layout: Agnes Weitzhofer, Alois Kandler
Illustrationen: Graham Wiseman
Satz: A3 Werbeservice GmbH
Umschlagfotos: iStockphoto/Damir Cudic, Stockphoto/lightkey

Schulbuchvergütung/Bildrechte: © Bildrecht/Wien
Alle Ausschnitte mit Zustimmung der Bildrecht/Wien

Der Verlag hat sich bemüht, alle Rechtsinhaber ausfindig zu machen. Sollten trotzdem Urheberrechte verletzt worden sein, wird der Verlag nach Anmeldung berechtigter Ansprüche diese entgelten.

ISBN 978-3-7058-9475-4
ISBN 978-3-7058-1456-4 (Set Buch + E-Book)

Für die Arbeit im Rahmen der **Neuen Oberstufe** (NOst) stehen **Hilfestellungen** für die Kompetenzmodule 3 + 4 im E-Book und auf der Verlagswebsite zur Verfügung.

Zusätzliche Materialien zum Schulbuch im **E-Book**!
Aktuelle Infos zur Aktivierung unter:
www.scook.at/materialien

Working with English in Context

English in Context 6. Student's Book ist der zweite Band der bewährten Lehrwerk-Reihe für Englisch an allgemein bildenden höheren Schulen. Das Lehrwerk orientiert sich am Oberstufen-Themenpool und am AHS-Lehrplan 2017 sowie an den Vorgaben für die Standardisierte Kompetenzorientierte Reifeprüfung (SRP). Es führt in zwei Kompetenzmodulen mit insgesamt 6 Topics und einer Vielfalt an authentischen Text- und Hörmaterialien sowie abwechslungsreichen Aufgabenstellungen und durch die Vermittlung wichtiger Skills, Kompetenzen und Lernstrategien zur Niveaustufe B1 des GERS.

Aufbau

Die insgesamt 6 Topics sind auf die Semester bzw. Kompetenzmodule 3 und 4 verteilt.
Jedes Topic ist wie folgt aufgebaut:

- **Lead-In** (Doppelseite) leitet das Topic ein, bietet einen Überblick zu den **Lernzielen** und soll z. B. mit Übungen wie *Think – Pair – Share* für das Topic interessieren und aktivieren.

- **Words in Context** (Doppelseite) erschließt und festigt mit einem Textimpuls und Übungen zu *Wordpower, Wordfields, Collocations* etc. den Grundwortschatz des jeweiligen Topics.

- Je **3 Units** eröffnen in den Abschnitten **A/B/C** mit einer abwechslungsreichen Auswahl an Lese- und Hörimpulsen unterschiedliche Aspekte eines Topics – eine Stärke der Reihe. Dabei wird gezielt auf die Vorentlastung von längeren Lesetexten geachtet (*pre-reading questions*, Üben von *skimming /scanning* etc.).

- In der **Randspalte** wird Vokabular zum jeweiligen Text auf Englisch erklärt; *Language Help* bietet dort hilfreiche Redemittel zur Bewältigung der Aufgabenstellungen, *Tips*, Hinweise auf typische Fehler (*Trouble Spot*) und Verweise in den Companion.

- **Grammatik** (als Vorbereitung auf *Language in Use*) fließt wo notwendig und passend ein; die Verweise in die *Language Practice* des dem Student's Book beigelegten Companion regen zum selbstständigen Nachschlagen und Wiederholen an.

- Die **vier Fertigkeiten** (Hören, Sprechen, Lesen und Schreiben) werden über vielfältige Übungs- und Sozialformen trainiert und gefestigt (unterstützt von der *Skills Practice* im Companion), wobei bereits von Anfang an auch mit testformatähnlichen Beispielen und Textsorten (zu erkennen an der orangen Nummerierung mit Linie) an die SRP herangeführt wird.

- Im Sinne der **Lernerautonomie** zeigen **Can-do statements** (nach Skills und Kompetenzen, dem GERS-Niveau zugeordnet) pro Unit und ein **Self-Assessment** (*Check Your Progress*; Doppelseite mit testformatähnlichen Beispielen) am Ende jedes Topics den Lernfortschritt auf.

Symbole

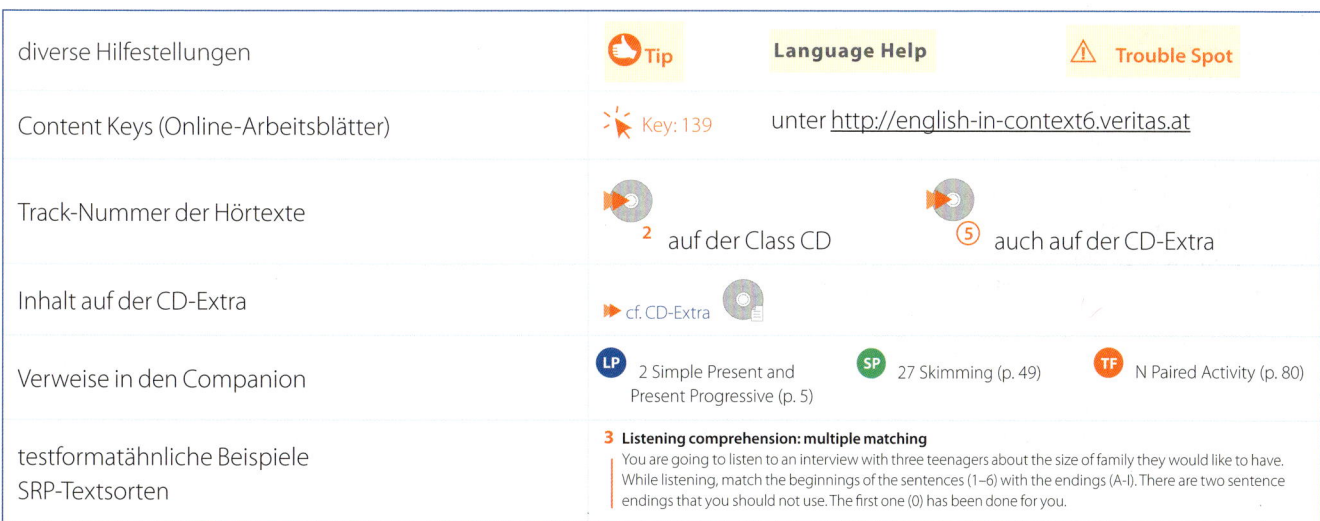

diverse Hilfestellungen	👍 **Tip** **Language Help** ⚠ **Trouble Spot**
Content Keys (Online-Arbeitsblätter)	Key: 139 unter http://english-in-context6.veritas.at
Track-Nummer der Hörtexte	**2** auf der Class CD **⑤** auch auf der CD-Extra
Inhalt auf der CD-Extra	▶ cf. CD-Extra
Verweise in den Companion	**LP** 2 Simple Present and Present Progressive (p. 5) **SP** 27 Skimming (p. 49) **TF** N Paired Activity (p. 80)
testformatähnliche Beispiele SRP-Textsorten	**3 Listening comprehension: multiple matching** You are going to listen to an interview with three teenagers about the size of family they would like to have. While listening, match the beginnings of the sentences (1–6) with the endings (A–I). There are two sentence endings that you should not use. The first one (0) has been done for you.

Weitere Elemente

- **Partner Pages**
- ergänzende **Online-Materialien** (Webquests), aufrufbar über 3-stellige Content Keys: http://english-in-context6.veritas.at
- **Extra** Aufgabenstellungen und **Mini-Projekte**
- **Landeskundliche** Informationen

Progression

Zwischen Band 5 und 6 gibt es eine spürbare Progression:

Über das Format *Grammar in Use* werden auch in Band 6 einzelne **Grammatik-Strukturen** noch punktuell wiederholt (und können im Companion gezielt aufgefrischt und trainiert werden).

Beim **Writing** greift Band 6 die Textsorten E-Mail und Blog aus Band 5 auf. Im Kompetenzmodul 3 liegt der Schwerpunkt auf dem Bericht, im Kompetenzmodul 4 auf dem Artikel; im Kompetenzmodul 4 gibt es auch eine erste Einführung ins Essay-Writing (Vorgriff auf Kompetenzmodul 5).

CD-Extra (Inhalte)

- ausgewählte **Hörübungen** (.mp3) aus dem Student's Book, zum Nachhören für daheim
- sämtliche **Partner Pages** zum Student's Book
- **Wordlists** (.docx, .pdf), chronological and alphabetical, zum Nachschlagen und individuellen Bearbeiten der Vokabeln

Content Key – wie nutzen?

Key: 735   In diesem Buch finden sich auf einigen Seiten Content Keys: Sie verweisen auf zusätzliche Inhalte im Internet. Dazu auf dem PC die Webadresse mit dem jeweiligen Content Key eingeben, z. B. http://english-in-context6.veritas.at/key/735

Ausführliche Informationen unter http://veritas.at/key

Die Inhalte sind auch über das E-Book zugänglich.

Jetzt **E-Book** zum Schulbuch aktivieren!

Zusätzliche Materialien zum Schulbuch im **E-Book**!

Aktuelle Infos zur Aktivierung unter:

www.scook.at/materialien

Neue Oberstufe (NOst)

Für die Arbeit im Rahmen der Neuen Oberstufe (NOst), konkret für die Kompetenzmodule 3+4, stehen **Hilfestellungen** auf der Verlagswebsite und im E-Book zur Verfügung.

Language and Skills Practice im Companion (ISBN 978-3-7058-9470-9)

Auf nachhaltigen Kompetenzerwerb und Skillstraining legt die Reihe von Beginn an sehr viel Wert – das Student's Book wird hier durch den Companion mit den Abschnitten *Language Practice* (grammar, vocabulary, communication), *Skills Practice* (study, listening, speaking, reading, wiriting), *SRP Text Types* und *SRP Test Formats* optimal ergänzt: Er soll den SchülerInnen die gesamte Oberstufe hindurch als Nachschlagewerk dienen.

Er ist dem *English in Context 5. Student's Book* beigelegt, ist aber auch unter o.a. ISBN separat erhältlich.

Language and Skills Practice im Training (BNR 165.621 [Anhang])

Eine konsequente Vertiefung und nachhaltige Festigung der sprachlichen Strukturen und Skills kann mit *English in Context 6. Training* erzielt werden.

Sämtliche Hörübungen auf der Class CD bzw. im E-Book zum Hören in der Klasse.

Have fun with English in Context!

Die Autoren und das Beraterteam

Contents ☀ Key: 343

3. Semester/Kompetenzmodul 3 text type: report

| Topic 1 | The Web of Communication | 10 |

UNIT 1	Connecting through the Internet	14
A	Online Pressure	14
B	An Online Hoax	16
C	Risky Behaviour	17
CAN-DO STATEMENTS		19

UNIT 2	To Talk or Not to Talk?	20
A	Meeting the Stepmother	20
B	A New Kind of Connectedness?	22
CAN-DO STATEMENTS		24

UNIT 3	Creative Communication	25
A	Expressing Yourself through Poetry	25
B	Presenting Yourself Creatively	26
CAN-DO STATEMENTS		27

| CHECK YOUR PROGRESS 1 | | 28 |

| Topic 2 | Violence and Crime | 30 |

UNIT 4	Violence in Popular Culture	34
A	If It Bleeds, It Leads	34
B	How Do Violent Video Games Affect Us?	36
C	The Hunger Games	38
CAN-DO STATEMENTS		41

UNIT 5	Crime and Prevention	42
A	Graffiti – Vandalism or Art?	42
B	Knife Crime Campaign	44
C	The Agony of the Needle	45
CAN-DO STATEMENTS		49

UNIT 6	Bullying and Conformism	50
A	Bullying at School	50
B	Gangs: the Alternative Family	53
CAN-DO STATEMENTS		54

| CHECK YOUR PROGRESS 2 | | 55 |

Contents

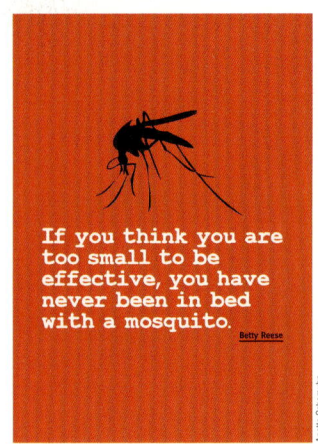

If you think you are too small to be effective, you have never been in bed with a mosquito. **Betty Reese**

Topic 3	Making a Difference	58
UNIT 7	**It's Your Turn**	**62**
A	What Role Will You Play?	62
B	Take a Chance	64
C	'How Could the World Let these Children Die?'	66
CAN-DO STATEMENTS		**68**
UNIT 8	**Can I Help?**	**69**
A	If I Can Stop One Heart from Breaking	69
B	Bread on the Water	70
CAN-DO STATEMENTS		**77**
UNIT 9	**Applying for Volunteer Work**	**78**
A	Two Job Descriptions	78
CAN-DO STATEMENTS		**81**
CHECK YOUR PROGRESS 3		**82**

4. Semester/Kompetenzmodul 4 text type: article

Topic 4	Our Changing Planet	84
UNIT 10	**The Scientist's View**	**88**
A	What Is Global Warming?	88
B	Species Extinction and Human Activity	90
CAN-DO STATEMENTS		**93**
UNIT 11	**Different Points of View**	**94**
A	Countdown for Our Planet	94
B	Climate Change	95
CAN-DO STATEMENTS		**98**
UNIT 12	**Searching for Solutions**	**99**
A	Think Globally, Act Locally	99
B	Greener Travel	101
C	Discussing a Current Affairs Topic	102
CAN-DO STATEMENTS		**104**
CHECK YOUR PROGRESS 4		**105**

Topic 5	**Migrants and Minorities**	**108**
UNIT 13	**What Is Migration?**	**112**
A	The New Slave Trade?	112
B	Warsaw on the Thames	113
C	The Pendulum Effect	115
CAN-DO STATEMENTS		117
UNIT 14	**Migrants as Minority Groups**	**118**
A	"It's Not All Take, Take, Take"	118
B	Writing an Essay *(Vorgriff auf 5. Semester)*	120
CAN-DO STATEMENTS		122
UNIT 15	**The Downside of Migration**	**123**
A	Black Hoodie	123
CAN-DO STATEMENTS		124
CHECK YOUR PROGRESS 5		**125**
Topic 6	**A Good Read**	**128**
UNIT 16	**The Curious Incident of the Dog in the Night-Time**	**132**
A	Opening Lines	132
B	Who Is Telling the Story?	132
C	The Author and the Narrator	134
CAN-DO STATEMENTS		136
UNIT 17	**The Absolutely True Diary of a Part-Time Indian**	**137**
A	Opening Lines	137
B	'A Very Autobiographical Novel'	137
C	Penelope's Dreams	139
CAN-DO STATEMENTS		141
UNIT 18	**Looking for Alaska**	**142**
A	Opening Lines	142
B	Getting to Know the Narrator	142
C	Miles and Alaska	144
CAN-DO STATEMENTS		147
CHECK YOUR PROGRESS 6		**148**
PARTNER PAGES	cf. CD-Extra	
Language for Tasks ('Operatoren')		150
Answer Key zu Check Your Progress		152
Übersichten: Content Keys, CD-Extra		153–154

ingimage.com

Fotolia.com/Michael Flippo

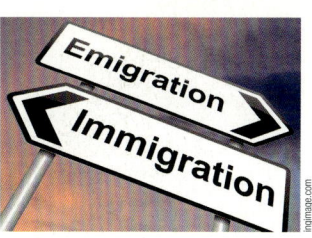

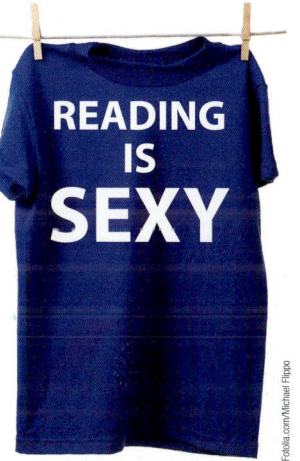

1 The Web of Communication

SP 12 Working with Pictures (p. 38)

1 Working with pictures

a Work with a partner. Agree on a caption for each of the eight photos.

b Put the photos into groups. Point out which of the photos have something in common. Share your ideas with your partner.

2 Thinking about a title

a Work with a partner. What does the title of this Topic make you think of? What different meanings can the word web have?

b Look at the photos again and think of a common title for them.

c Collect your ideas in class and choose the best or most original title.

In this topic you will learn about …

- how we communicate (WiC)
- modern forms of communication (Unit 1)
- communication in the family (Unit 2)
- presenting yourself creatively (Unit 3)

A

Soz yr dog
dd. :-(
C u sn,
X Anne

Fotolia.com/DesignNic

B **Employers use Facebook when hiring**

Some employers say they use the website to check
you out before they hire you. […] Employers also
search websites like MySpace and Friendster, so
Career Services warns students to be careful about
what they put on the Web. You never know who
might be looking.

Mari Fagel: Employers use facebook when hiring.
In: Northwestern News Network, April 19, 2006

© Randy Glasbergen.
www.glasbergen.com

C

"Dear Andy: How have you been?
Your mother and I are fine. We miss you.
Please sign off your computer and come
downstairs for something to eat. Love, Dad."

Randy Glasbergen

D Chris Tarantino goes online to learn about her
daughters' school day.

New York Times, May 4, 2008

Fotolia.com/Kalib Kozakiel

6

soz *(text message abbr)* sorry
dd *(text message abbr)* died
employer person or company
that gives people jobs
hire sb. give sb. a job
Career Services organization
that gives advice about jobs

Anette Schamuhn

3 Working with different texts

a Work in groups of four. Each choose a different one of the texts above and make notes:
- How did you react when you first read the text?
- What does it reveal about the way people use modern media today?

b Share your ideas in the group.

c What problems of modern means of communication do you think will be mentioned in this
Topic?

4 Collecting communication terms

Write an A–Z of different terms to do with communication. Add new words and phrases as you
go through this Topic.
A: advertisement, B: blog, C: chat room, D: …

Words in Context

 24 Increase Your Word Power Online (p. 18)

> ⚠ **Trouble Spot**
>
> **mobile (phone)** *(BE)* = **cellphone**
> *(esp. AE)*
> Not: ~~handy~~

 27 False Friends (p. 22)

> ⚠ **Trouble Spot**
>
> im Internet = **on the Internet**
> im Internet surfen = **surf the Internet/Net**

You Can't Not Communicate  **Key: 722**

Whenever we transmit information of any kind, we are communicating. Writing and speech are the most obvious means of communication, but we can also communicate our thoughts and feelings through music, dance, poetry, or any other art form. You should choose carefully how you communicate, though, as there are certain conventions to follow. Just as it can be considered rude to send a text message to express your condolences, using your mobile phone in public can be seen as being rude when you speak loudly and annoy others. In conversation with strangers, on the other hand, silence is considered awkward, leading to the necessity of making conversation, or small talk.

Technological advances have made connecting to like-minded strangers as easy as keeping in touch with friends and family. All we have to do is go on the Internet, read a blog, update our online profile on social networking sites such as Facebook, MySpace or Twitter, chat, send emails or simply use a mobile phone to talk or text. Many social networking sites are growing in popularity. Thus, surfing the Net allows us to contact others with the same interests or the same friends. It brings people together who may never have met otherwise. At the same time, these social networks also allow others to post information about us on the Internet – whether it is good or bad, true or not.

Whenever we speak, we not only send a verbal message, but at the same time transmit a non-verbal message through our body language or facial expressions. We send non-verbal messages even when we don't speak, for example when we are simply listening to someone else talk. In short: you can't not communicate. However, communication, or interaction, will only be successful if at least two people with a shared space are involved. In other words, they must have something in common, e.g. belong to the same family, be friends, go to the same school, speak the same language. As a rule, communication is easy and straightforward. Look at the diagram below. A, the sender, speaks to B, the recipient. A wants to communicate something to B: this is A's intended meaning. What B actually understands is the perceived meaning. This may, but must not necessarily, be the same as A's intended meaning.

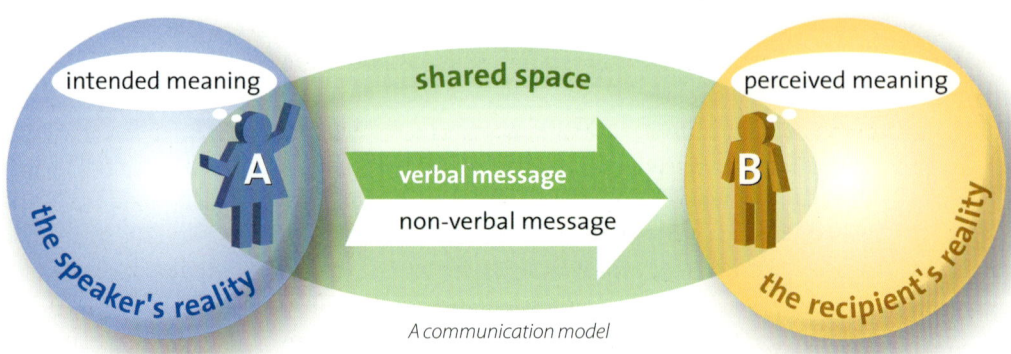

A communication model

1 A communication model

Look at the model of what happens during interaction above and match the definitions (1–8) with the terms from the model (a–h).

1 the person listening
2 the person speaking
3 what the two people communicating have in common
4 the world a person lives in and the way he or she sees it
5 the words the person speaking uses
6 what the person listening understands
7 body language and facial expressions
8 what the person speaking means

a verbal message
b the person's reality
c the speaker
d perceived meaning
e the recipient
f intended meaning
g shared space
h non-verbal message

2 Matching nouns and verbs

LP 25 Collocations (p. 20)

a Make collocations with the verbs and nouns below. Use *a/an* or *the* before the nouns.
Be careful: Some nouns might need no article at all!

1 necessary	6 create	11 surf	a conversation	f small talk
2 access	7 have	12 go on	b information	g text message
3 change	8 make	13 update	c Internet	
4 check out	9 receive	14 use	d mobile phone	
5 collect	10 send	15 write	e profile	

b Choose five of the collocations from **a** and write sentences with them.

3 Matching nouns and adjectives

a Match each group of adjectives (or adjectivally used nouns) with a noun from the right.

1 hidden/double/perceived/intended/literal/…   a information
2 useful/secret/detailed/correct/background/…   b language
3 important/urgent/phone/text/error/…   c meaning
4 foreign/first/official/native/body/sign/…   d message

b Choose two collocations from each group and write sentences with them.

4 Language in Use: word formation

Some words are missing from the text. Use the words in brackets to form a word that fits in the gap (1–10). Write your answers in the spaces provided. The first one (0) has been done for you.

TF I Word Formation (p. 77)

One problem with personal (0) ___ (communicate) is that the person you are talking to, or texting or sending an email to, does not always understand what you want to say. Even if you are only taking part in a simple (1) ___ (converse), often the perceived meaning that the (2) ___ (receive) understands may be different from your (3) ___ (intend) meaning. It is even more difficult if the two (4) ___ (speak) don't have a shared space: (5) ___ (interact) is always improved if the non-verbal (6) ___ (messenger), such as body language and (7) ___ (face) expressions can be taken into account as well. Many texts that are (8) ___ (send) on mobile phones only contain a few syllables or abbreviations, but they are still able to (9) ___ (transmitter) a large amount of (10) ___ (inform).

0	*communication*
1	
2	
3	
4	
5	
6	
7	
8	
9	
10	

Singing to find a mate is so old-fashioned!

A Online Pressure

Have you ever missed lessons without your parents knowing?
Have you ever got a bad mark in a test and not told your parents?
Talk about how you would like it if your parents had ways of finding out about this.

Getty Images/rubberball/White Packert

SP 30 Reading Non-Fiction (p. 50)

SP 4 Taking Notes (p. 32)

1 Looking at both sides

With a partner, you will read and work on a newspaper article about online programs called Edline, ParentConnect or PowerSchool which allow parents to check their children's grades and daily progress at school anytime.

Partner B: Look at the page provided by your teacher.

a Partner A: Read the following extract from the *New York Times* article and make notes on the following:

- reasons why parents check grades:
_____
_____

- effect of programs on …
  parents: _____
  pupils: _____
  schools: _____

pressure [ˈpreʃə] feelings of anxiety caused by the need to behave in a particular way
devastatingly [ˈdevəsteɪtɪŋli] causing a lot of damage
fondly in a way that shows affection
recall sth. remember sth.
adolescence [ˌædəˈlesns] puberty
subterfuge [ˈsʌbtəfjuːdʒ] *(fml)* secret and dishonest behaviour
be a given *here:* part of everyday life
fool sb. trick sb. into believing sth. that is not true
do away with sth. take sth. away
sly intending to trick sb.
all-consuming taking up all your time or energy
conclusively without any doubt
impact [ˈ- -] powerful effect
boon blessing
sufficiently [səˈfɪʃntli] as much as necessary
cancel sth. decide that sth. already arranged will not take place

At an age when teenagers increasingly want to manage their own lives, many parents use these programs to tighten the grip. College admission is so devastatingly competitive, parents say, they feel compelled to check online grades frequently. [...]

Paradoxically, many parents who regularly check their children's grades online fondly recall that during their own adolescence, subterfuge was a given. 'I'll admit it,' said Chris Tarantino, Emily's mother. 'I got satisfaction in fooling my parents.'

Programs like Edline do away with that sly pleasure. But Mrs. Tarantino, a PowerSchool fan, said the stakes had changed drastically. Academic pressure a generation ago was not nearly as all-consuming.

It is difficult to demonstrate conclusively what impact these programs have on school performance, because of all the variables. Anecdotally, principals report that the programs have motivated otherwise hard-to-reach parents and students. They have helped some middle-school boys, in particular, become better organized.

'Edline opens up communication between parents and teachers,' said Ron Jones, the principal at Huth Middle School, which has a 90-percent minority student population, in Matteson, Ill., a middle-class Chicago suburb. 'It helps keep the children minding their Ps and Qs.'

The software can certainly be a boon to working parents. And divorced parents can log on without having to contact each other. [...]

In Noblesville, Ind., after a survey indicated that parents felt sufficiently informed by PowerSchool and subsequent email exchanges with teachers, the middle-school principal canceled parent-teacher conferences this spring and gave the time back to classes.

Jan Hoffman: I Know What You Did Last Math Class. In: http://www.nytimes.com, May 4, 2008

b Now summarize your text to Partner B, using your notes.

c Your partner will read you six words or phrases from your text. Match each of the words or phrases to one of these definitions:

- put (more) pressure on sb./sth. _____
- what is at risk _____
- pressure to get good grades at school _____
- how students do at school _____
- describes a situation in which students compete against each other _____
- be careful about what one says or does (i.e. say 'please' and 'thank you') _____

d Now swap roles and read the words and phrases below to your partner.

- college admission (l. 2)
- feel compelled to do sth. (l. 3)
- gifted-and-talented program (l. 11)
- monitor one's records (l. 14)
- snoop (l. 19)
- slip up (l. 21)

e Role-play: A high-school pupil is arguing with his/her father/mother about online programs. Look at your role card. Can you agree with your partner on how much to use them?

Partner A

- You are the parent of a high-school pupil and you are worried that your child is not doing well enough at school. You want to check his/her grades every day. Use these arguments:
- high academic pressure
- pupils work harder
- better communication with teachers
- more time for school work

2 Looking at adverbs

Look at these adverbs from the article. What function does the adverb have in each case?

At an age when teenagers <u>increasingly</u> ▶ want to manage their own lives …

Adverb	modifies verb	modifies adjective	refers to sentence ✔
increasingly (l. 1)	*want*		
devastatingly (l. 2)			
frequently (l. 3)			
paradoxically (l. 4)			✔
fondly (l. 4)			
drastically (l. 8)			
anecdotally (l. 11)			
better (l. 13)			✔

LP 23 Adverbs of Manner (p. 17)

3 Language in Use: banked gap-fill

Some words are missing from the text below. For each gap, choose the correct word (A–K) from the list. There are two extra words that you should not use. Write your answers in the spaces provided. The first one (0) has been done for you.

TF J Banked Gap-Fill (p. 78)

Many parents check their children's grades (0) ___ because they are (1) ___ worried about how they are achieving at school. They say that the pressure to succeed at high-school has changed (2) ___ . (3) ___ , these are the same parents who (4) ___ remember fooling their own families when they were children. (5) ___ , pupils are not as much in favour of these online programs as their parents, and they (6) ___ denounce them on social networking websites for snooping on them. The schools cannot say (7) ___ how much things have improved, but many pupils, especially boys, are now much (8) ___ organized.

A better	D dramatically	G funnily	J permanently
B bitterly	E evenly	H happily	K surprisingly
C daily	F exactly	I obviously	

0	1	2	3	4	5	6	7	8
C	___	___	___	___	___	___	___	___

Language Help

- Dear Mr/Mrs …
- I am writing to you because …
- Teachers will find that …
- For parents it will be easy to …
- Students will also benefit from …, because …
- However, I would like to point out that …
- On the other hand, …
- One other disadvantage is that …
- Finally, I would like to say …
- Yours sincerely …

TT 2 Formal Email (p. 60)

SP 30 Reading Non-Fiction (p. 50)

hoax [həʊks] act intended to make sb. believe sth. that is not true, esp sth. unpleasant

insult ['- -] sth. that is said to offend sb.

sob (v) cry

closet ['klɒzɪt] (esp. AE) a small room or a space in a wall used for storing things

joined at the hip (infml) inseparable friends

drift apart lose contact

prescribe sth. for sb. to tell somebody to take a particular medicine

minor ['maɪnə] sb. who is under 18 years old

mess with sb. do sth. to sb. that may be harmful

profanity-laden [prə'fænəti,leɪdn] (fml) full of bad language

4 Writing: formal email

Write an email to the head teacher of a school using *Edline* or *PowerSchool*.
In your email you should:
- present arguments in favour of online programs
- consider arguments against online programs
- make suggestions on how to use the programs wisely.

Write about 200 words.

B An Online Hoax  Key: 191

Before reading the following article, think what an online hoax and an online character could be.

Megan Meier died believing that somewhere in this world lived a boy named Josh Evans who hated her. He was 16, owned a pet snake, and she thought he was the cutest boyfriend she ever had.

Josh contacted Megan through her page on MySpace.com, the social networking website, said Megan's mother, Tina Meier. They flirted for weeks, but only online – Josh said his family had no phone. On October 15, 2006, Josh suddenly turned mean. He called Megan names, and later they traded insults for an hour.

The next day, in his final message, said Megan's father Ron Meier, Josh wrote, 'The world would be a better place without you.'

Sobbing, Megan ran into her bedroom closet. Her mother found her there, hanging from a belt. She was 13.

Tina Meier with pictures of her daughter Megan

Six weeks after Megan's death, her parents learned that Josh Evans never existed. He was an online character created by Lori Drew, then 47, who lived four houses down the street in this rapidly growing community 35 miles northwest of St. Louis.

In seventh grade, Megan Meier had tried desperately to join the popular crowd at Fort Zumwalt West Middle School, only to be teased about her weight, her mother said. At the beginning of eighth grade last year, she transferred to Immaculate Conception, a nearby Catholic school. Within three months, Ms. Meier said, her daughter had a new group of friends, lost 20 pounds and joined the volleyball team.

At one time, Lori Drew's daughter and Megan had been 'joined at the hip', said Megan's great-aunt Vicki Dunn. But the two drifted apart, and when Megan changed schools, she told the other girl that she no longer wanted to be friends, Ms. Meier said. […]

Because Ms. Drew had taken Megan on family vacations, she knew the girl had been prescribed antidepression medication, Ms. Meier said. She also knew that Megan had a MySpace page.

Lori Drew (right) and her daughter

Ms. Drew had told a girl across the street about the hoax, said the girl's mother, who requested anonymity to protect her daughter, a minor.

'Lori laughed about it,' the mother said, adding that Ms. Drew and Ms. Drew's daughter 'said they were going to mess with Megan.' […]

Other youngsters who had linked to Josh's MySpace profile joined the increasingly bitter exchange and began sending profanity-laden messages to Megan, who retreated to her bedroom. No more than 15 minutes had passed, Ms. Meier recalled, when she suddenly felt something was terribly wrong. She rushed to the bedroom and found her daughter's body hanging in the closet.

Christopher Maag: A Hoax Turned Fatal Draws Anger but No Charges.
In: http://www.nytimes.com, November 28, 2007

1 **1 Reading comprehension: sequencing**

a Put the following events (A–M) into the order in which they took place. There is one extra event that you should not use. Write your answers in the spaces provided. The first one (0) has been done for you.

Key: 922

A Lori Drew invents the boy Josh who is in love with Megan.
B Megan transfers to a Catholic school and no longer wants to be friends with Lori Drew's daughter.
C Josh and Megan flirt for weeks.
D Megan starts at Fort Zumwalt West Middle School.
E Megan's parents learn that Josh Evans was an online character created by Lori Drew.
F Megan tells Lori Drew's daughter about Josh.
G Josh tells Megan that the world would be a better place without her.
H Other youngsters also send mean messages to Megan.
I Megan is friends with Lori Drew's daughter.
J Megan hangs herself in her closet.
K Lori Drew tells a neighbour that they are planning to 'mess with Megan'.
L Josh suddenly turns mean.
M Josh contacts Megan through her page on MySpace.

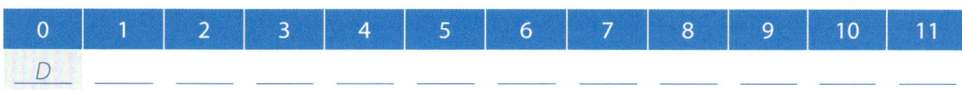

0	1	2	3	4	5	6	7	8	9	10	11
D											

b Why do you think Ms Drew wanted to 'mess with' Megan (l. 33)?

2 Your reactions

Make notes on how you felt as you read the text. Describe how you reacted to a partner.

Language Help

- The text made me angry/sad/upset/… because …
- I found it interesting/surprising/shocking/…
- I was speechless because …
- I couldn't believe it when …
- I felt sorry for … (when/because) …

C Risky Behaviour

The interview you are going to listen to presents research carried out by Dr Megan Moreno from the University of Wisconsin on references to sex, drugs and violence in MySpace profiles.

1 Working with words

Before you listen, match the words on the left to the definitions on the right.

1	substance abuse		clever
2	savvy		the act of killing yourself
3	disclose sth.	1	the use of drugs in a harmful way
4	mortality		have an effect on sth.
5	homicide		sb. who frightens weaker people via the Internet
6	suicide		death
7	boast (v)		encourage sth.
8	cyberbully		show off
9	foster sth.		a message of warning
10	cautionary message		murder
11	influence sth.		give sb. information about sth.

2 Listening: true/false

Listen and decide whether the statements (1–7) are true (T) or false (F) and put a cross (✖) in the correct box. The first one (0) has been done for you.

		T	F
0	According to new research, more than 50% of teenagers who use the social networking site MySpace have posted information about sex, drugs or violence.	✖	☐
1	The top three causes of death for teenagers are substance abuse, murder and suicide.	☐	☐
2	The researchers only looked for evidence of tobacco, alcohol and drug abuse in the MySpace profiles.	☐	☐
3	Some teenagers post information on risky behaviours because they want to see how other teenagers react to them before they try them out.	☐	☐
4	The negative consequences of posting information depend on the reasons the teenagers have for doing so.	☐	☐
5	The information can attract unwelcome attention from cyberbullies, sexual predators, future employees or educational institutions.	☐	☐
6	Profiles containing information on risky behaviours encourage other teens to accept this kind of behaviour as normal.	☐	☐
7	It's not possible for adults to influence teenagers' behaviour online.	☐	☐

3 Positive and negative aspects of social networking sites

a In groups of four, do a placemat activity. In your corner of the placemat, write down positive and negative aspects of social networking sites such as Facebook or MySpace.

b Talk about your lists in your group. Write the two most positive and the two most dangerous aspects in the middle of your placemat.

c Compare your results with those of other groups. Would you change your four central ideas now?

SP 2 Brainstorming (p. 30)

4 Working with posters

Make a poster or flyer warning teenagers of the risks of sharing information about themselves on social networking sites like MySpace. Hang up your posters in the class and vote on which one is the best. Use some of the phrases to help you:

SP 12 Working with Pictures (p. 38)

Keep … !

Avoid … !

Don't put any(thing) … !

Don't let (anybody) … !

Watch out for … !

Be careful of … !

my profile/ friends

privacy/security settings

5 Writing: report

An international media project has asked for reports on the use of communication technology by teenagers and you have decided to take part. As a first step you have interviewed 50 students and taken these notes:

TT 4 Report (p. 64)

Complete the sentence: 'I use … to chat with others every day.'	
texting	33
voice calls – mobile phone	19
social network website	17
instant messages	11
land lines	9
emails	3
none of the above	7

Language Help

- This report aims to compare …
- I have carried out a survey of …
- The results of the survey are as follows: …
- The most/least popular means of communication is/are …
- Another technology that is often used is …
- By contrast, …
- One possible reason for this is (that) …
- It is also very likely that …

Based on your notes, write your report. You should…

- inform the readers about the results of your interviews
- compare the popularity of the different technologies
- suggest possible reasons for the results

Write about 200 words. Divide your report into sections and give them headings.

CAN-DO STATEMENTS

		Part / Ex	✔
👂	I can understand the main points of radio news bulletins and simpler recorded material on topics of personal interest delivered relatively slowly and clearly. (B1/5)	C / Ex 2	☐
📖	I can understand the main points in short newspaper articles about current and familiar topics. (B1/1)	A / Ex 1 B/ Ex 1–2	☐
	I can skim short texts (for example news summaries) and find relevant facts and information (for example who has done what and where). (B1/8)	B / Ex 1	☐
😊😊	I can maintain a conversation or discussion but may sometimes be difficult to follow when trying to say exactly what I would like to. (B1/1)	L-I / Ex 1–3 A / Ex 1e C / Ex 3	☐
👄	I can express and respond to feelings such as surprise, happiness, sadness, interest and indifference. (B1/2)	B / Ex 2	☐
	I can give or seek personal views and opinions in an informal discussion with friends. (B1/6)	L-I / Ex 1–3 C / Ex 3	☐
	I can agree and disagree politely. (B1/6)	A / Ex 1e	☐
	I can give detailed accounts of experiences, describing feelings and reactions. (B1/1)	L-I / Ex 3 B / Ex 2 C / Ex 3	☐
	I can paraphrase short written passages orally in a simple fashion, using the original text wording and ordering. (B1/7)	A / Ex 1b	☐
✏️	I can write simple connected texts on a range of topics within my field of interest and can express personal views and opinions. (B1/1)	A / Ex 4 C / Ex 5	☐

A   Meeting the Stepmother

Have you ever been in a situation in which you did not know what to say? What kind of situation was that? How did you or the others behave?

The father of Julia and Jason Taylor has left the family for another woman, Cynthia. Read this extract about the first meeting between father and son after the separation.

29 Reading Fiction (p. 50)

Hi, Dad.'

'Oh!' Dad's expression was a mountaineer's, the moment his rope snaps. 'Jason. I didn't expect you to –' Dad'd been going to say 'to be at home' but he changed his sentence. 'I didn't hear you.'
'I heard the car.' Obviously. 'Mum's at work.' Dad knew that.
'She left some things for me. I've just come to pick them up.'
'Yeah. She said.'

A moon-grey cat strolled into the garage and settled down on a cushion of potatoes.

'So ...' Dad said. 'How's Julia?'

Dad meant *Does Julia hate me*? But not even Julia could answer that. 'She's ... fine.'

'Good. Good. Say hi from me.'

'Okay.' *Tell her yourself, why don't you*? 'How was Christmas?'

'Oh ... fine. Quiet.' Dad looked at the pyramid of bin-bags. 'Horrendous. For obvious reasons. Yours?'

'Mine was horrendous too. Are you growing a beard, Dad?'

'No, I just haven't ... maybe I will. I don't know. Are the Richmond relatives all well?'

'Aunt Alice's as you'd expect, all clucky 'cause of ... y'know.'

'Of course.'

'Alex just played on his BBC computer. Hugo's smarmy as ever. Nigel's doing quadratic equations for fun. Uncle Brian ...' Finishing the sentence about Uncle Brian was hard work.

'... got drunk as a lord and prattled on about me?'

'Dad, is Uncle Brian an idiot?'

'He can *act* like one.' Something's unknotted in Dad. He looks hollow and unhappy but he's definitely more peaceful. 'But how someone acts isn't what they are. Not necessarily. Best not to be too judgemental. Maybe there's stuff going on you don't know about. You know?'

I do know.

The horriblest part was, being friendly to Dad makes me feel disloyal to Mum. However much they *say* 'We both still love you', you do have to choose. Words like 'maintenance' and 'best interests' don't leave you alone. A figure sat in the sky-blue Jetta. 'Is ...' I didn't know what to call *her*.

'Cynthia drove me over, yes. She'd like to say hello, if ...' (a mad organist thumped my panic chords) '... if you'd like to.' A pleading note bent Dad's voice. 'Would you?'

'Okay.' I didn't want to. 'Okay.'

Outside the cave of the garage, rain fell so lightly it wasn't even falling. Before I'd got to the Jetta, Cynthia'd got out. She's not a big-boobed bimbo or an evil-eyed witch.

She's frumpier than Mum, *any* day, and mousier. Brown hair in a bob, brown eyes. She doesn't look a *thing* like a stepmother. Which is what she'll be, by and by.

---

mountaineer sb. who climbs mountains as a sport
snap (v) break
horrendous [hɒ'rendəs] terrible
clucky (infml) wanting to take care of sb. too much, like a mother hen
smarmy (infml) too polite in a way that is not sincere
prattle on about sth./sb. talk a lot about unimportant things
judgemental [dʒʌdʒ'mentl] judging people and criticizing them too quickly
maintenance ['meɪntənəns] *here:* money that sb. must pay regularly to a former wife, husband or partner, esp. when they have had children together
Jetta type of car ('Volkswagen')
pleading begging
big-boobed (slang) with big breasts
bimbo (infml, disapproving) usu. a young woman who is sexually attractive but not very intelligent
frumpy dressed in an old-fashioned way

⚠ **Trouble Spot**
look unhappy (adj)
smile unhappily (adv)

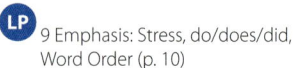
9 Emphasis: Stress, do/does/did, Word Order (p. 10)

'Hallo, Jason.' The woman Dad'd rather spend the rest of his life with than Mum looked at me like I had a gun pointed at her. 'I'm Cynthia.'

'Hi. I'm Jason.' This was very, very, *very* weird. Neither of us tried to shake hands. In the back of her car was a BABY ON BOARD sticker. 'You've got a baby?'

'Well, Milly's more of a toddler now.' If you just heard her voice next to Mum's, you'd say Mum's posher. 'Camilla. Milly. Milly's father – my ex-husband – we're already ... I mean, he's not on the scene. As they say.'

'Right.'

Dad watched his future wife and his only son from his ex-garage.

'Well.' Cynthia smiled unhappily. 'Come and visit whenever you want, Jason. Trains go to Oxford from Cheltenham, direct.' Cynthia's voice is less than half the volume of Mum's. 'Your dad would like you to. He *really* would. So would I. It's a big old house we're in. There's a stream at the end of the garden. You could even have your –' (she was about to say 'your own bedroom'.) 'Well, you're welcome, any time.'

All I could do was nod.

'Whenever it suits.' Cynthia looked at Dad.

'So how –' I began, suddenly scared of having nothing to say.

'If you –' she began in the same second.

'After you –'

'No, after you. Really. You go ahead.'

'How long' (no grown-up's ever made me go first) 'have you known Dad?' I'd meant the question to sound breezy but it came out all Gestapo.

'Since we were growing up,' Cynthia was working hard to iron out any extra meanings, 'in Derbyshire.'

Longer than Mum, then. If Dad'd married this Cynthia in the first place, instead of Mum, and if they'd had a son, would it have been me? Or a totally different kid? Or a kid who's half me?

David Mitchell: Black Swan Green. London: Hodder & Stoughton 2006 © David Mitchell

toddler child who has just learned to walk
posh (BE, infml) here: belonging to a high social class
breezy cheerful and relaxed
iron sth. out ['aɪən] get rid of sth.

⚠ **Trouble Spot**
How long have you known Dad?
Not: ~~How long do you know Dad?~~

LP 5 Present Perfect for 'time up until now' (p. 7)

TF G True/False Justify (p. 75)

1 Reading comprehension: true/false justify

First decide whether the statements 1–9 are true (T) or false (F) and put a cross (✗) in the correct box. Then identify the sentence in the text which supports your decision. Write the first four words of this sentence in the space provided. There may be more than one correct answer; write down only one. The first one (0) has been done for you.

	Statements	T	F	
0	Jason's father came to the house because he thought his wife was out.	✗		*Dad knew that*
1	Jason's sister, Julia, hates her father for leaving the family.			
2	Jason thinks his father's character has changed somehow.			
3	Jason feels uncomfortable talking to his father.			
4	Jason's father doesn't really mind whether Jason wants to meet Cynthia or not.			
5	Jason doesn't believe that his father will marry Cynthia.			
6	Cynthia is unhappy about meeting Jason.			
7	Jason's father helps to keep the conversation between Jason and Cynthia going.			
8	Jason doesn't know what to say to Cynthia.			
9	Jason tries hard not to sound angry when he is talking to Cynthia			

LP 3 Simple Present to Talk about Texts (p. 6)

2 Working with the text

a Write a short description of the situation in your own words. (60–70 words)

b Look at lines 1–32. Find one example from the text for each of the following:
- how Jason feels about his father
- how his father feels about Jason

c What makes the communication between father and son so difficult?

d Look at lines 37–62. Collect all the information in the text on Cynthia. Who provides this information? What effect does it have on you, the reader?

3 Adjectives or adverbs?

a Find the following adjectives in lines 22–26 of the text: unhappy, friendly, disloyal. Which words do they relate to? Why are these verbs followed by an adjective and not an adverb? Which other verbs can be followed by an adjective?

b Choose the correct adjective or adverb to complete the sentences. Cross out the wrong word. The first one (0) has been done for you.

The small dog looked (0) harmless/~~harmlessly~~ enough but it stared at me (1) *angry/angrily* when I opened the garage door and saw it sitting in the corner. For some reason, I felt really (2) *uncomfortable/uncomfortably* about being in the same place with it, but it seemed (3) *stupid/stupidly* to turn around and leave. 'Good dog,' I said, but my voice sounded (4) *hollow/hollowly* and I was (5) *scared/scaredly* of frightening it. Suddenly, the light went out and my mouth tasted (6) *bitter/bitterly* in the darkness. Where was the dog now? I felt (7) *careful/carefully* for the light switch with my hand and looked around (8) *slow/slowly* for the way back out. The fresh air smelled (9) *sweet/sweetly* when I got out into the garden, but I could hear the dog barking from the garage. A car sounded its horn (10) *noisy/noisily* from the street and I jumped. Why did everything seem so (11) *scary/scarily*? What was (12) *wrong/wrongly* with me?

c **EXTRA** Continue the story using your own adjectives and adverbs. Write about 70 words.

SP 44 Creative Writing (p. 58)

4 Creative Writing
Choose one of the following tasks – **a** or **b**:

a You are Jason. Write an email to your father in which you tell him everything that remained unsaid during your conversation? Will you be angry with him or understanding? Will you want to keep in touch?
When you have finished your email, swap it with a partner. What might Jason's father reply to him? Write his email to Jason. Will he tell him everything that remained unsaid during the conversation? Will he just feel sorry for his son? Will he try to explain openly why he left the family for another woman?

b You are Cynthia. Describe meeting Jason (ll. 43–70) from your point of view.
I was waiting in the car when I saw Jason come over to me. I got out of the car …

B A New Kind of Connectedness?

3

1 Listening for gist
Listen once only and choose the sentence that best describes the situation.

SP 19 Listening for Gist (p. 45)

a An interviewer and a researcher from the 'Pew Internet and American Life Project' are t[alking] about whether people think modern communications have improved their family live[s].

b An interviewer and a researcher from the 'Pew Internet and American Life Project' are talkin[g] about which means of communication a modern family uses most.

▶ ▶ ▶

c An interviewer and a professor of Sociology are talking about the effects of modern communications technology on family life.

d An interviewer and a professor of Technology are talking about how to improve communication between workers on factory assembly lines.

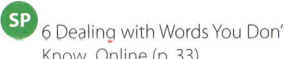

The Simpsons:
family togetherness, ca. 2000

2 Working with words

Look at the words and phrases below. You have heard them now at least once during the interview. Try to guess their meaning, either ...

● from the context of the sentence, or
● from a part of the word that you already know.

Only look up the underlined words in a dictionary (online) if you can't guess what they mean.

1 to <u>evaluate</u> sth. in a study
2 a <u>variety</u> of tools
3 to <u>dispel</u> a myth
4 <u>assembly</u> line workers
5 an old-fashioned <u>notion</u>
6 a <u>respondent</u> to a survey
7 <u>reliance</u> on digital tools
8 <u>fear-mongering</u> critics
9 my <u>spin</u> on the data
10 a 2:1 <u>ratio</u> of people in favour
11 a <u>substitute</u> for sth. else
12 to <u>blur</u> the <u>distinction</u> between two things

LP 24 Increase Your Word Power Online (p. 18)

SP 6 Dealing with Words You Don't Know Online (p. 33)

SP 8 Using a Dictionary (p. 34)

⚠ **Trouble Spot**
complement = Ergänzung
compliment = Kompliment

3 Listening comprehension: short answers

Listen again and answer the questions using a maximum of four words. Write your answers in the spaces provided. The first one (0) has been done for you.

TF F Short Answers (p. 72)

0 Instead of creating isolation, what effect are the Internet and mobile phones having on families?

bringing them closer together

1 According to the survey, which household type has the highest rate of technology usage?

2 What do families use to connect with each other?

3 Which myth do the results of the research dispel?

4 What new type of communication is taking place in familes using the new technology?

5 What times during the week do families spend a lot of time together?

6 How does the Internet add to communication among family members?

7 How many people say the Internet is a good thing rather than a bad thing?

8 What negative effect do people say technology has on their family lives?

TF M Individual Long Turn (p. 80)

4 Speaking: individual long turn

SP 12 Working with Pictures (p. 38)

- Compare the pictures.
- Discuss how communication between families has changed during the last decades.
- Suggest ways in which schools, parents and pupils could communicate better using modern technology.

5 Doing a project

Work in groups of three or four. Prepare a (PowerPoint?) presentation on which means of communication people use and how often they use them.

Think about which areas you want to cover first:

SP 15 Doing a Project (p. 41)

SP 22 Giving a Presentation (p. 46)

- groups of people (friends, family members, parents, grandparents, … ?)
- types of communication (mobile phone, smart phone, email, Facebook, Twitter, …?)
- how often they are used (per hour, per day, per week, … ?)

Interview the people and collect the information. Talk in your groups about the best way to present the information (bar chart, pie chart, line graph, … ?)

CAN-DO STATEMENTS

		Part / Ex	✔
👂	I can understand the most important elements of radio programmes and sound recordings when they deal with current events or my interests. (B1/5)	B / Ex 1 B / Ex 3	☐
📖	I can understand longer, relatively simple literary texts on themes that are familiar to me (e.g. modern popular literature). (B1/3)	A / Ex 1	☐
	I can find information that I need to solve a specific task in various longer texts or text sections. (B1/8)	A / Ex 1	☐
👀	I can ask and answer questions on familiar themes without preparation. (B1/5)	B / Ex 5	☐
	I can give information about myself, my family or my professional life in an interview situation. (B1/7)	B / Ex 5	☐
👄	I can give a prepared straightforward presentation, which can be followed easily and which I can make interesting for my listeners. (B1/3)	B / Ex 4	☐
✏️	I can write simple, private correspondence, e.g. letters and emails. (B1/5)	A / Ex 4	☐
	I can summarize the most important information in a text that deals with a theme I am familiar with. (B1/10)	A / Ex 2	☐

A Expressing Yourself through Poetry ⚡ Key: 984

In this section, you will experience how writing poetry can be a means of expressing your thoughts and feelings.

How To Eat a Poem

Dont be polite.
Bite in.
Pick it up with your fingers and lick the
juice that may run down your chin.
It is ready and ripe now, whenever you are.

You do not need a knife or fork or spoon or
plate or napkin or tablecloth.

For there is no core
or stem
or rind
or pit
or seed
or skin
to throw away.

Eve Merriam: How to Eat a Poem. In: A Sky full of Poems. Yearling 1967 © 1964, 1970, 1973,
1986 by Eve Merriam

napkin piece of cloth or paper used at meals for cleaning your lips and fingers
core hard central part of the fruit that contains the seeds
stem long thin part of a plant from which the leaves or flowers grow
rind [rind] thick skin of some fruits
pit *(AE)* stone-like, large seed of some fruit

1 Poems for everyone
What do you expect when you read the title of the poem below?
What metaphor does the poem make use of?
Perhaps its message can help you when writing your own poem.

2 Creative writing: poem
Look at the following three poems.
Choose one as a model to write a poem about yourself. If you don't want to write about yourself, choose another person or topic.
Then have a partner guess who or what the poem is about (or keep it to yourself).

SP 44 Creative Writing (p. 58)

a A **poem skeleton** offers you the basic structure of a poem and leaves it up to you to fill it out. The title and last line are the same.

> *Charlotte the shy*
> I am the colour of *winter.*
> If I was a sound, *I would be a whisper.*
> Many people think *I'm not even there,* but *I am.*
> If I was a garden, *I would be overgrown and wild, a secret hiding place.*
> I taste of *winter.*
> I dream of *freedom* and one day *I will fly.*
> My friends say I *'m a closed book.*
> My mother doesn't want me to *become an astronaut,* yet I *still dream on.*
> If I was a book, *my cover wouldn't give away much.*
> I hope that one day *I will be able to do anything I want.*
> *Charlotte the shy*

⚠ **Trouble Spot**
She doesn't want me to …
Not: ~~She doesn't want that I …~~

b In a **biography poem**, what is said in each line is fixed, but fewer words are given, leaving a bit more room for creativity than the poem skeleton.

1 *Barack*	(first name)
2 *Charismatic, determined, powerful*	(three descriptive adjectives)
3 Who loves *his country*	Who loves …
4 Who wants *change to come*	Who wants …
5 Always *working,* never *giving up*	Always …, never …
6 Obama	(last name)

Language Help

- The poem has no/little/a great/ a powerful effect (on me).
- It's powerful/moving/bizarre/…
- When they all speak together, I …/it's …
- It made me thoughtful/…
- It made me think that …

c Of the three types of poem, the **rondo** is the most open form. It consists of eight lines. Lines 1, 4 and 7 are the same, as are lines 2 and 8. Because of the repetition, these five lines are the most important.

> 1 Life wasn't easy
> 2 When I was a young boy
> 3 I had to leave my home country
> 4 Life wasn't easy
> 5 Before I took a chance
> 6 And music and dance changed my life
> 7 Life wasn't easy
> 8 When I was a young boy

3 Writing is …

④ a Listen to four Native American teenagers present their own poem for the 11th International Youth Poetry Slam Festival in Washington, D.C. What is the poem about?

b What effect does this poem have on you?

c What do you like about it? What would you do differently when presenting your poem? Consider tempo, articulation, etc.

convey sth. communicate sth.
innocent not having done sth. wrong
antidote sth. that takes away the effects of sth. unpleasant
absolution formal statement that sb. is forgiven for what he/she has done
boundary (real or imaginary) dividing line
continuous happening or existing for a period of time without interruption
claw at sth. scratch or tear sth. with claws or fingernails

B Presenting Yourself Creatively

In this section, you will learn how to 'sell yourself' to people your age in an informal situation, such as trying to get a flat share.

1 Getting it right

Hi there,

I'm Linda. I don't like pizza, like everybody else does. I'm 16 years old. I have a sister, Pam – she's a real pain, I can tell you!! Don't get me wrong, I like her, but most of the time she's just a pain. My dad lives in London with his second wife, Anna. Anna is 26. When my dad said he was leaving us for a woman 15 years younger than him, I thought that was gross, but Anna is cool, and so is London. I love going clubbing there. To be honest I'm not really into studying, but I do love Maths, although most of my friends say Maths sucks. I had a dog once, but it died – like they sometimes do. I don't really know what else to write, so I'll sign off now. If you want to get back to me, send me an email to

a Read Linda's text and make notes on the following:

- how she expresses herself
- whether or not she has structured her text well
- who she might have written it for
- what kind of impression she gives of herself

b Now note down some information about yourself that you could use to present yourself to somebody your own age that you have not yet met. Structure your notes as well as you can. You will need them in exercise **2a**.

2 Putting together an application

SP 15 Doing a Project (p. 41)

a Imagine one of the following situations and how you would present yourself. Collect some ideas. Use the notes you made in **1b**.

- A TV station wants to produce a musical with teenage amateurs and you want to apply for an audition. You don't have to be a professional singer, dancer or actor, but you have to be able to express yourself creatively.
- You plan to go abroad for some work experience or to spend a term at a university and have found a shared flat. Your potential flatmates ask you to send them information about yourself so they can see whether or not you would fit in.

b Share your ideas with your partner and give each other feedback:
What is good? What could be improved? What could be added?

c Choose a medium, then prepare your application. Bear in mind that the medium you choose also says something about you. Here are some suggestions:

SP 11 Keeping a Portfolio (p. 36)

1 **A dossier** (folder or computer-assisted presentation) including e.g.
- a text in which you introduce yourself and photos showing you doing what you are good at or something that characterizes you,
- other texts you have written (about yourself), e.g. some poems, a rap or anything else you made up yourself,
- descriptions or photos of creative projects or performances you have taken part in.

2 **A video**
- How long should the video be? It has to be long enough to say something about you, but shouldn't bore your audience.
- Should there be other people in it apart from you?
- Should you do all the talking? Should friends/teachers/family say something about you? Should there be a 'narrator'?
- Do you need a script or music?

d In class, decide how you can best organize a presentation of the different applications.

SP 22 Giving a Presentation (p. 46)

CAN-DO STATEMENTS

		Part / Ex	✔
🎧	I can understand the main points of anecdotes, stories, acted scenes, poems or songs. (B1/3)	A / Ex 3	☐
📖	I can understand simple poems on themes that are familiar to me. (B1/3)	A / Ex 1 A / Ex 2	☐
👀	I can express and give reasons for my opinion in conversations and discussions. Furthermore, I can agree or politely disagree and make other suggestions. (B1/6)	B / Ex 2b	☐
👄	I can describe myself and my interests in a short, interesting but creative presentation.	B / Ex 2c	☐
✍	I can write a short simple creative text about myself and my interests. (B1/2)	B / Ex 2c	☐

1 Listening comprehension: multiple matching

You are going to listen to a recording about a Vietnamese immigrant family in the USA and how they learned to communicate through songs. While listening, match the beginnings of the sentences (1–6) with the sentence endings (A–I). There are two more sentence endings than you need. Write your answers in the spaces provided. The first one (0) has been done for you.

B Multiple Matching (p. 72)

0   At the uncle's birthday party …
1   The speaker's family has difficulty with …
2   The uncle was sad because …
3   The family discovered that …
4   The family showed their sympathy with the cousin by …
5   An aunt finished the uncle's song when …
6   The speaker sang a song about …

A   … each guest had to sing a karaoke song.
B   … everyone cried a lot.
C   … he was too upset to continue.
D   … helping a friend in difficulties.
E   … his marriage had come to an end.
F   … joining in the refrain of 'Delilah'.
G   … reciting a poem about love.
H   … talking openly about emotions.
I   … they could express their emotions through singing.

0	1	2	3	4	5	6
A	___	___	___	___	___	___

2 Language in Use: editing

You are going to read a text about social media. In most lines of the text there is a word that shows not to be true. Write that word in the space provided. Indicate the correct lines with a tick (✔). There are two examples (0, 00) at the beginning.

L Editing (p. 79)

What is meant by 'social media'?		
Social media are a relatively new phenomenon, one which did emerged with the	*did*	0
development of the interactive World Wide Web and other communication	✔	00
technologies such as mobile phones. Earlier forms of communication over in the	___	1
internet, such as email, are not truly social media because really they are only	___	2
open to the sender and the recipient – however nobody else can join the	___	3
conversation.	___	4
There are many different forms of the social media, such as internet forums, blogs,	___	5
wikis, social networks, podcasts, websites for sharing of photos or videos, and	___	6
virtual game worlds. Three of the biggest, most successful examples so far are	___	7
Facebook, with 900 million active users, Wikipedia, an online encyclopedia which	___	8
containing over 3.5 million articles, all created and edited by it's its own readers,	___	9
and World of Warcraft, a fantasy game with around 11 million players.	___	10
What all forms of social media have in common together is the idea that ordinary	___	11
individuals can create their own self online material, rather than waiting for	___	12
companies to create material for them. Furthermore too, they can easily set up	___	13
online communities to share this material. Social media have become a way to	___	14
of express our identity, build relationships, have conversations and share ideas.	___	15

3 Speaking: paired activity

You have decided to organise a money-raising event for a charity. There will be a sponsored 20-kilometre walk, followed by a barbecue party at your local sports club. You want to persuade as many people as possible to take part.

Discuss the following means of communication and the role they could play to advertise the event:

- Facebook
- Twitter
- WhatsApp
- email
- website

At the end of your discussion, try to come to an agreement on which three of them are likely to attract the most people to take part.

TF N Paired Activity (p. 80)

charity organization that works to help other people

4 Writing: blog entry

Write a blog entry about how you use digital media (Internet, email, text messages, social networking websites, etc.) during a normal day.

- Describe the media you use and how often you use them.
- Explain how your life would be different if you didn't have these digital media.
- Speculate on whether it would be better or worse without them.

Write about 150 words.

TT 3 Blog Entry (p. 63)

5 Language in Use: word formation

Read this text about young people and social networking sites. Some words are missing from the text. Use the words in brackets to form a word that fits in the gaps (1–12). Write your answers in the spaces provided. The first one (0) has been done for you.

TF I Word Formation (p. 77)

When young people use the internet and (0) ___ (society) media, they should follow a few simple rules. First of all, they should keep their passwords private (even from their friends). Seondly, they should use the (1) ___ (private) tools available on social networking sites to protect their (2) ___ (person) information. These settings give a (3) ___ (use) the ability to control who they share content with, for example photos can be made visible only to Friends or to the Public.

Some young people often don't understand the (4) ___ (important) of thinking before they post something online. Some people exploit the (5) ___ (anonymous) that some online communities offer, but they should remember that this is not an excuse for bad or anti-social (6) ___ (behave). Sometimes online messages can be (7) ___ (understand) and what may start out as a harmless joke for one person, can turn out to be extremely (8) ___ (embarrass) or hurtful for another individual. They should always make sure that they ask permission from other people before (9) ___ (post) pictures of them online.

Finally, young people should know how to report abusive comments or (10) ___ (legal) activity on social networking sites. If young people have concerns about (11) ___ (cyberbully) then they should speak to a trusted adult as well as saving the evidence, and even use the tools available to block other users. Although there is a lot of (12) ___ (compete) among young people to be active in social networks, following these simple rules can make sure they are a safe place for young people to spend their time.

0	*social*
1	
2	
3	
4	
5	
6	
7	
8	
9	
10	
11	
12	

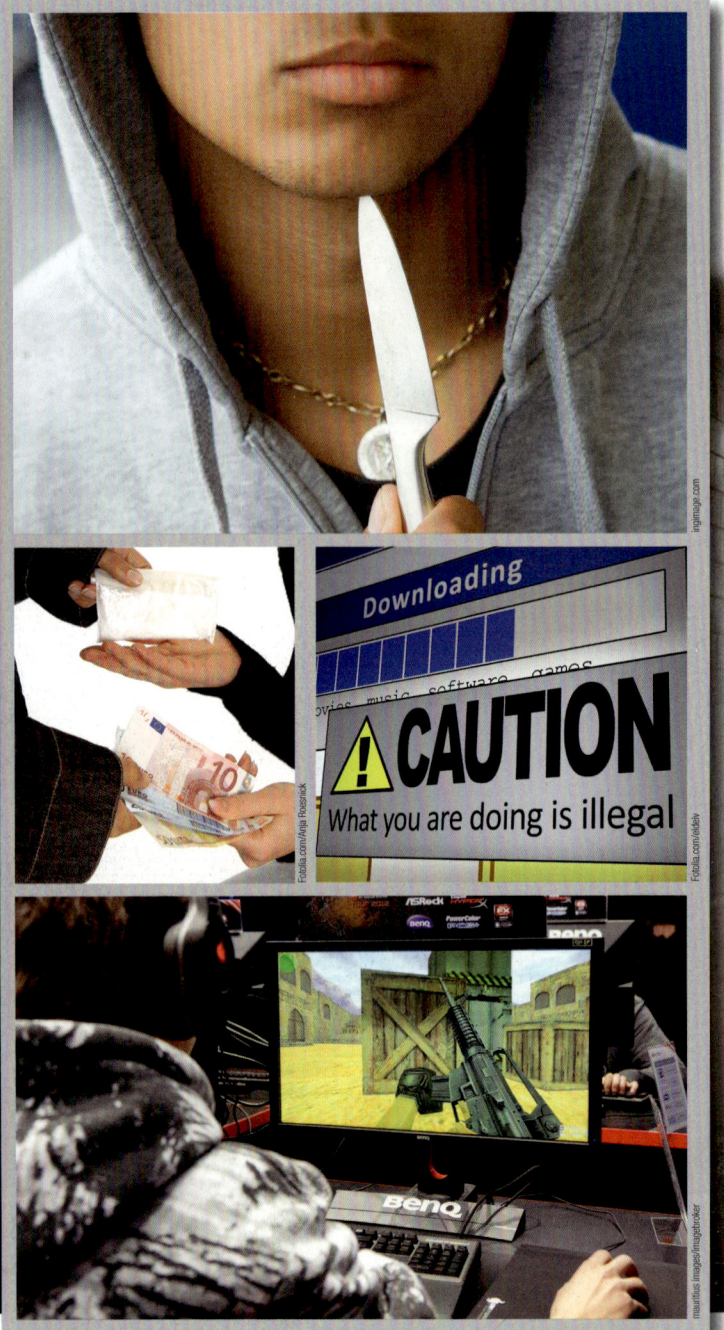

Language Help

- **drug dealing** selling drugs
- **gang** illegal group
- **internet piracy** copying files illegally
- **video game** game played on a computer etc.
- **weapon** sth. used to hurt sb.

LP 1 Modal Verbs (p. 5)

SP 12 Working with Pictures (p. 38)

1 Working with photos

Work in groups of five. Each person chooses a photo and makes notes:

a How could the picture relate to this topic's themes of 'violence' and 'crime'?
Note down as many connections as you can.

_____

_____

_____

b Look through the topic and match the photo with one or more relevant texts. One photo does not match any of the texts.

_____

c Share your ideas with your group.

In this topic you will learn about …

- crime statistics: perceptions and reality (WiC)
- violence in TV news, games and literature (Unit 4)
- crime and prevention (Unit 5)
- bullying and conformism (Unit 6)

Despite the headlines, schools are safer than they used to be
http://www.upi.com, March 4, 2012

LA gangs take over UK streets
The Sun, April 15, 2010

Riots blamed on poor parenting
The Sun, March 27, 2012

Pirates cost the music industry £1 billion
http://www.mirror.co.uk, December 17, 2011

Recorded crime falls by 12%
The Guardian, April 24, 2008

School taken over by street gangs
The Mail Online, April 5, 2012

Britain tops European crime league
The Telegraph, February 6, 2007

record sth. to write sth. down and store it for later use
take sth. over take control of sth.
gang group of people who come together to fight others etc.
league group of people/teams/countries combined for a particular purpose
riot violent protest by a crowd of people
migrant ['maɪɡrənt] person who moves from one area or country to another, especially in order to find work

Fotolia.com/lassedesignen

2 Working with news headlines

a Read the headlines. Which seem to be about bad news and which about good news? Are any of them neutral?

b Which of the headlines make you want to read the story? Choose two headlines and tell your partner why you chose them.

3 Mind mapping

Start a mind map on the subject of 'violence and crime'. Add new concepts as you work through this topic.

 1 Mind Mapping (p. 30)

Language Help

- The headline caught my eye because …
- I expect it's a story about …
- It would be interesting to know more about …
- The headline suggests that …
- When I read it, I wondered if …

Crime – Fiction and Reality

There seems to be a growing gap between public perceptions of crime and the reality. Surveys from across the world show that, in most developed countries, crime of most types is falling steadily.

However, other research shows that in those same countries, fear of crime is rising. To take the UK as an example: in the 15 year period from 1995 to 2010, the crime rate fell by nearly 50%. That dramatic fall has to be a good reason to be less worried about crime. Yet in 2010, 66% of people still thought that crime nationally was increasing.

Perhaps the media are to blame for our fear of crime. Sensational headlines about horrific crimes sell newspapers, increase TV ratings and earn internet clicks. To put it simply: crime pays – if you're in the media business.

The fear of crime changes our behaviour and may even affect our health. Fearful of being attacked on the streets, more and more people stay indoors, avoid public spaces and worry about their children's safety – unless they are sitting safely in front of the TV set or computer screen. As a result, we get less exercise and have less social interaction.

Unfortunately, social isolation and lack of exercise are real killers in our society. The suicide rate* in Austria is nearly 50 times the murder rate*, and an inactive lifestyle puts us at risk of many diseases.

The kind of crime that most people are worried about is violent crime, yet the probability of being hurt or killed in an act of violence is low. In 40% of 'violent' crime nobody is actually injured and in two-thirds of incidents the injury is not serious enough to require any medical treatment. Murder is one of the least common types of violent crime.

Perhaps we feel that society is growing less safe because we are exposed to a lot of fictional aggression through our entertainment preferences: video games involve increasingly explicit violence – and gameplay is becoming more immersive and realistic as computer technology improves. Detective series on TV are no longer content to concentrate on police officers and criminals – they also show pathologists cutting open dead bodies.

Nevertheless, we shouldn't confuse fiction with reality: in our society, there has never been a safer time to be alive.

23.8 per 100,000 people (WHO)

0.51 per 100,000 people (Eurostat)

1   Word power: antonyms

One way to build your word power is by learning pairs of antonyms or opposites. Find opposites of these words from the text. Use your (online) dictionary if you need to.
Be careful: the correct antonym will sometimes depend on the context in which a word is used. There may also be more than one possible solution.

 24 Increase Your Word Power Online (p. 18)

 8 Using a Dictionary (p. 34)

1   fiction headline   _reality_
2   fall (v) (line 2)   _____
3   steadily (line 3)   _____
4   increase (v) (line 11)   _____
5   sensational (line 13)   _____
6   fearful of (line 16)   _____
7   avoid (line 17)   _____
8   public (line 17)   _____

9 safety (line 18) _____
10 safely (line 18) _____
11 result (line 19) _____
12 inactive (line 21) _____
13 violent (line 23) _____
14 serious (line 25) _____
15 improve (line 30) _____

2 Language in Use: editing

You are going to read a text giving advice to US tourists in Austria. In most lines of the text there is an unnecessary word. Write the unnecessary word in the space provided after each line. Some lines are correct. Indicate these lines with a tick (✔). There are two examples at the beginning.

 **TF** L Editing (p. 79)

Advice for U.S. travelers in Austria

Austria has one of the lowest crime rates in Europe, and violent crime is rare.	✔	0
However, crimes which involving theft of personal property occur. Most crimes	*which*	00
involving U.S. citizens are crimes of opportunity such as theft of the personal	___	1
belongings.	___	2
The U.S. Embassy receives reports of theft on public transportation lines,	___	3
especially just on the lines going into and out from the city center. Keep your	___	4
personal belongings somewhere being safe and always take precautions while	___	5
you are on public transportation and in public places such as example cafés	___	6
and tourist areas.	___	7
Don't buy counterfeit and pirated goods, when even if they are widely	___	8
available. Not only is it illegal to bring these goods back into the United States,	___	9
by buying them you may also be breaking local law too.	___	10
Foreigners breaking Austrian laws, even by mistake, may be arrested and	___	11
deported or put in the prison. The penalties for using or dealing illegal	___	12
drugs in Austria are severe, so anyone who caught with illegal drugs can	___	13
had expect a long prison sentence.	___	14

take precautions do sth. to avoid future problems

Adapted from: http://travel.state.gov

3 Analysing a chart · Key: 250

Describe and analyse the chart in 100–120 words.

SP 13 Working With Charts and Graphs (p. 39)

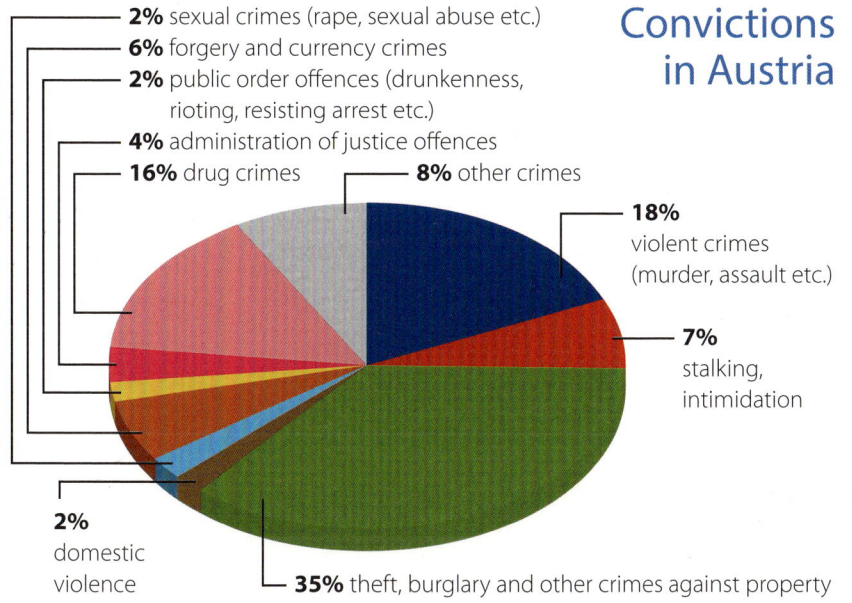

2% sexual crimes (rape, sexual abuse etc.)
6% forgery and currency crimes
2% public order offences (drunkenness, rioting, resisting arrest etc.)
4% administration of justice offences
16% drug crimes
8% other crimes

Convictions in Austria

18% violent crimes (murder, assault etc.)

7% stalking, intimidation

2% domestic violence

35% theft, burglary and other crimes against property

Data from: Statistik Austria, Verurteilungsstatistik 2015

Language Help

- The chart is derived from …
- Relative to … we can see that …
- … per cent of crimes concern …
- … is a major/minor factor in the overall crime figures.
- The commonest types of crime are …
- … helps to put … in perspective.
- … fears of … are justified/ unjustified.

UNIT 4   Violence in Popular Culture

A If It Bleeds, It Leads

Violent crime has been declining in the USA for 20 years, yet the single most-reported topic on TV news is crime, particularly stories about murders, shootings, and other violence. In this essay extract, journalism student Anuradha Kher comments on this situation.

SP 7 Paraphrasing (p. 33)

1 Preparing to read

a Look at the photos above. What do you think the saying 'If it bleeds, it leads' means? Paraphrase it in a sentence.

_____

_____

b Compare sentences with your partner. Do you agree on the meaning?

TF E Multiple Matching (p. 73)

2 Reading comprehension: multiple matching

Read the text on page 35, then choose the best heading (A–I) for each section (0–6). There are two extra headings that you should not use. The first one has been done for you.

A A diet of sex and violence
B A failed experiment
C An average TV news report
D Disappointed with news reporting
E Driven by viewers' demands

F Living in fear of crime
G Statistics prove the point
H The viewers want to know
I Unsuitable for younger viewers

0	1	2	3	4	5	6
C	____	____	____	____	____	____

SP 30 Reading Non-Fiction (p. 50)

SP 28 Scanning (p. 50)

3 Reading for detail

1 What topics does the newscast on News Three cover?
2 How does the anchor encourage viewers to keep watching when the programme breaks for commercials?
3 What did Matthew Kerbel try to show in his book?
4 How did the findings of Rocky Mountain Media Watch support Kerbel's conclusions?
5 In what way did Mediascope contradict Kerbel's conclusions?
6 What happened to the Chicago TV channel when it stopped sensationalizing the news? *(2 things)*
7 Why didn't this surprise George Knapp? *(3 reasons)*

SP 1 Mind Mapping (p. 30)

4 Working with words: mind map

Add a new branch 'Crime in the news' to your mind map (see page 31)

0 *An average TV news report*

A typical evening newscast on local television begins like this: "Hi, I am XX. Next on News Three: Angry parents go searching for answers after two students were accused of raping another in a South Philadelphia classroom and the man who killed a woman and taped her final moments apologizes to her family."

Then the newscast breaks for commercials. Anchor: "Well, later in the broadcast, scary stories about breast implants haven't stopped the rush to get them. We'll have a special report. And it can happen at any time, without warning. We'll tell you what it is."

1 _____

Switch on local television news in any part of the country, and one is most likely to hear some version of this example. Crime, violence and sex stories almost always take the lead in any news, especially on local news. There is no debate about whether a story that bleeds should lead in a local evening newscast. "Without a doubt, that is the mantra in local TV newsrooms across America," says Matthew Kerbel, media watcher and author of the book If It Bleeds, It Leads, in which he uses footage of local news from all over the US to prove the point in his title.

2 _____

Kerbel, who was a news writer for local television in New York, left disillusioned with the way news was being sensationalized. "'If it bleeds, it leads' is a term that was and is openly used by editors and reporters in television," he says.

3 _____

Kerbel's observation is also proved in studies about local television. For example, in the late 1990s, a Denver-based media monitoring group Rocky Mountain Media Watch analyzed tapes of local evening news programs that aired on 100 television stations in 35 states. Among other things, this is what they found:

A full 30% of the news was devoted to crime.
- Coverage of government came in a distant second at 11%.
- Environmental stories accounted for 2% of the local TV news time.
- Poverty received 1.8% of air time.
- Unions and labor overall got 1.6%.
- Civil rights netted 0.9%

4 _____

But contrary to Kerbel's point, some studies suggest that crime reporting has risen dramatically in newsrooms across America not because TV station executives intentionally sensationalize news but because the audience demands it. According to a report by Mediascope, a non-profit media research and policy organization: "Market research suggests that stories of crime and violence increase newscasts' ratings." This finding drives news directors to deliver crime-related stories to their audiences.

5 _____

In 2001, a struggling Chicago news channel tried to reverse its fortunes by switching its late news program to basic, no-frills, old-fashioned journalism in place of the usual crime-and-mayhem, disaster and scary health reports that fill almost every local newscast in the country. Within months, the news program's rating had sunk to a much lower level than that of the format it had replaced. After only nine months, the show was replaced with a newscast like most others on the country's commercial television stations.

6 _____

"Experiments like these have always bombed," says George Knapp, Chief Reporter at KLAS, a local TV station in Las Vegas. "Unfortunately, news is not always cheery, and there is death and violence around us every day, and yes, people want to know about it."

Abridged from: Anuradha Kher: On local television, if it bleeds it leads. In: http://mediacrit.wetpaint.com, November 5, 2007

---

newscast news show
accuse sb. of sth. claim that sb. has done sth. (wrong or illegal)
rape sb. force sb. to have sex
anchor studio presenter in a news show
breast implant sth. put into a woman's breasts to make them bigger
rush when a lot of people want to do sth. quickly
bleed lose blood
take the lead/lead be the first, most important story
mantra phrase that is constantly repeated
footage filmed material
monitor watch closely
air be shown on TV
be devoted to sth. be about sth.
coverage of sth. news about sth.
account for X% of sth. take X% of sth.
air time how long sth. is on TV/radio
union organization to protect workers' rights
labor workers in general
rating how many people watch a show
no-frills uncomplicated
mayhem chaos
bomb (infml) fail
cheery optimistic, happy

⚠ **Trouble Spot**
program (AE) = Sendung
channel = Programm

 22 Giving a Presentation (p. 46)

5 Speaking: group discussion

Work in groups of four or five students. Each person writes down a brief description in English of a news item he/she remembers from the last seven days.

One student collects all of the notes and reads them out. Discuss: can you see any patterns about the sort of news that your group finds interesting or memorable?

6 EXTRA Research, analysis and presentation

Austria has one of the lowest crime rates in the world, so you would expect much less violence on TV news in Austria than in the USA. Is that really the case?

Work in groups. Each group member analyzes one evening's newscasts on Austrian TV like in section 3 of the text. What does your analysis show? Does the saying 'If it bleeds, it leads?' apply to Austrian news reporting too?

Present the results of your analysis as graphs or pie charts. Report back to the class what you found out.

B How Do Violent Video Games Affect Us?  Key: 606

Do violent video games make people more violent? You are going to listen to a report on this question by US radio station NPR on its Morning Edition news show.

1 Preparing to listen
Match the meanings (a–l) to the words (1–12).

1	response	a	action or feeling produced in answer to sth.
2	brain	b	do, say or feel sth. in answer to sth.
3	throat	c	feeling sorry when sb. is unhappy or hurt
4	respond	d	injury, hurt or damage
5	mean (adj.)	e	make sb. less sensitive
6	desensitize	f	organ of the body inside the head that controls thought and feeling
7	behaviour	g	tube inside the neck through which food and air are taken into the body
8	trivial	h	unable to feel
9	objectionable	i	unimportant
10	harm (n)	j	unkind
11	compassion	k	unpleasant, making people angry
12	numb	l	what sb. does

6

2 Listening for gist

Listen to the broadcast. Where do these people stand on the question 'Violent games – harmful or not? 'Write a tick (✔) in the correct column.

SP 19 Listening for Gist (p. 45)

	'Very harmful'	'Slightly/Not harmful'	Neutral/No opinion
Shankar Vedantam			
Brad Bushman			
Chris Ferguson			

3 Listening comprehension: sentence completion (short answers)

Now listen again and complete the sentences using a maximum of four words. Write your answers in the spaces provided. The first one (0) has been done for you.

TF C Short Answers (p. 72)

0	Most experiments on the effects of video game violence use two ___.	*groups of students*
1	One group plays a violent game and the other group ___.	
2	Dr Bushman measured his subjects' emotional responses by ___.	
3	In this first test, he found that the group who had played violent games ___.	
4	In this second test, he found that the group who had played violent games were ___.	
5	However, Dr Ferguson says that the changes caused by these experiments are ___.	
6	He thinks it is wrong to mix up video games and ___.	
7	Both scientists ___ in their families.	

4 Classroom discussion

What is your opinion:

SP 23 Taking Part in a Classroom Discussion (p. 47)

- Are violent video games harmful or not?
- Are there types of violence which are never acceptable in a game?
- Is the PEGI ratings system (see text "Video game ratings" on page 38) useful and effective?

Before you start, make notes to back up your opinion.

_____

_____

_____

_____

_____

Choose a discussion leader. He/She will make sure that everyone gets a chance to express an opinion. The rules: no-one can speak more than **twice** until **everyone** has spoken **once**.

informed based on facts
suitable of the right kind for the situation
appropriate of the right kind for the situation
context situation
innuendo suggesting sth. without actually saying or showing it
gambling winning and losing money by guessing what will happen
explicit shown clearly
defenceless not able to protect oneself

Video game ratings

Pan European Game Information (PEGI) is a European video game content rating system established to help European consumers make informed decisions on buying computer games with logos on games boxes.

PEGI has five age categories.

3: Suitable for ages 3 and older. May contain mild violence in an appropriate context for younger children, but no bad language is allowed.

7: Suitable for ages 7 and older. May contain mild, cartoon-style violence, sports, or elements that can be frightening to younger children.

12: Suitable for ages 12 and older. May contain violence in a fantasy setting, mild bad language, mild sexual references or innuendo, or gambling (but never for real money).

16: Suitable for ages 16 and older. May contain explicit violence, sexual references or content, bad language, gambling, or drug use.

18: Suitable for ages 18 and older. May contain graphic violence, including 'violence towards defenceless people' and 'multiple, motiveless killing', strong sexual content, vulgar language, gambling (never for real money), drug use, or discrimination.

http://en.wikipedia.org/wiki/Pan_European_Game_Information unter der Lizenz CC-BY-SA
http://creativecommons.org/licenses/by-sa/3.0/deed.de

SP 1 Mind Mapping (p. 30)

5 Working with words: mind map

Add a new sub-branch 'Video games' to the branch 'Violence' in your mind map (see page 31).

SP 34 Structuring a Text (p. 52)

TT 2 Formal Email (p. 60)

6 Writing: formal email

A group Society Against Violent and Aggressive Games in Europe (SAVAGE) wants the European Parliament to introduce a new, strict law to ban all violent video games (PEGI 12 and 18 ratings) for young people under 18 in all EU countries.

You like to play video games, so you decide to write an email to the European Parliament to give your opinion about this suggestion. In your email, you should:

- explain why you are writing
- analyze the effect of violent video games on players
- state whether a ban on violent games will be effective in your opinion

Write around 250 words.

C The Hunger Games

picturedesk.com/Murray Close/Everett Collection

The Hunger Games is a novel for young adults. It is set in a future where the USA no longer exists and the Capitol rules North America, now the country of Panem. Each year, the Capitol selects a boy and girl aged 12–18 from the 12 Districts to fight to the death on live television in the Games. The heroine, 16-year-old Katniss Everdeen, volunteers to take the place of her younger sister Primrose (Prim) as a competitor ('tribute') in the latest Games.

This first book in the Hunger Games trilogy has received several awards but has been frequently criticized for being too violent and sexually explicit for its age group. In 2012 it was made into a film.

In the following extract on page 39f, Katniss' 12-year-old ally and friend Rue is killed by another competitor.

1 Preparing to read

a Have you seen the film or read the book?

b If you have: find someone in the class who hasn't, and tell him/her about it. Did you like it?
If you haven't: find someone in the class who can tell you about it.

2 Reading for detail
Read the text carefully and answer these questions.

1 What has happened just before this extract (two events)?
2 Why does Katniss find it difficult to sing for Rue?
3 What do we learn about Katniss' family?
4 Why does Katniss leave the spear in Rue's body?
5 When Katniss says 'They'll have to show it,' who are 'they' and what will they have to show?

3 Interpreting the text
Answer two of the questions below in 50–80 words each.

1 Describe Katniss' actions in this extract. What aspects of her character do they show?
2 Explain in your own words what Katniss is trying to do by decorating Rue's body with flowers.
3 Comment on the use of the first person singular ('I') and the simple present tense in the extract: what effects does this use of language have?
4 What elements of this extract would be difficult to show in a film? What solutions can you think of?

The boy from District 1 dies before he can pull out the spear. My arrow drives deeply in to the centre of his neck. He falls to his knees and halves the brief remainder of his life by yanking out the arrow and drowning in his own blood. I'm reloaded, shifting my aim from side to side, while I shout at Rue, "Are there more? Are there more?"

She has to say no several times before I hear it.

Rue has rolled to her side, her body curved in and around the spear. I shove the boy away from her and pull out my knife, freeing her from the net. One look at the wound and I know it's far beyond my capacity to heal. Beyond anyone's, probably. The spearhead is buried up to the shaft in her stomach. I crouch before her, staring helplessly at the embedded weapon. There's no point in comforting words, in telling her she'll be all right. She's no fool. Her hand reaches out and I clutch it like a lifeline. As if it's me who's dying instead of Rue.

"You blew up the food?" she whispers.

"Every last bit," I say.

"You have to win," she says.

"I'm going to. Going to win for both of us now," I promise. I hear a cannon and look up. It must be for the boy from District 1.

"Don't go." Rue tightens her grip on my hand.

"Course not. Staying right here," I say. I move in closer to her, pulling her head on to my lap. I gently brush the dark, thick hair back behind her ear.

"Sing," she says, but I barely catch the word.

Sing? I think. Sing what? I do know a few songs. Believe it or not, there was once music in my house, too. Music I helped make. My father pulled me in with that remarkable voice – but I haven't sung much since he died. Except when Prim is very sick. Then I sing her the same songs she liked as a baby. Sing. My throat is tight with tears, hoarse from smoke and fatigue. But if this is Prim's, I mean, Rue's last request, I have to at least try. The song that comes to me is a simple

spear [BE: spɪəʳ] weapon with a sharp metal point on a long stick
arrow thin stick with a sharp point that is shot from a bow
remainder rest
yank pull violently
drown die because of water/blood in one's lungs
shove push roughly
wound [wuːnd] injury, hole in sb's skin
heal make healthy again
shaft wooden handle of a spear
clutch hold tightly
lap flat area between a person's stomach and knees when sitting
remarkable very unusual (esp. unusually good)

▶▶▶

lullaby, one we sing fretful, hungry babies to sleep with. It's old, very old I think. Made up long ago in our hills. What my music teacher calls Sa mountain air. But the words are easy and soothing, promising tomorrow will be more hopeful than this awful piece of time we call today.

I give a small cough, swallow hard, and begin:
> Deep in the meadow, under the willow
> A bed of grass, a soft green pillow
> Lay down your head, and close your sleepy eyes
> And when again they open, the sun will rise.
> [...]

For a moment, I sit there, watching my tears drip down on her face. Rue's cannon fires. I lean forward and press my lips against her temple. Slowly, as if not to wake her, I lay her head back on the ground and release her hand.

They'll want me to clear out now. So they can collect the bodies. And there's nothing to stay for. I roll the boy from District 1 on to his face and take his pack, retrieve the arrow that ended his life. I cut Rue's pack from her back as well, knowing she'd want me to have it, but leave the spear in her stomach. Weapons in bodies will be transported to the hovercraft. I've no use for a spear, so the sooner it's gone from the arena the better.

I can't stop looking at Rue, smaller than ever, a baby animal curled up in a nest of netting. I can't bring myself to leave her like this. Past harm, but seeming utterly defenceless. To hate the boy from District 1, who also appears so vulnerable in death, seems inadequate. It's the Capitol I hate, for doing this to all of us.

Gale's voice is in my head. His ravings against the Capitol no longer pointless, no longer to be ignored. Rue's death has forced me to confront my own fury against the cruelty, the injustice they inflict upon us. But here, even more strongly than at home, I feel my impotence. There's no way to take revenge on the Capitol. Is there?

Then I remember Peeta's words on the roof. "Only I keep wishing I could think of a way to … to show the Capitol they don't own me. That I'm more than just a piece in their Games." And for the first time, I understand what he means.

I want to do something, right here, right now, to shame them, to make them accountable, to show the Capitol that whatever they do or force us to do there is a part of every tribute they can't own. That Rue was more than a piece in their Games. And so am I.

A few steps back into the woods grows a bank of wild flowers. Perhaps they are really weeds of some sort, but they have blossoms in beautiful shades of violet and yellow and white. I gather up an armful and come back to Rue's side. Slowly, one stem at a time, I decorate her body in the flowers. Covering the ugly wound. Wreathing her face. Weaving her hair with bright colours.

They'll have to show it. Or, even if they choose to turn the cameras elsewhere at this moment, they'll have to bring them back when they collect the bodies and everyone will see her then and know I did it. I step back and take a last look at Rue. She could really be asleep in that meadow after all.

"Bye, Rue," I whisper. I press the three middle fingers of my left hand against my lips and hold them out in her direction. Then I walk away without looking back.

Suzanne Collins: The Hunger Games. Scholastic 2008, S. 168ff. © Suzanne Collins

---

hoarse hurting when one speaks
fatigue being tired
fretful unable to rest
soothing making one feel calm, taking away pain
willow type of tree
pillow what one puts under one's head in bed
temple top part of the face
retrieve take back
hovercraft vehicle that floats just above the ground
vulnerable easy to hurt
ravings mad speech
cruelty hurting someone unnecessarily
impotence lack of power
take revenge on sb. for sth. do sth. bad to sb. because of sth. bad they did to you
accountable having to take responsibility for one's actions
weed plant that grows where it shouldn't
blossom flower

4 Working with words: meaning from context

SP 6 Dealing with Words You Don't Know (p. 33)

a Find these words in the text. Use the context to work out what they mean.

1 halve (l. 2) _____
2 crouch (v) (l. 9) _____
3 lullaby (l. 26) _____
4 meadow (l. 31) _____

5 fury (l. 49) _____
6 revenge (l. 51) _____
7 shame (v) (l. 55) _____
8 wreath (v) (l. 61) _____

b Compare answers in a group. The group then reads its answers to the class.

5 Writing: blog comment

TT 3 Blog Entry (p. 63)

You read this extract from a review on the youngbookcritics.com website.

> The Hunger Games is a great book and I loved reading it. But I'm 17 and I wouldn't want my little sister to read it. She's only 12 and this book is waaaay too violent for kids that age!
>
> *Jodie17*

You decide to post a comment on the review, based on the extract you have just read. In your blog comment you should …

- describe the level of violence in the extract
- explain the relevance of violence for the plot
- state your opinion on whether the book is suitable for young teenage readers

Write about 200 words.

CAN-DO STATEMENTS

		Part / Ex	✔
👂	I can understand the main points in interviews, reports and presentations. (B1/2)	B / Ex 2, B / Ex 3	☐
	I can understand, fundamentally, native speakers when they speak clearly and directly about subjects familiar to me and use standard language. (B1/4)	B / Ex 2, B / Ex 3	☐
📖	I can get the essential information from simple newspaper and magazine articles that are clearly structured. (B1/1)	A / Ex 3	☐
	I can understand longer, relatively simple literary texts on themes that are familiar to me (e.g. modern popular literature). (B1/3)	C / Ex 2, C / Ex 3	☐
	I can recognize the essential conclusions in clearly structured argumentative texts. (B1/4)	A / Ex 2	☐
	I can find information that I need to solve a specific task in various longer texts or text sections. (B1/8)	C / Ex 2	☐
👀	I can begin, maintain and end a conversation about subjects familiar to me. (B1/1)	A / Ex 6	☐
	I can express and give reasons for my opinion in conversations and discussions. Furthermore, I can agree or politely disagree and make other suggestions. (B1/6)	B / Ex 4	☐
👄	I can give a prepared straightforward presentation, which can be followed easily and which I can make interesting for my listeners. (B1/3)	A / Ex 7	☐
	I can describe and interpret graphs in simple, connected sentences. (B1/8)	A / Ex 7	☐
✍️	I can write simple stories, essays and creative texts. (B1/2)	C / Ex 5	☐
	I can describe my personal impression of stories and books, films and plays. (B1/3)	C / Ex 5	☐
	I can write simple, private correspondence, e.g. letters and emails. (B1/5)	B / Ex 6	☐

UNIT 5   Crime and Prevention  **Key: 288**

A Graffiti – Vandalism or Art?

Graffiti is a common sight in towns and cities around the world. Is it a trivial problem or a serious crime – or is it art? Opinions are divided.

1 Reading: taking notes
With a partner, you will read and work on an essay about graffiti.
Partner B: look at the page provided by your teacher
Partner A: Read the essay below about graffiti in Los Angeles, USA.
Take notes on the following aspects:
- What the authorities are doing
- Negative effects of graffiti on the community
- Reasons not to prosecute graffiti sprayers
- Positive potential of graffiti
- Ways to reduce the problem of illegal graffiti

Vandalism or Art? Debate over graffiti arises as an LA tagging crew is busted

Nineteen members of the notorious group known as BDS or "Big Dog's Crew" were arrested on Wednesday, bringing an end to a six-month investigation. The group was named as one of the crews causing major damage to MTA (Metropolitan Transportation Authority) property throughout Los Angeles County in July.

bust sb. (AE infml) arrest *(see below)*
notorious well known for doing bad things
crew *(infml)* gang
arrest sb. take sb. prisoner with the authority of the law
violation here: breaking
adamant unwilling to change one's mind
gravity seriousness
victim sb. who is harmed by a crime
juvenile person under 18
resources things like money, time, labour which are available to do sth.
recruit employ
white collar *(adj)* related to people who work in offices
tagger person who writes his/her initials or pseudonym everywhere
outlet way of expressing one's feelings
beneficial having a good effect
beautification making sth. beautiful
promote encourage
corporate of large companies
arguably it could be argued
detrimental harmful

Although graffiti is not a violent crime, it is a clear violation of the law, and the LAPD is adamant about the gravity of these acts. Sgt. Chris Meadows of the Sheriff's Transit Services Bureau stated. "Graffiti vandalism is not a victimless crime. It brings fear to the community and someone, usually taxpayers, has to pay to clean it up. We take it very seriously."

Of the individuals arrested, four were juveniles; all of the suspects were arrested on suspicion of vandalism and participating in a criminal street gang. It is estimated that over the past few years there have been over 500 acts of vandalism, costing approximately $200,000 to clean and repair.

While these are surprisingly high numbers, many argue that too many of the LAPD's resources are wasted on these crimes. The arrests on Tuesday required involvement from over 200 officers. In addition, 11 agencies and separate police departments were recruited to assist in the bust, while white collar crimes costing taxpayers and governments far more than $200,000 were going unnoticed.

Others argue that taggers are not criminals, but artists who simply lack the proper outlet to express what could be a beneficial beautification to the Los Angeles landscape. Some believe that graffiti itself is not vandalism, but art which makes the city much more visually interesting. A possible solution is for the County to employ some of the tagging crews for public arts projects, using their talents for good, so that they would not need to vandalize property.

Providing legal outlets for street artists, perhaps even promoting relationships between tagging crews and companies seeking artists, would free up police to focus on violent crimes, and corporate crimes which arguably are much more detrimental to society. But, perhaps taggers would continue to commit crime, regardless of their involvement in legal art ... the debate will rage on.

Matthew Harang: Vandalism or Art? Debate over graffiti arises as an LA tagging crew is busted.
In: http://www.thepolicytree.com/

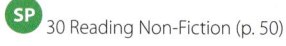 30 Reading Non-Fiction (p. 50)

2 Collaborative mind map

a Tell your partner the main points you found out from your text.

b Work with your partner to construct a mind map on 'graffiti', using information from both of the texts. Start like this:

SP 1 Mind Mapping (p. 30)

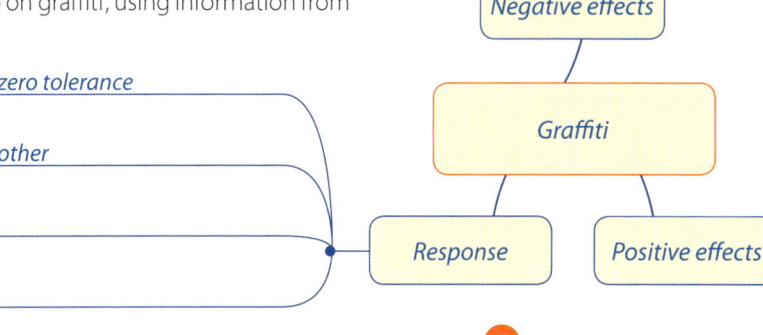

zero tolerance

other

Negative effects

Graffiti

Response

Positive effects

3 Speaking: individual long turn
- Compare the pictures.
- Evaluate the graffiti situation in your area.
- Suggest ways to reduce illegal graffiti.

TF M Individual Long Turn (p. 80)

Fotolia.com/bighorn

Fotolia.com/pics

4 Language in Use: word formation
You are going to read a text about the street artist Banksy. Some words are missing from the text. Use the words in brackets to form a word that fits in the gap (0–9). Write your answers in the spaces provided at the end of the text. The first one (0) has been done for you.

TF I Word Formation (p. 77)

Banksy

The (0) ___ **(argue)** whether graffiti sprayers are (1) ___ **(vandalism)** or artists is full of (2) ___ **(contradict)**. Nowhere are these clearer than in public attitudes to the (3) ___ **(succeed)** but anonymous street artist 'Banksy'.

Banksy is (4) ___ **(fame)** for his images which are displayed on public surfaces such as tube station walls. Art galleries have held exhibitions of his work. If you were (5) ___ **(luck)** enough to have a Banksy image on the wall of your house, you could make a lot of money selling photos of it.

Yet 'Banksy' is a pseudonym and the artist's (6) ___ **(identify)** is a secret. If his real name were known, he might be arrested for his criminal – or (7) ___ **(art)** – activities.

Just how good is Banksy? Some say that he is very (8) ___ **(talent)**, but others (9) ___ **(critic)** him because he copies the work of other artists or because his technique, stencilling, is 'cheating' and not 'proper' graffiti.

IF GRAFFITI CHANGED ANYTHING IT WOULD BE ILLEGAL

Alamy/M.J.S.

stencilling spraying paint onto a surface through a hole in a sheet of paper

0	*argument*	
1	_____	5 _____
2	_____	6 _____
3	_____	7 _____
4	_____	8 _____
		9 _____

⚠ **Trouble Spot**
lucky = glücklich (wenn man Glück gehabt hat)
happy = glücklich (fröhlich)

B Knife Crime Campaign

Great Britain has a problem with knife crime: many young people carry knives, and deaths from knife wounds are increasing. Advertising campaigns have been launched in response.

1 Preparing to listen

a Match the meanings (a–i) to the expressions (1–9).

1 crack down on sth.	a bad treatment
2 stab sb.	b deal with (a problem)
3 consequence	c disagreement, argument
4 abuse (n)	d failure to look after sb.
5 neglect (n)	e make sth. stronger
6 curb sth.	f push the point of a knife or other weapon into sb.
7 bolster sth.	g react harshly to (a crime or bad behaviour)
8 dispute (n)	h reduce (a problem)
9 tackle (v)	i result of an action

b Study exercise **2** carefully. What is the key information you need to listen for?

TF B Multiple Matching (p. 72)

7

2 Listening comprehension: multiple matching

You are going to listen to an interview with police officer Mark Simmons and youth campaigner Camilla Batman-Ghelidja about a police advertising campaign against knives.

You will hear the recording twice. While listening, match the beginnings of the sentences (1–7) with the sentence endings (A–J). There are two sentence endings that you should not use. The first one (0) has been done for you. After the second listening, check your answers.

0 Londoners are shocked that …
1 Commander Mark Simmons is confident that …
2 Mrs Batman-Ghelidja thinks that we should ask ourselves why …
3 In her view, the answer is that …
4 The employees of Kids' Company are working to …
5 Mrs Batman-Ghelidja doesn't believe that …
6 The new weapon on the street is not knives, she claims, instead …
7 Instead of treating the symptoms, …

A … children feel the need to carry a knife.
B … damage young minds and lead to criminal behaviour.
C … dogs are being mistreated so that they can be used to attack opponents.
D … police stop and search teenagers who may be carrying knives.
E … so many people are dying in knife attacks.
F … support thousands of young people.
G … the campaign will have much effect on the crime rate.
H … the campaign will lead to less knife crime on the streets.
I … they don't feel safe without one.
J … we should find out the real problem and deal with that.

0	1	2	3	4	5	6	7
E							

> ⚠ **Trouble Spot**
> **abuse** (v) əˈbjuːz
> **abuse** (n) əˈbjuːs

SP 1 Mind Mapping (p. 30)

3 Working with words: mind map

Add words from this text to the branch 'Violence' in your mind map (see page 31).

4 Group brainstorming

Work in a group.

SP 2 Brainstorming (p. 30)

a What reasons do you think young people might give for carrying a knife? Try to think of as many reasons as you can.

b For every reason to carry a knife, find a convincing counter-argument.

5 Speaking: role play

Record a role play to be used as part of a campaign against knife crime.

Partner A: You discover that your friend carries a knife. Tell him/her your reaction to the news. Find out why, and try to persuade him/her to stop.

Partner B: Explain why you carry a knife. Respond to your partner's arguments.

6 Writing: analysing a picture

The knife bins were successfully launched in London's anti-knife crime campaign.

a Describe what you can see in the picture.

b Explain in your own words what the message is.

SP 12 Working With Pictures (p. 38)

c Comment on the campaign's effectiveness.

Alamy/Maurice Savage

C The Agony of the Needle  Key: 984

This article about heroin addiction was printed in the Australian newspaper The Age.

SP 30 Reading Non-Fiction (p. 50)

1 Reading for gist

Skim the text below, then choose the summary (a-c) which best describes the text.

SP 27 Skimming (p. 49)

a The text is about the relationship between a parent and her heroin addict son.

b The text is about Australia's failed drug policy and what should be done differently.

c The text is about the dangers of drug addiction and how anyone can become a drug addict.

JUDY Smith knew nothing about heroin until it had her only child, Daniel, in its grip.

She and her husband, Ray, had raised their son in a stable home and sent him to a leading Catholic boys' school in Sydney's eastern suburbs.

They were not blind to his bouts of low self-esteem and anxiety but believed he was building the foundations for a happy, successful life. A bachelor of fine arts from the University of New South Wales was proof.

What they did not know was that their 22-year-old son had been using heroin for three years, often in the family's home. Mrs Smith discovered this when she found a backpack on his bed. "His behaviour had become strange. I think deep down I probably knew what was going on but I was in denial," she said. "You don't want to accept this beautiful child, for whom you've done all the right things, is doing this sort of thing."

In the backpack she found two brown paper bags, which contained cotton wool and swabs, and a black plastic box filled with needles and injecting equipment. "All I could think is 'Oh God, oh God'. My heart started racing. That was the beginning of it."

In those first days, the Smiths tried reprimand and reason. "We were a respectable, middle-class family," she said. "This couldn't be happening to us."

grip strong hold
bout short period
self-esteem feeling that one has value
anxiety feeling anxious, scared
bachelor of fine arts university qualification in art
be in denial be unwilling to realize sth.
swab material used to clean a wound
reprimand telling sb. one strongly disapproves of their actions

▶▶▶

faith strong belief
paraphernalia pieces of equipment
surreal unreal in a dream-like way
habit *(here)* addiction
**ABC (Australian Broadcasting
  Corporation)** a TV company
supportive helping others
battle fight
come good recover from a bad
  situation
dig deep *(fig)* use all one's strength

But they realised – with the help of Family Drug Support – that it was "naive" to think they could cure their son immediately. Their first responsibility was to keep him safe. They put their faith in harm minimisation.

"I said, 'If you do not have clean needles, you let me know and we will get you clean needles'," Mrs Smith said.

Like many addicts, Daniel would buy drugs to last him for some time but use them quickly. "My grief counsellor said to me, 'Would you consider holding his drugs for him?' I said to her, 'I would do anything, anything'. I did a spreadsheet to try and keep track of his drugs. He had all the paraphernalia and he would disappear into the bathroom after I had given him a bag. I would say, 'You have four minutes. If you haven't called out that you are fine, I'm coming in'."

"It was surreal. I used to think I can't believe I am doing this. How could I tell anybody that we are doing this?"

For six years, Mrs Smith watched her son fight his habit. He was not a "junkie", she said – "how I hate that word" – but a gentle young man with an addiction. He held jobs at a pharmaceutical company and the ABC, she said, and was a valued employee. When her husband was diagnosed with non-Hodgkin lymphoma in 2010, she "could not have asked for a better, more supportive son".

Daniel Smith died on January 22 this year – alone in his car, outside the home of a drug dealer at Blackheath. He was 28.

"Daniel's big problem was that he would always use alone. His close friends weren't users. On the morning he died, I feel that if he had had somewhere to go – like a safe room in a hospital or an injecting centre – there would have been help for him," Mrs Smith said."He battled so hard, he was so brave – and he was coming good. He just needed more time."

Mrs Smith supports Family Drug Support, founded in 1997 by Tony Trimingham whose son, Damien, died of a heroin overdose. "I want to tell people: Your son or daughter or partner is not going to have a chance unless you walk beside them. If you dig deep, you can do it," she said.

Liz Hannan: Parents feel agony of needle and damage done. In: http://www.theage.com.au, May 19, 2012

2 Reading comprehension: multiple-choice

Read the text again, then choose the correct ending (A, B, C or D) for sentences 1–7. Put a cross (✘) in the correct box. The first one (0) has been done for you.

TF D Multiple-Choice (p. 73)

0 Judy Smith learned about the effects of heroin …
  A   when she started to take the drug. ☐
  B   when her son started to take the drug. ☐
  C   when her son was already addicted. ☒
  D   at school. ☐

1 Daniel …
  A   was happy and successful, but later became worried and depressed. ☐
  B   was often worried and depressed, but seemed to have a good future. ☐
  C   didn't complete his university studies because of depression. ☐
  D   dropped out of university without telling his parents. ☐

2 Judy discovered her son's heroin use when …
  A   she found him taking drugs. ☐
  B   she found drugs in his room. ☐
  C   she found equipment in his room for taking drugs. ☐
  D   she noticed the change in his behaviour. ☐

3 After the discovery, the Smith's first approach was to …
   A   ignore the problem.   ☐
   B   try to persuade Daniel to give up drugs.   ☐
   C   throw Daniel out of the family home.   ☐
   D   take away Daniel's drugs.   ☐

4 After contacting Family Drug Support, they realized that it was more realistic to …
   A   keep Daniel as safe as possible while he dealt with his habit.   ☐
   B   prevent Daniel from getting drugs.   ☐
   C   help Daniel to get enough drugs to manage his habit.   ☐
   D   get Daniel to reduce his drug use.   ☐

5 To reduce the chance of an overdose, Judy used to …
   A   hide Daniel's drugs from him.   ☐
   B   only give him a small amount of heroin at a time.   ☐
   C   only allow him four minutes alone in the bathroom.   ☐
   D   keep details of reliable drug dealers in a spreadsheet.   ☐

6 For six years, Daniel …
   A   managed to live a fairly normal life despite his addiction. ☐
   B   lost one job after another because of his addiction.   ☐
   C   looked after his sick father.   ☐
   D   didn't take drugs.   ☐

7 Daniel might have survived if he had …
   A   listened to his friends' advice not to take drugs.   ☐
   B   been able to take drugs in a safe environment.   ☐
   C   chosen another drug dealer.   ☐
   D   listened to his mother's advice not to go to the drug deal alone.   ☐

3 Working with words: mind map
Add a branch 'Drugs' to your mind map (see page 31).

SP 1 Mind Mapping (p. 30)

4 Working with words: prepositions
Choose the correct preposition to complete each sentence.

1   After smoking 40 cigarettes a day for 20 years, he was diagnosed _____ cancer.

2   Each day after school she would disappear _____ her bedroom and not come out for several hours.

3   Hopefully we can build the foundations _____ better treatment of drug addicts.

4   'I couldn't have asked _____ a better life, but somehow it all went wrong,' said the addict.

5   Rather than putting their faith _____ government programmes, the parents decided to start their own support group.

6   They knew very little _____ ecstasy before they caught their son with some tablets.

7   They sent their children _____ an expensive private school.

8   What are the risks of dying _____ an overdose?

9   When heroin addicts don't keep track _____ how much they have injected, they put their lives at risk.

10   When Leah started taking drugs, she was blind _____ the dangers.

5 Research and presentation: the fight against drugs

Many people argue that a strict zero tolerance policy on drug use causes more harm than it prevents. Some even want all drug use to be made legal.

a Here are some of the arguments for and against each approach. Put each argument in the best place in the table. The first one has been done for you.

	zero tolerance	decriminalization of users, not dealers	full legalization
arguments for	*B,*		
arguments against			

A   Alcohol and tobacco are also addictive drugs – but they are legal.
B   Even soft drugs have proven negative effects on health.
C   If drug use isn't a crime, how is it a crime to help someone to use drugs?
D   If users can't get drugs, they can't harm themselves.
E   It may make drug use much more common.
F   It takes drug profits away from criminal gangs.
G   The US War on Drugs has tried this for 40 years and it hasn't worked.
H   Users are only harming themselves, dealers harm others.

SP 14 Doing Research (p. 40)

b Use the Internet to research other arguments in favour of and against each approach, and examples from around the world of where each approach has been used.

c Report back to the class with what you found out in your research.

SP 13 Working with Charts and Graphs (p. 39)

TT 4 Report (p. 64)

6 Writing: report

The European Youth Parliament has invited young Europeans to comment on the drugs situation in their countries. You have obtained the chart below from the *Bundeskriminalamt*.

- Describe the results.
- Comment on what they show about young Austrians and drug crime.
- Suggest ways to discourage young Austrians from taking drugs.

Write about 250 words.

Drugs-related prosecutions in Austria

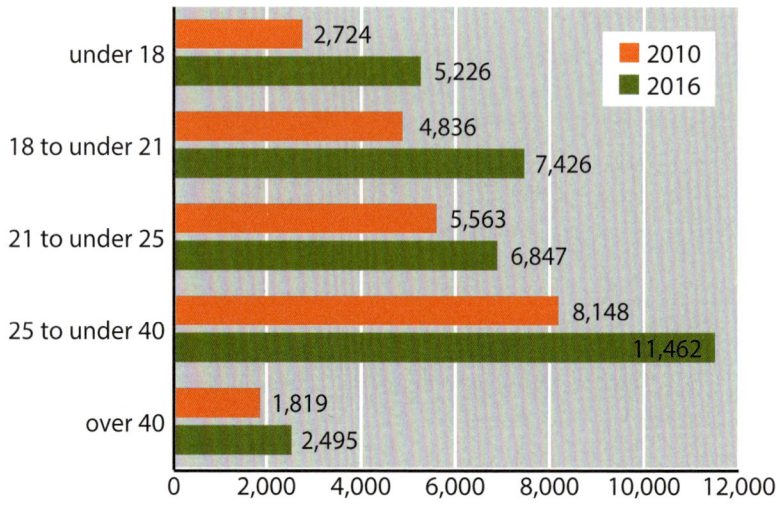

Data from: http://bundeskriminalamt.at/302/files/Suchtmittelbericht2016.pdf, p. 11

CAN-DO STATEMENTS

		Part/Ex	✔
👂	I can understand the main points in interviews, reports and presentations. (B1/2)	B/Ex 2	☐
	I can understand, fundamentally, native speakers when they speak clearly and directly about subjects familiar to me and use standard language. (B1/4)	B/Ex 2	☐
📖	I can get the essential information from simple newspaper and magazine articles that are clearly structured. (B1/1)	A/Ex 1	☐
	I can understand straightforward factual texts written for a wide audience on subjects related to my field and interest. (B1/2)	C/Ex1, C/Ex 2	☐
👀	I can express and give reasons for my opinion in conversations and discussions. Furthermore, I can agree or politely disagree and make other suggestions. (B1/6)	B/Ex 4	☐
	I can take on a role in a simulated everyday or professional situation and also improvise thereby. (B1/9)	B/Ex 5	☐
👄	I can give a prepared straightforward presentation, which can be followed easily and which I can make interesting for my listeners. (B1/3)	C/Ex 5	☐
	I can describe pictures and tell stories with the help of key words or illustrations. (B1/5)	A/Ex 3	☐
✏️	I can write reports or simple articles on events, experiences of a general or a professional nature. These texts may be intended for different media or different personal or professional purposes. (B1/1)	C/Ex 6	☐
	I can write simple descriptive texts on basic themes and problems that I am familiar with from school (e.g. technology, natural sciences, economics, language and literature). (B1/4)	B/Ex 6	☐

UNIT 6 Bullying and Conformism

A Bullying at School

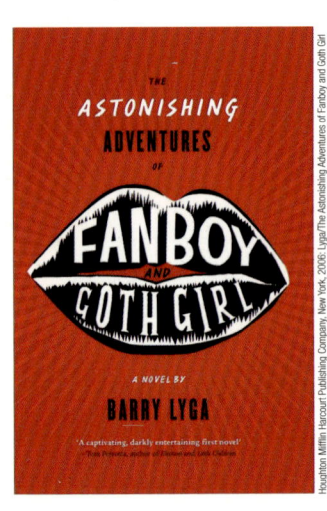

You are going to read an extract from 'The Astonishing Adventures of Fanboy and Goth Girl', a novel by Barry Lyga. The first-person narrator 'Fanboy' is an outsider at his school, where the 'jocks' push him around and the girls ignore him.

1 Reading for gist

Most of this passage (book chapter 3) is about Fanboy's 'inner world': his thoughts about a fantasy scenario, his general situation and his relationship with his mother. However, it is also about an unpleasant incident in the gym.

Find and mark the lines where the real world intrudes on his inner world, through the actions and speech of others.

FOR SOME REASON (IT'S NOT IMPORTANT), South Brook High School has been taken hostage. Mike Lorenz, Jason Benatovech, Pete Vesentine, and Ronnie Warshaw are all dead with bullets in their heads. Todd Bellanger has been shot, too, but he's not dead, just writhing in pain and crying. I note with some satisfaction that Mark Broderick is also among the deceased.

I'm hiding in the computer lab, and that's when I realize that everyone is being herded towards the gym. Cal is with them, and he looks angry and scared all at once. I realize that with a single distraction Cal would be able to disarm one of the bad guys and probably rescue everybody (even the ones who don't deserve it).

From the computer lab, I'm able to hack into the bell system, which is all automated. I can kick off the distraction and save everyone.

And that's when my arm explodes.

I look around. My fantasy of the school invasion has to be put on hold. (It's a good fantasy, and I add more details each time I relive it.) What the hell just happened to –

Again. Pain. Erupting in my right shoulder. I rock to one side with the force of the blow and bite my lip to keep from crying out.

I'm in gym class, or, as the idiots who teach it insist on calling it, "Physical Education." "Education," as if they're teaching us something other than the utterly useless skills of volleyball, flag football, and pushups.

And my personal favorite (I'm being sarcastic), dodge ball. What genius invented this game? What unrelentingly stupid jackass decided that it was a good idea to take a cluster of people with widely varying body types, strength levels, and skill sets (to say nothing of ever-shifting moralities and ethics), and then encourage them to *hit each other* with a ball?

I always try to get out early and easily – a glancing shot off my leg or shoulder. So I was standing in the Dead Zone of the game, whiling away "Physical Education" in my fantasy world, when the pain hit me.

And again.

I look over. The only other person in the dodge ball Dead Zone with me is Mitchell Frampton, a big stupid junior with shaggy blond hair that hangs over his eyes. He's grinning a dumb grin, his lower lip dried and cracked as he chews on it, and then he hits me again, in the exact same spot. My shoulder feels like it could just detonate, dropping my arm to the floor.

"Pussy," he says. "Pussy. Whatcha gonna do? Pussy." And wham! Again. Same spot. Uncannily in the same damn spot. My vision goes red for a moment with pain.

SP 29 Reading Fiction (p. 50)

take sb. hostage kidnap sb.
writhe move around as if in pain
deceased dead
herd sb. move (a group of people) as if they were farm animals
disarm sb. take a weapon away from sb.
kick off start
put sth. on hold stop sth. until a later time
erupt explode like a volcano
pushup exercise in which you lie on the floor and use your arms to push your body upwards
dodge ball game similar to *Völkerball*
jackass *(AE infml)* stupid person
glancing when a bullet, ball, etc. hits sth. at an angle, not with full force
shaggy having a lot of untidy hair
detonate explode
pussy *(AE vulgar slang)* weak person

Why is he doing this? I don't even know him. I've never even *talked* to him before. I look around quickly. No one's watching. On the gym floor, everyone's busy being physically educated by firing rubber balls around, what fun. The two gym teachers (sorry, *physical educators*) are standing off in a corner, talking and gesturing to each other, totally useless, not even watching the

Ow! Again!

Not even watching what's going on. I want to yell, but no one would hear me unless I screamed bloody murder at the top of my lungs and then I'd just be another wimp, another

Again!

tattletale. I'd be the crybaby, the momma's boy, the pussy, the weakling, the

Again!

victim. Let's see, what else have I been called over the glorious years? How about –

Again!

"Please stop," I say to him.

"Make me." Again. Again. Same spot, over and over. It's as if a Mitchell Frampton's fist–size part of my arm has become a mass of raw meat and screaming nerve endings. "Make me."

I can't. He knows I can't. I'm a computer geek, a comic book geek, a study geek. Even in the Fast-Track classes, I'm apart. To complete the stereotype-made-flesh that is me, I'm also half a head shorter than most guys my age, and while I'm not a ninety-pound skeletal weakling, my body is, in some ways, like one of those armature dolls, all straight, uninterrupted lines, uncut by any sort of evident muscle tone. I've got my South Brook High gym T-shirt on, and that's it as far as armor goes.

"Just ignore them," my mother used to tell me, when I was a kid, when I was younger, when the other kids would tease and make fun. "Why do you care what they think? Just ignore them and they'll go away."

They didn't go away, though. She was wrong about that. And the more I told her about them, the less she wanted to hear, and even when I was a kid, I could tell that she didn't want to hear about it. She had other things to worry about. She had to leave my dad and run off with her boyfriend, and for some reason she decided to add to the complications by dragging me along, too. Dragging me along, then ignoring me when I told her the other kids were making fun of me, were tormenting me, and what great advice: "Ignore them." So I did, even though they didn't go away, and pretty soon there was nothing to say, nothing to do, because how are you supposed to suddenly stand up to them after years of silence and nothing? Besides, I *can't* get in trouble. I just can't. I have one thing going for me: my brains. My ticket out. And college means transcripts, so unlike the rest of these idiots, my permanent record actually means something.

[...]

I stand there and stare straight ahead while Mitchell Frampton giggles and keeps hitting that *same damn spot.* And I realize that someone else does see. Someone sitting up on the bleachers at the far side of the gym. Someone dressed in black, with black hair, the face just a white blur. Watching.

Good. At least someone sees.

Barry Lyga: The Astonishing Adventures of Fanboy and Goth Girl. Houghton Mifflin Harcourt 2007 © Barry Lyga

wimp *(infml)* weak person
tattletale *(AE infml)* sb. who accuses another person of doing sth. wrong
crybaby *(infml)* childish person who cries easily
geek *(infml)* person who is intellectual and has no social skills
Fast-Track *(AE)* classes for more able students
skeletal having only bones, no fat or muscle
armature doll simple human figure used in art classes
armor *(AE)* hard, protective clothing
tease sb. try to annoy sb. by calling names etc.
torment sb. annoy, upset sb.
transcript *(here)* permanent record of a student's education
giggle laugh quietly
bleachers *(AE)* raised seats

2 Reading: true, false or not given

Read the text again, then decide whether the statements (1–9) are true (T), false (F) or not given (NG) in the text. Put a cross (✖) in the correct box. The first one (0) has been done for you.

		T	F	NG
0	In his fantasy, Fanboy imagines that he helps Cal to rescue other students.	✖	☐	☐
1	Physical education is usually Fanboy's favourite lesson.	☐	☐	☐
2	Whenever the class has to play dodge ball, Fanboy tries to lose quickly.	☐	☐	☐
3	Mitchell Frampton is older than Fanboy.	☐	☐	☐
4	The gym teachers are not paying attention to the students' behaviour.	☐	☐	☐
5	Fanboy finds even the Fast-Track classes too easy.	☐	☐	☐
6	Fanboy's mother was concerned when he told her about bullying at school.	☐	☐	☐
7	He doesn't feel that he can stand up to bullies now because he hasn't done it before.	☐	☐	☐
8	He doesn't want to get into trouble because he wants to go to college.	☐	☐	☐
9	He feels embarrassed when he realizes that someone else is watching Mitchell hit him.	☐	☐	☐

3 Interpreting the text

Answer three of the questions below. Take notes. Then write 40–50 words each.

1 How does Fanboy's fantasy help him to deal with school?
2 What is Fanboy's attitude to gym class?
3 What strategy does Fanboy have for dealing with bullying?
4 Why does Fanboy feel powerless to stop Mitchell Frampton?
5 In what ways does he set himself apart from the other students at his school?
6 Describe Fanboy's relationship with his mother.

4 Discussion

Work in small groups. Look again at how Fanboy reacts to Mitchell Frampton's bullying. What else could he have done?

a Brainstorm options for Fanboy.
Example: *shout loudly so that the other students and the teachers can hear*

b Think through the probable consequences of each option.
Example:
A: If he had shouted loudly, the teachers would have punished Mitchell.
B: Yes, but the other students would have called Fanboy a wimp.

 15 Conditional Sentences Type III (p. 13)

 3 Blog Entry (p. 63)

5 Writing: blog entry

You are the person in black who watches the incident described in this passage. That evening, you write an entry about it in your blog, without mentioning the names of the people involved.

In your blog entry, you should …
- describe the incident from your point of view;
- explain how you feel about it;
- justify whatever you decide to do, or not to do, about the incident.
Write about 200 words.

B Gangs: the Alternative Family

We hear and read a lot in the media about the problems associated with gangs: organized crime, drugs,
violence, etc. Yet there is less discussion about why young people join gangs, and what they get from
gang membership.

1 Preparing to listen

a Match the meanings (a–i) to the expressions (1–9).

1	accept sb.	a	informal word for 'friend'
2	community	b	easily hurt
3	dysfunctional	c	help
4	identify sb.	d	group of people amongst whom one lives
5	independent	e	not working well
6	mate	f	not needing help
7	skill	g	ability to do sth.
8	support	h	recognize who sb. is
9	vulnerable	i	treat sb. as welcome

b Discuss with a partner.

- What do young people need from their families?
- Could a gang ever be an 'alternative family'? If so, in what ways?

2 Listening comprehension: multiple-choice

You are going to hear a news report about gangs in London. While listening, choose the
correct ending (A, B, C or D) for sentences 1–8. Put a cross (✘) in the correct box. The first one (0)
has been done for you.

TF A Multiple-Choice (p. 71)

0 According to Ian Congreve …
  A children join gangs when they run away from home. ☐
  B children join gangs because they are looking for a 'family'. ☒
  C most gang members have bad relationships with their families. ☐
  D most gang members come from poor families. ☐

1 Ian Congreve …
  A lives in a Salvation Army hostel. ☐
  B works with the Salvation Army. ☐
  C used to be in a gang. ☐
  D leads a gang. ☐

2 Of the residents at Springfield Lodge …
  A all are young men in gangs. ☐
  B most have been gang members. ☐
  C all have come from families that have failed in some way. ☐
  D most want to join a gang. ☐

3 Gang culture is popular because …
  A gang members find that they are treated well by the rest of the gang. ☐
  B if you are in a gang, people respect you. ☐
  C gang members have the chance to get involved in organized crime. ☐
  D it's not safe to be on the streets unless you're a gang member. ☐

4 Many of the young men …
  A see their parents as friends, not parents. ☐
  B see their parents as part of the problem. ☐
  C don't want their parents to know where they are. ☐
  D never knew their parents. ☐

▶▶▶

5 Ian Congreve attributes the lack of family relationships to …
  A poor communication skills and too much time spent alone. ☐
  B a lack of interest on the part of the parents. ☐
  C the fact that the parents never gave their children anything. ☐
  D parents giving children bad advice. ☐

6 Young men come to Springfield Lodge because …
  A they have nowhere else to go. ☐
  B they have no friends that they can stay with. ☐
  C they see that they need to change their lives. ☐
  D the police send them there. ☐

7 The Salvation Army wants …
  A more money to support vulnerable children. ☐
  B more help for broken families. ☐
  C more work to identify families which need help. ☐
  D more beds in hostels like Springfield Lodge. ☐

8 The Seeds of Exclusion report …
  A blames parents for failing to help their children. ☐
  B shows that there is a strong link between homelessness and poor
      family relationships. ☐
  C calls on the government to do more to help young people. ☐
  D shows that almost half of young people no longer respect their parents. ☐

SP 1 Mind Mapping (p. 30)

3 Working with words: mind map
Add words from this text to the branch 'Gangs' in your mind map (see page 31).

CAN-DO STATEMENTS

		Part / Ex	✔
👂	I can understand the main points in interviews, reports and presentations. (B1/2)	B / Ex 2	☐
	I can understand, fundamentally, native speakers when they speak clearly and directly about subjects familiar to me and use standard language. (B1/4)	B / Ex 2	☐
	I can understand the most important elements of radio programmes and sound recordings when they deal with current events or my interests. (B1/5)	B / Ex 2	☐
📖	I can understand longer, relatively simple literary texts on themes that are familiar to me (e.g. modern popular literature). (B1/3)	A / Ex 1, A / Ex 2, A / Ex 3	☐
	I can find information that I need to solve a specific task in various longer texts or text sections. (B1/8)	A / Ex 2, A / Ex 3	☐
👀	I can begin, maintain and end a conversation about subjects familiar to me. (B1/1)	B / Ex 1b	☐
	I can express and give reasons for my opinion in conversations and discussions. Furthermore, I can agree or politely disagree and make other suggestions. (B1/6)	A / Ex 4	☐
✏️	I can write simple stories, essays and creative texts. (B1/2)	A / Ex 5	☐

CHECK YOUR PROGRESS 2

1 Reading comprehension: multiple-choice

TF D Multiple-Choice (p. 73)

Read the text on page 42 again. Choose the correct answer (A, B, C or D) for questions 1–6.
Put a (✘) in the correct box. The first one (0) has been done for you.

Fotolia.com/pics

0 What is 'Big Dog's Crew'?
   A A gang which sprays graffiti in shopping malls in Los Angeles. ☐
   B A police investigation team in Los Angeles. ☐
   C A gang which sprays graffiti on public transport property. ✘
   D Gang members who attacked graffiti sprayers. ☐

1 What is the attitude of the Los Angeles Police Department (LAPD) towards graffiti?
   A It is not really a crime. ☐
   B It can lead to violent crime. ☐
   C It is illegal and cannot be ignored. ☐
   D It is a waste of taxpayers' money to arrest graffiti sprayers. ☐

2 Who where the people who were arrested?
   A Mostly adolescents. ☐
   B People who may be in an illegal gang. ☐
   C Known criminals. ☐
   D Vandals who have caused damage costing $200,000. ☐

3 Why do some people criticise the LAPD for their anti-graffiti action?
   A It takes too long to catch the graffiti sprayers. ☐
   B It costs too much to catch the graffiti sprayers. ☐
   C There is no proof that Big Dog's Crew was involved. ☐
   D There are more important crimes which are not being investigated. ☐

4 Why do others argue that graffiti should not be considered a crime?
   A The graffiti is more interesting to look at than bare walls. ☐
   B Many of the graffiti sprayers are professional artists. ☐
   C It does not hurt anyone. ☐
   D Tagging is a good outlet for youths who want to do something creative. ☐

5 What alternative solution to the problem of graffiti has been suggested?
   A Give the graffiti sprayers a job cleaning up graffiti. ☐
   B Give the graffiti sprayers proper artistic training. ☐
   C Give the graffiti sprayers a job making street art. ☐
   D Employ real artists to make the city beautiful. ☐

6 What might happen if graffiti sprayers had legal projects to work on? ☐
   A They might earn money instead of costing the city money. ☐
   B The police might have officers available for more important work. ☐
   C Violent crime might increase. ☐
   D Professional street artists might move to the city looking for work. ☐

 C Short Answers (p. 72)

2 Listening comprehension: short answers

You are going to listen to part of a recording for UK schools about legal and illegal drugs. Answer the questions (1–6) using a maximum of four words. The first one (0) has been done for you.

0   Why should prescription drugs not be modified for recreational purposes?
1   What do recreational drugs do?
2   What effect do heroin and cocaine have on your brain?
3   Why are heroin and cocain particularly dangerous?
4   What effect may drug addiction have on a person's diet?
5   What effects did the researchers look at in 2006 when they classified drugs?
6   Which drugs mentioned are among the five most dangerous?

0   *dangerous, illegal*
1   _____
2   _____
3   _____
4   _____
5   _____
6   _____

 L Editing (p. 79)

3 Language in Use: editing

You are going to read a text about guns in the USA. In most lines of the text there is an unnecessary word. Write the unnecessary word in the space provided after each line. Some lines are correct. Indicate these lines with a tick (✔). There are two examples at the beginning.

Fotolia.com/Les Cunliffe

America's love affair with the gun		
Gun control is are amongst the most difficult issues in the USA. The right to	*are*	0
own a gun and defend oneself seems to be central to the American identity.	✔	00
Guns enabled the early settlers to protect them themselves from native	_____	1
Americans (whose own land they were taking), animals and foreign armies.	_____	2
Citizens took the responsibility for their self-defence. This 'Wild West'	_____	3
mentality is still evident in the USA today. The importance of guns also	_____	4
comes from the role of hunting in American culture. In the nation's early	_____	5
years, hunting was essential for food and today yet it remains popular in	_____	6
many parts of the country.	_____	7
Part of the reason which this issue goes around in circles is that it is difficult	_____	8
to establish a causal link between guns and violence. Those ones who	_____	9
demand gun control point out that guns are involved in to the vast majority	_____	10
of fatal violent crimes in the US, yet they cannot prove that the guns cause	_____	11
the violence. There does seems to be no way of calculating the role gun	_____	12
culture plays in the comparison to poverty, education, mental illness,	_____	13
alcohol and unemployment.	_____	14
However, the impact of America's gun culture can be being seen	_____	15
everywhere. When movies appear on television, sex is censored, but	_____	16
shootings are shown in it's graphic detail. Metal detectors are used in	_____	17
government buildings and even schools to prevent people on entering	_____	18
with weapons.	_____	19
There is no any national gun register in the USA, so it is impossible to know	_____	20
exactly how many of guns are in circulation or who has them. The FBI	_____	21
estimates there are more than 200 million guns in civilian hands.	_____	22

4 Speaking: paired activity

TF N Paired Activity (p. 80)

There has been a shooting at an American high school recently. At the home of the person responsible, the police found weapons and a large number of violent video games. You and your partner decide to write an article for a youth magazine calling for a ban on violent video games. Discuss the following aspects:

- players can't tell the difference between fantasy and reality
- the games make players more violent and aggressive
- players who are addicted to games don't have "real" friends
- the games teach people to use violence to solve their problems
- violent games give potential murderers a chance to practice

Agree on the best three arguments for your article.

5 Writing: report

TT 4 Report (p. 64)

You are at a Junior High School in the USA, where there have been several cases of cyberbullying in recent weeks. The school principal has asked students to prepare a report on the topic, using the following information:

Percentage of 12–17 year old middle and high school students in the U.S. who were cyber bullied between July and October 2016, by type of cyber bullying

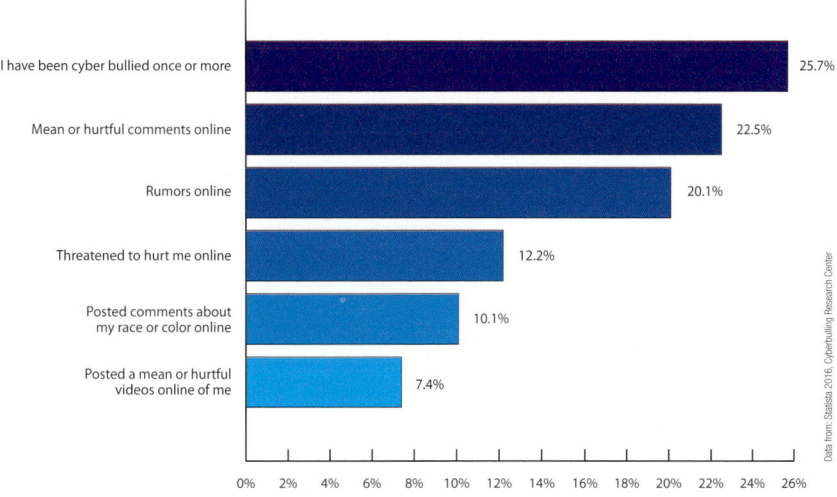

I have been cyber bullied once or more	25.7%
Mean or hurtful comments online	22.5%
Rumors online	20.1%
Threatened to hurt me online	12.2%
Posted comments about my race or color online	10.1%
Posted a mean or hurtful videos online of me	7.4%

Data from: Statista 2016, Cyberbullying Research Center

In your report you should …

- point out the current situation that the statistics show
- comment on the different forms of cyberbullying
- suggest ways in which cyberbullying could be reduced among teenagers

Write about 250 words.

3 Making a Difference

WHAT **YOUNG PEOPLE** ARE SAYING

unicef

www.unicef.org/voy/news   The bimonthly newsletter of Voices of Youth

> *I feel this world has let us down, but we can't sit around and complain all day. Children all over the world are dying, and the worst thing is that help comes too late or never arrives at all.*
>
> Jomo, South Africa

> *There are enough resources in the world for all, but the wealth is so unfairly distributed – some have nothing while others have far too much. If we all stand together, we CAN make a difference.*
>
> Siri, Norway

> *Education is the best way to end poverty, unemployment and ethnic conflicts. It shouldn't be a dream for education to be free. If a country can spend huge amounts of money on missiles, why not spend it on helping people instead?*
>
> Meera, India

Picture 1-4: Inginiage.com; 5: MEV Verlag/Susanne Kracke; 6. Corbis/ImageShop

---

let sb. down to fail to help sb. when they expect it

complain say you are unhappy about the way things are

distribute sth. [dɪ'strɪbjuːt] *here:* divide sth.

poverty ['pɒvəti] state of being very poor

unemployment state of not having a job

huge amounts of a lot of

missile [*BE:* 'mɪsaɪl; *AE:* 'mɪsl] rocket

Language Help

- I think the worst problem in Siri's country is …, so …
- Jomo is angry because …
- I think it's difficult for us to …, but we should …

 35 Expressing Opinions (p. 28)

---

1 Young people's worries

a Work in groups of three. Each study one of the statements above and identify what the person is worried about. What do you already know about that person's country? Which of these issues might play a role: famine, health, war, education, racial conflicts, pollution, the gap between rich and poor?

b What issues are you worried about – in your town, your country or abroad? Make a list.

c Are Siri, Meera and Jomo's worries different from or the same as yours? Discuss and explain.

In this topic you will learn about ...

- ways of getting involved   **(WiC)**
- deciding how to help   **(Unit 7)**
- helping in small ways   **(Unit 8)**
- applying for a volunteer job   **(Unit 9)**

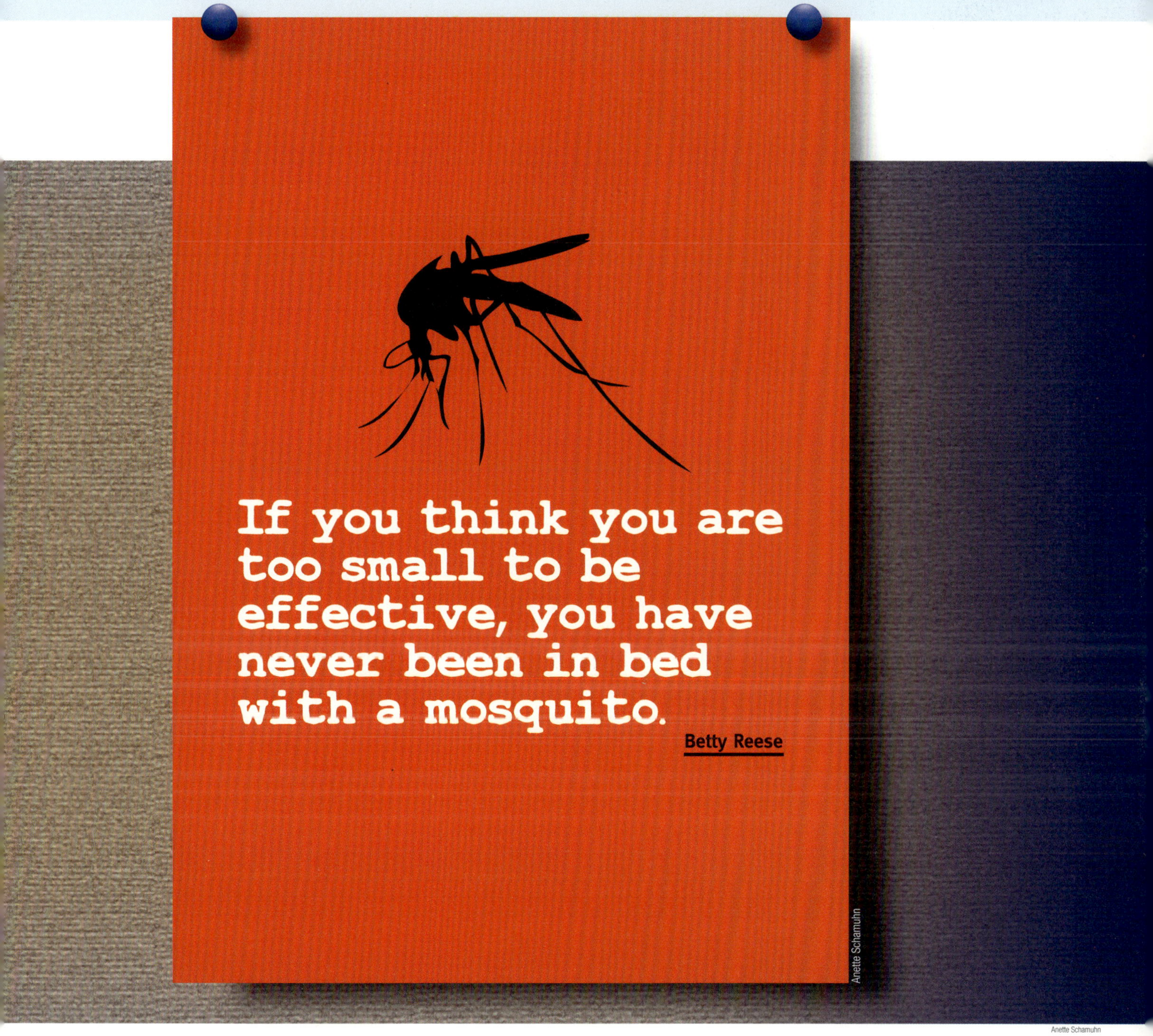

If you think you are too small to be effective, you have never been in bed with a mosquito.

Betty Reese

Anette Schamuhn

Anette Schamuhn

2 Working with posters

a Explain what you think this poster means.

SP 12 Working with Pictures (p. 38)

b Is the poster effective? How does it get its message across? Think about the drawing of the mosquito, the colours, …

c Discuss your list from **1b** with a partner. Decide together on one global issue that you would like to draw people's attention to with an English poster like the one above.

d Make a poster about the issue with your partner. Display it in the classroom. Walk round and discuss the posters.

Getting Involved

LP 24 Increase Your Word Power Online (p. 18)

Schools in English-speaking countries usually offer extra-curricular activities, and they encourage kids to 'get involved'. Students join school clubs and participate in school sports, and as they get older, they often join voluntary organizations. These groups perform a service to the community, like cleaning up a park, doing the shopping for an elderly person, or raising money for a homeless shelter; or they may get involved in more political activity, like making and putting up posters to promote a particular cause – a campaign to stop smoking, for example.

I AM AN ACTIVIST

GET INFORMED
GET INSPIRED
GET OUTRAGED
GET ACTIVE

Anita Roddick, founder of The Body Shop and lifelong activist

When they leave school, many young people take time off before starting university. This is known as a gap year. While some 'gappers' use this time to travel or to pursue their hobbies, many enjoy doing volunteer work during this time, often abroad.

Young international volunteers mostly spend their time working in developing countries. There they do social work (e.g. helping to bring health care to rural areas or teaching children to read) or help on construction projects (e.g. building schools or clinics, or bringing clean water to poor communities) or ecological projects (e.g. planting trees or showing local farmers how to save water). Some serve in places that have been hit by natural disasters such as earthquakes, tsunamis or tropical storms.

While most volunteers work quietly to make a difference in their small corner of the world, activists want to change the world – or at least people's thinking and/or behaviour. Activists hope to achieve social or political change. To do so, they lobby politicians, advertise for their cause or stage protests to draw people's attention to their cause.

But why do people want to help others by volunteering or donating money to a charity? Well, there are rewards for this sort of commitment. Research has proved that when we help other people, we feel better ourselves: do good, feel good!

1 Think – pair – share: ways of getting involved

a Think: Collect different ways of getting involved that are mentioned in the text. Add your own ideas.

b Pair: Compare notes with a partner. Discuss which ways of getting involved would be practical for people your age in Austria.

c Share: With another pair, agree on the three most practical ways of getting involved and report to the class.

2 Analysing a poster

Analyse the main elements of the poster above: the photo and the words. Comment on the effectiveness of the poster.

SP 12 Working with Pictures (p. 38)

3 Working with words: word families

a Add the missing words to the chart below. Some of the words you need are in the text on p. 104; you can find the others in your (online) dictionary.

LP 31–32 Word Formation (p. 24)

LP 33 Word Stress (p. 26)

SP 8 Using a Dictionary (p. 34)

Abstract noun	Noun: person	Verb	Adjective
activity			active
		advertise	————
campaign			————
charity	————	————	
	politician	————	
thought			
	volunteer		

b Now use words you have added to the chart in **3a** to complete this text.
Many schools, parents and _____ **1** organizations, such as Oxfam and Greenpeace, try to encourage young people to do _____ **2** work in their spare time. Volunteers are necessary to help _____ **3** for change on important global issues. Many charities only have a small staff of full-time _____ **4** and they could not continue their work if people didn't _____ **5** to help. TV and newspaper _____ **6** are one way of drawing attention to a particular issue, but charities also have to lobby _____ **7** who they _____ **8** might be influential in achieving their goals. The _____ **9** of social change can be very difficult and demanding and charities need to _____ **10** all the resources they can.

4 Collocations

a Match verbs on the left to phrases on the right to form collocations from the text on page 104.

LP 25 Collocations (p. 20)

1	achieve	a	a hobby
2	do	b	money for a charity
3	donate	c	money to a charity
4	draw	d	sb.'s attention to a cause
5	join	e	school sports
6	participate in	f	social or political change
7	pursue	g	social or voluntary work
8	raise	h	time off before university
9	take	i	a voluntary organization

b Which verbs from the text go with these phrases?
1 _____ a political protest
2 _____ politicians for support
3 _____ a particular cause
4 _____ involved in an activity
5 _____ your time doing sth.

5 Writing: report

a First of all, do a class survey: How many students take part in extra-curricular activities or are members of a club? Which clubs/activities are the most popular? (Think of sports clubs, the volunteer fire brigade, the town/village band, …) How many hours a week do people spend on their activity? Why do they do an activity? (Why not?)

SP 17 Conducting a Survey (p. 42)

b Now write a report for the principal of your school about extra-curricular activities in your class.
- Describe what activities your classmates do.
- Explain why some people do not do any at all.
- Suggest one or two ways in which students could be encouraged to "get involved".

Write about 200 words.

SP 32 The Stages of Writing (p. 51)

SP 34 Structuring a Text (p. 52)

TT 4 Report (p. 64)

UNIT 7 It's Your Turn

A What Role Will You Play?

The following extract is taken from the Commencement Address given by Barack Obama at the University of Massachusetts Boston on 2 June 2006.

TF E Multiple Matching (p. 73)

1 Reading comprehension: multiple matching

One <u>adjective</u> and one <u>noun</u> are missing from each paragraph of the text. Choose the correct word (A–J) for each gap (1–9). Write your answer in the space provided. The first one (0) has been done for you.

adjectives

A black   B diverse   C free   D precarious   E radical

nouns

F belief   G home   H justice   I power   J prosperity

0	1	2	3	4	5	6	7	8	9
F	___	___	___	___	___	___	___	___	___

Commencement Address
[kəˈmensmənt] speech at a US university ceremony where students are given their diplomas

built on defiance of the odds
[dɪˈfaɪəns] based on a refusal to accept defeat

set off start

daring brave

unfailingly simple notion always simple idea

pursue sth. try to achieve sth.

doubt sth. [daʊt] not believe sth.

attend college go to college

diverse [daɪˈvɜːs] mixed

City on a Hill *(biblical)* a place that is easily seen and, figuratively, a shining example

unlikely not probable

occur [əˈkɜː] happen

No Irish Need Apply Irish people not wanted for a job

pelt sb. with rocks throw stones at sb.

Red Sox Boston's baseball team

sign sb. arrange for sb. to sign a contract

Jackie Robinson first famous African American baseball player

bring sth. about make sth. happen

liberate sb. free sb.

prosperity state of being successful, especially in making money

Alamy/Zuma Wire Service

America is an unlikely place – it's a country built on defiance of the odds; on a (0) ___ in the impossible. And I remind you of this because as you set off on your own lives of success and achievement, it's now your turn to help keep it this way. It's your turn to keep this daringly (1) ___ but unfailingly simple notion of America alive – that no matter where you're born or how much your parents have; no matter what you look like or what you believe in, you can still rise to become whatever you want; still go on to achieve great things; still pursue the happiness that you hope for. [. . .]

Now, there may be some who doubt that much has changed – those who doubt that things are better today than they were yesterday. For those who believe that, take a look at this class of 2006. More than half represent the very first members of their family ever to attend college. In the most (2) ___ university in New England, I look out at a sea of faces that are African-American and Hispanic-American and Asian-American and Arab-American and Anglo-American. I see students who've come here from over 100 different countries, believing like those first settlers that they too could find a (3) ___ in that City on a Hill – that they too could find success in the unlikeliest of places.

All this has occurred in the midst of a city where *No Irish Need Apply* signs once hung from stores. All of this in a city where, just thirty years ago, buses of (4) ___ students were pelted with rocks as they pulled into schools in South Boston, where the Red Sox were once the team who refused to sign the great Jackie Robinson.
But the problem isn't that we haven't made progress – we have. The problem is that the progress still isn't good enough. There is more work to be done, more (5) ___ to be had, there are more barriers to break down. And now it's your generation's turn to bring those changes about.

The last century was undoubtedly the American century. Our victory over Fascism and Communism liberated millions. At home, we built a shared (6) ___ that created the largest middle-class in history. Ours was a nation of liberators; of (7) ___ people; of prosperous people – and the world took notice.

▶ ▶ ▶

But today, just a few years into the twenty-first century, we've already found ourselves in a different and sometimes (8) ___ position. As revolutions in communications and technology have broken down barriers across the world, it's given more (9) ___ to both our competitors and to our enemies.

No longer can we assume that a high-school education in Boston is enough to compete for a job that can easily go to the college-educated in Bangalore or in Beijing. No more can we count on employers to provide health care and pensions and job training when their bottom lines know no borders. Never again can we expect the oceans that surround America to keep us safe from attacks on our own soil.

Barack Obama: University of Massachusetts at Boston Commencement Address, June 2, 2006

competitor [kəmˈpetɪtə] sb. who competes with sb. else in business
assume sth. [əˈsjuːm] think or accept that sth. is true
provide sth. give sth., offer sth.
pension [ˈpenʃn] money paid by the government or a company when sb. stops working
bottom line here: the amount of profit a company makes
soil earth, country

2 Understanding the message

a Read the text again and take notes on each paragraph; try to give each paragraph a heading.

b Now write one sentence about each paragraph, using the words from exercise **1**.

c Use some of the phrases on the right to link your sentences into one paragraph summarizing the message of the extract.

3 Working with words: word families

a Which verbs and adjectives belong to these abstract nouns from the text? Use your (online) dictionary for help if you need to.

	Abstract noun	Verb	Adjective
1	achievement	*achieve*	*achievable*
2	assumption		
3	belief		
4	competition		
5	defiance		
6	education		
7	liberation		
8	prosperity		
9	success		

b The abstract nouns in the list have the following suffixes: *-ment, -tion, -ition, -ance, -ation, -ity*. How many different suffixes are there in the list of adjectives?

c Progress is both a verb and an abstract noun. Look up the correct pronunciation in your (online) dictionary. Find at least six other words in the text where the verb and abstract noun forms are the same.

4 Talking

Barack Obama's speech continues like this: "So what does this mean for you? What role will you play in meeting these challenges? I do not pretend to have all the answers. […] But perhaps I can offer a few suggestions that may be useful along the way."

a Discuss with a partner: Do you think the challenges Obama describes are the same or different for young Austrians?

b What advice do you think Barack Obama is going to offer his listeners in the next part of his speech? Explain your choice.

Language Help

- Obama starts off by …-ing …
- He emphasizes / points out that …
- He goes on to say that …
- He describes how …
- He contrasts … and …

 4 Taking Notes (p. 32)

 35 Linking Ideas (p. 53)

SP 8 Using a Dictionary (p. 34)

B Take a Chance  Key: 313

 21 Quantifiers (p. 16)

challenge a difficult task
I do not pretend I do not claim
on the brink of almost in a new situation
community organizer local social worker
low-income neighborhood *(AE)* part of a town/city where poor people live
law school legal faculty at a university
Wall Street financial centre of New York
deal with sth. solve a problem
steel plant steel works

beat-up *(infml)* scratched and damaged
(not) a living soul (not) anybody
appreciate sth. [əˈpriːʃieɪt] be grateful for sth.
words of wisdom wise words
talk sb. out of doing sth. persuade sb. not to do sth.

 4 Taking Notes (p. 32)

 C Short Answers (p. 72)
 20 Listening for Detail (p. 45)

1 Listening and taking notes

a Make sure you know the meaning of all the words listed on the left. Then read the questions in exercise **2**.

b Listen to the second half of Obama's speech and take notes under the following headings:

Obama's preferred job: _____

Friends' and relatives' advice: _____

Job offer: _____

Trip to Chicago: _____

Obama's advice: _____

2 Listening comprehension: short answers

Now listen again and answer the questions using a maximum of 4 words. Write your answers in the spaces provided. The first one (0) has been done for you. (Your notes in **1b** will help you.)

0 What did Barack Obama want to work as after university?
1 Where did he want to work?
2 Who thought he should go to law school?
3 What were his friends applying for?
4 Who offered him a job?
5 Why were there problems in that area?
6 What sort of work did the man in the motel recommend to Obama?
7 Why didn't he take anybody's advice?
8 What advice does he give to his listeners?

0 *as a community organizer*
1 _____
2 _____
3 _____
4 _____
5 _____
6 _____
7 _____
8 _____

3 Language in Use: banked gap-fill

Read this text about young people and political activity. Some words are missing from the text. For each gap, choose the correct word (A–O) from the list. There are two extra words that you should not use. Write your answers in the spaces provided. The first one (0) has been done for you.

TF J Banked Gap-Fill (p. 78)

It's something you often hear in shops and pubs: an older person complaining about today's "younger (0)___ ": they wear strange clothes and listen to awful music, their friends have no (1)___ and are probably high on ecstasy all the time. What the older people often forget, though, is that their own (2)___ used to say exactly the same things about them many years ago.

Young people's social interaction is so (3)___ different nowadays that people who grew up without smartphones and the worldwide web cannot (4)___ them having any political interests or ambition. However, just because we can't see something doesn't mean that it doesn't (5)___ at all: many young people have found a new political forum on the Internet. For all the (6)___ things we hear about the Internet, for example cyberbullying, there are a lot of positive (7)___ that have completely changed the way young people participate in (8)___ . Activists start online petitions or upload videos to YouTube to (9)___ particular campaigns; young people tweet about politicians and events as well as rockstars and the (10)___ fashions; they "like" Greenpeace and Amnesty International and are "friends" of charities on Facebook; above all, (11)___ can be organized on social network websites so (12)___ that old political campaigners will probably turn green with envy.

envy wanting sth. that sb. else has

A aspects
B demonstrations
C effective
D efficiently
E exist
F fundamentally
G generation
H imagine

I latest
J manners
K negative
L parents
M promote
N recognize
O society

0	1	2	3	4	5	6	7	8	9	10	11	12
G	___	___	___	___	___	___	___	___	___	___	___	___

4 Working with words: collocations

Use the verbs in the box to complete collocations from Obama's speech. Sometimes more than one answer is possible.

> apply ▪ change ▪ follow ▪ give ▪ have ▪ make ▪ meet ▪ offer ▪ play ▪ put ▪ take ▪ talk

1 _____ a role		7 _____ sb. a piece of advice
2 _____ an idea		8 _____ the world
3 _____ a challenge		9 _____ a name for oneself
4 _____ for a job		10 _____ sb.'s advice
5 _____ sb. out of work		11 _____ a path
6 _____ sb. a job		12 _____ sb. out of doing sth.

5 Speaking: individual long turn

Talk about the topics below. Try to use some of the phrases from exercise **4**.
- Compare the pictures.
- Explain some of the social problems in your area and suggest ways to solve them.
- State your own opinion: How important is it for young people to help the community?

 M Individual Long Turn (p. 80)

C 'How Could The World Let These Children Die?'

On 7 June 2007, Bill Gates, founder of Microsoft, gave a speech at Harvard University's Commencement Ceremony. In it he explained how we can 'turn caring into action' and why, as a rule, we don't.

SP 19 Listening for Gist (p. 45)

1 Listening strategies

a Read the following statements. Do you think they are true or false? Write your answers in the first column.

		True/False?	True/False?
1	Bill and Melinda Gates have to think about charity differently to other people because they have so much money.		
2	Malaria and hepatitis B are serious health problems in the USA.		
3	The disease rotavirus kills 50,000 children in the USA every year.		
4	Most vaccinations (Impfung) cost $1.		
5	Bill Gates doesn't agree that some lives are more worth saving than other lives.		
6	Children in the Third World suffer and die because their parents have no economic or political power.		

intervention action or activity to improve a situation
revolting extremely unpleasant
subsidize give money to help pay for sth.

b Now listen to the first part of the speech and look at your answers in **1a**: Were any of your answers wrong? If so, write the correct answer in the second column.

c Compare your answers in class: Which answers did you change after listening to the speech. Why?

2 Working with words

a Match the words (1–14) from the second half of Bill Gates' speech to the synonyms or paraphrases in the box.

> able to be stopped or avoided ▪ able to continue for a long time ▪ an attempt to do sth.
> difficult ▪ a large and difficult project ▪ deliberate and controlled ▪ injustice ▪ opposite of
> problem ▪ way of dealing with sth.

1	approach _____	8	barrier _____
2	inequity _____	9	complexity _____
3	conscious _____	10	solution _____
4	effort _____	11	enterprise _____
5	sceptic _____	12	advent _____
6	tragedy _____	13	preventable _____
7	optimistic _____	14	sustainable _____

SP 6 Dealing with Words You Don't Know (p. 33)

SP 8 Using a Dictionary (p. 34)

b Which words are left over? Why do you think that is? Look them up in your (online) dictionary if you don't know their meaning.

c "The barrier to change is not too little caring; it is too much … ." Which word do you think is missing? Discuss with a partner what Bill Gates will say in the next part of his speech.

3 Listening comprehension: multiple-choice

Now listen to the second part of Bill Gates' speech. Choose the correct answer (A, B, C or D) for questions 1–5. Put a (✗) in the correct box.

11

TF A Multiple-Choice (p. 71)

1 According to Bill Gates, to reduce injustice in the world we have to …
   A meet the needs of the poor. ☐
   B make profit for businesses. ☐
   C win votes for politicians. ☐
   D all of the above. ☐

2 Bill Gates says that the challenge of changing the world …
   A cannot ever be fully achieved. ☐
   B will be achieved very soon. ☐
   C is hardly worth starting. ☐
   D is something people don't care about. ☐

3 He claims that people don't act to help when tragedies occur because …
   A their hearts are broken. ☐
   B they care too much. ☐
   C they don't know what to do. ☐
   D they know they can't help. ☐

> **determine sth.** find out sth.
> **determined** having decided to do sth. and not letting oneself be stopped

4 Gates criticizes the fact that …
   A people try to find out why planes crash. ☐
   B people can't see what the real problems are. ☐
   C there is news on the TV 24 hours a day. ☐
   D the Internet has made the world more complex. ☐

5 People ignore the millions who are dying because …
   A they are only interested in new problems. ☐
   B the media doesn't cover the story at all. ☐
   C they don't think it is a problem at all. ☐
   D they don't want to see a problem that they don't know how to solve. ☐

4 Grammar in Use: conditional sentences
Complete the sentences with the correct form of the verb in brackets.

1 If you had a few dollars a month to donate to a cause, where _____ (you/spend) it?
2 If you believe that every life is equal, it _____ (be) revolting to learn that some lives are more worth saving than others.
3 The children wouldn't have died if the governments _____ (subsidize) the medicines.
4 If their parents had a political voice, they _____ (not live) in such poverty.
5 Politicians _____ (acted) to help the poor if they had had a voice in the system.
6 We _____ (reduce) inequity in the world if we find a sustainable solution.
7 If the officials _____ (be) honest, they would have said that other things were more important.
8 We _____ (not find) a solution until we recognize what the problem really is.
9 If the media _____ (cover) the story better, we wouldn't be able to ignore it so easily.
10 We _____ (change) the world if we make a conscious effort to do so.

5 EXTRA Making a speech

a Write your own speech of 2–3 minutes about something you would like to change. You can use some of the stylistic devices that Barack Obama and Bill Gates used in their speeches, for example:
- speaking to the audience directly (using 'you' or imperatives)
- inversion (putting the auxiliary before the subject in a statement)
- repetition (using a word or phrase several times for effect)

b Write prompt cards with not more than three or four words on each one. Practise your speech with a partner, then present it to the class.

CAN-DO STATEMENTS

LP 13 Conditional Sentences: Type I (p. 12)

LP 14 Conditional Sentences: Type II (p. 12)

LP 15 Conditional Sentences: Type III (p. 13)

⚠ **Trouble Spot**

spenden = **donate**
spend = (Geld) ausgeben, (Zeit) verbringen

LP 27 False Friends (p. 22)

Language Help

- May I remind you, …
- So what does this mean for you?
- Don't let people …
- Never again can we expect …
- No longer can we assume …

LP 10 Emphasis: Inversion (p. 10)

Intro:
helping children
…

Situation:
poverty, disease
…

Projects:
fresh water, schooling
…

		Part / Ex	✔
👂	I can understand the main points in interviews, reports and presentations. (B1/2)	B / Ex 1 C / Ex 3	☐
	I can understand the most important elements of radio programmes and sound recordings when they deal with current events or my interests. (B1/5)	B / Ex 1 C / Ex 3	☐
📖	I can recognize the essential conclusions in clearly structured argumentative texts. (B1/4)	A / Ex 2	☐
	I can find information that I need to solve a specific task in various longer texts or text sections. (B1/8)	A / Ex 1 A / Ex 2	☐
💬	I can begin, maintain and end a conversation about subjects familiar to me. (B1/1)	A / Ex 4	☐
	I can express and give reasons for my opinion in conversations and discussions. Furthermore, I can agree or politely disagree and make other suggestions. (B1/6)	A / Ex 4	☐
👄	I can give a prepared straightforward presentation, which can be followed easily and which I can make interesting for my listeners. (B1/3)	B / Ex 4 C / Ex 4	☐
	I can describe pictures and tell stories with the help of key words or illustrations. (B1/5)	B / Ex 4	☐
✏	I can write reports or simple articles on events, experiences of a general or a professional nature. These texts may be intended for different media or different personal or professional purposes. (B1/1)	WiC / Ex 5	☐

A If I Can Stop One Heart from Breaking

> If I can stop one heart from breaking,
>   I shall not live in vain;
> If I can ease one life the aching,
>   Or cool one pain,
> Or help one lonely person
>   Into happiness again,
> I shall not live in vain

Emily Dickinson: If I can stop one heart from breaking.
In: The Complete Poems, 1925

in vain for nothing
ease the aching ['eɪkɪŋ] stop the
   pain

1 Talking about the poem

a State the main idea of the poem in one sentence. Read the poem again out loud.

b Compare your sentence with your partner's. Do you agree with the main idea of the poem?

2 Talking about the pictures

 12 Working with Pictures (p. 38)

a Work in groups of four. Each describe one picture to the other members of the group.
   - Who are the people? (How old are they? What are they wearing?)
   - What is the situation? (Where are they? What are they doing?)
   - What do you think the people might be saying?

b Have you ever been in a situation where you needed help or had to help someone?
Describe the situation.

c Choose your favourite picture. Look for a line or phrase in the poem that fits it and explain why
to the group.

B Bread on the Water

SP 29 Reading Fiction (p. 50)

This short story by David Lubar describes one event in the life of a teenage boy in a typical US small town.

Read each part of the short story. Make sure you can answer the questions in the margin before you read the next part.

sermon ['sɜːmən] a talk on a religious subject, given by a religious leader during a service

be doomed be in trouble or danger

pew [pjuː] bench in a church

piñata [pɪnˈjɑːtə] (from Spanish) figure decorated with coloured paper and filled with sweets

feed sb. some knuckles ['nʌklz] (infml) hit sb. in the mouth

be on a roll (infml) be in good form and unstoppable

split (infml) here: leave

destitute of sth. ['destɪtjuːt] (fml) completely without sth.

be needful to sb. (old-fashioned) be needed by sb.

doth [dʌθ] (old-fashioned) does

Doth Vader ['veɪdə] reference to Darth Vader, a character in the 'Star Wars' series of films

smack sb. hit sb.

shrug move the shoulders up and down

banish sb. from a place force sb. to leave a place

exodus (biblical) situation in which many people leave a place at the same time

transgression (fml) sin, wrongdoing

consolation sth. that makes you feel better when you are unhappy

Scripture ['skrɪptʃə] religious writings

It's going to be a long sermon,' Andy whispered to me.

'Yeah, we're doomed.' I could tell we were in trouble all the way from the back pew. Pastor Donald had stuck so many little colored slips of paper in his Bible, it looked like a piñata. He wasn't the sort of preacher who'd share a couple short verses and set us free to enjoy the day. He really liked to hammer home his messages. 5

'Turn with me to Romans twelve,' Pastor Donald said.

Andy started to snicker. 'Romans twelve, Christians nothing,' he whispered.

'Ssshhh.' I gave him an elbow and looked around. Mrs. Skeffington, three pews ahead and over to the left, was glaring at us. So were Mr. and Mrs. Linden, over on the right. [...]

Pastor Donald started to read out loud. 'Verse twenty tells us, if your enemy is hungry, feed him.' 10

'Feed him some knuckles,' Andy said, lifting his face from his hands.

I checked out my parents, up front. They hadn't looked back. Not yet. Neither had Andy's parents. If I could just get Andy to calm down, everything would be okay. 'Just cut it out,' I said. 'All right?'

No such luck. Andy was on a roll. And Pastor Donald was about to hand him even better 15 material to work with. After a brief visit with the Good Samaritan in Luke, and a short hop through Ecclesiastes, he landed squarely in James, chapter two, verse fifteen.

'If a brother or sister be naked ...'

'If a sister be naked, I'm staying,' Andy said. 'If a brother be naked, I'm splitting.'

'... and destitute of daily food ...' 20

'I thought destitutes made good money.' He scratched his head. 'Hold it. I think I got my 'tutes mixed up.'

'And one of you say unto them, Depart in peace, be ye warmed and filled; notwithstanding ye give them not those things which are needful to the body; what doth it profit?'

'Doth?' Andy said, stretching it out wetly like Daffy Duck. 'Doth who? Doth Vader?' He looked 25 at me and raised one eyebrow. 'Be ye warm, Tommy?'

As I reached over to smack Andy, the shadow of Assistant Pastor John fell across us.

'Out,' he whispered, pointing at the door with one hand and clutching the edge of the pew with the other. I could almost hear the wood splintering beneath his grip.

'I wasn't doing anything,' I said. 30

His index finger curled in, joining the rest of his fist. 'Out. Both of you.'

Questions on part 1 (ll. 1–40)

1 Where does the story take place?
2 When does it take place?
3 Who are the main characters?
4 What happens and why?

Andy shrugged and slipped past me. I followed him toward the door, hoping nobody noticed that we'd just been banished from church. As I glanced back, I saw that Mrs. Skeffington was following our exodus with the gloating satisfaction of someone who has just seen her worst enemy caught stealing money from the collection plate. No doubt, she'd make sure that my 35 parents didn't remain uninformed of my transgression.

My only consolation was the sight of Pastor Donald's Bible, which still had enough slips in it to fuel a small fire. I was going to miss a ton of Scripture.

I could still hear Pastor Donald as the door closed behind me, 'We are here to help others. Friend, enemy, brother, sister, neighbor, stranger – it doesn't matter.' [...] 40

It felt good to be free.

'So, whatcha want to do?' Andy asked when we'd walked down the steps to the street.

'I want to snap your head off,' I said.

45 'Now that's not very Christian.' Andy pointed over his shoulder. 'You should spend more time in church.'

'Look who's talking.' I wanted to be angry, but what the heck – it was a beautiful autumn day, cold and crisp, without a cloud in the sky. And my fate was at least an hour and a half away. Between the sermon and the singing, church wouldn't get out until eleven. I slipped into my
50 jacket.

Andy was already walking toward the center of town. 'What do you feel like doing?' I asked when I'd caught up with him.

'I don't know. How much money you got?'

I looked through my wallet. 'Enough for a couple orders of fries and some shakes,' I said. 'But
55 not enough for a cruise to the Bahamas.'

'Guess we'll have to settle for the fries.' Andy checked his own wallet. 'I think I can upgrade our meal in the direction of a couple burgers.'

We headed toward the Bridgeview Diner. When we were half a block away, I noticed a guy huddled in the entrance of a small office building across the street. He noticed me, too. He stood
60 and headed toward us in a way that reminded me of how my cat acts when I open the fridge.

'Man, he's going to ask for spare change,' I said. His hand was already out. I hated dealing with bums.

'I never give them money,' Andy said.

I was glad to hear that. I figured they probably just spent it on booze.

65 Sure enough, the guy reached us before we could get to the door of the diner. I took a step back. He looked pretty grubby. His wool plaid jacket was so worn that the squares were all the same color. I dropped my gaze and found myself staring at shoes that had split on the sides and were now wrapped with twine.

'Could you boys spare some money? I haven't eaten in a while.' His voice was so quiet I almost
70 couldn't make out the words.

Before I could tell him to leave us alone, Andy said, 'I'd be happy to buy you some food. You want a meal? Come with us.'

I glanced at Andy, surprised. But then I figured out what he was doing. He was calling the guy's bluff. That was brilliant. The bum didn't want food. He wanted our money so he could go buy
75 a bottle of cheap wine. No way he'd come with us.

'After you,' Andy said, holding the door open.

The guy went in. Man, I'd have bet a million bucks he'd have walked away from the offer. I figured Andy would back off now, but he followed the man right in. I didn't. I was used to Andy doing what he wanted. I'd seen him do stuff at school – like talk with the kids who everyone
80 else made fun of. But this was way over the top. Whoever the joke was on, it wasn't funny.

I thought about splitting. No way I wanted to eat with this guy. I glanced at my watch. It was too early to go back to church. Besides, I couldn't ditch Andy. He'd stuck with me a couple times when it would have been more fun to take off. And he was the only one from our school who'd visited me back when I'd had my appendix out. On the other hand, I'd never made him share a
85 meal with a bum. 'Let's just get it over with,' I muttered as I went through the door.

fate a bad thing that happens to sb.
bum (AE, offensive) homeless person
booze (infml) alcohol
grubby dirty
twine strong string
call sb.'s bluff to see if sb is brave enough to do sth. that they are threatening to do
ditch sb. (infml) get rid of sb. you no longer want to be with
appendix Blinddarm

Questions on part 2
(ll. 41–85)
1 Where do the boys want to go next?
2 Who do they meet?
3 How does Tommy feel?
4 What does Tommy do in the end?
5 Why does he act this way?

⚠ **Trouble Spot**
It's our treat. = Wir bezahlen.
treat sb. = jdn. einladen (z. B. in einem Restaurant bezahlen)
invite sb. = jdn. einladen (z. B. zu einer Party)

LP 26 One German Word, Two English Translations (p. 21)

fancy elegant
booth a place to sit in a restaurant with two long seats with a table between them
spring for sth. (AE, infml) pay for sth.
be broke (infml) have no money
sigh let out a long, deep breath to show that you are disappointed, sad, tired, etc
jock (AE, infml) boy or man who is good at sports
whiskers (pl) hair that grows on a man's face
nudge sb. push somebody gently, especially with your elbow
flat broke (infml) completely broke

⚠ **Trouble Spot**
wonder ['wʌndə] = sich fragen
sich wundern = **be surprised**

LP 27 False Friends (p. 22)

The place wasn't exactly fancy. Even so, the waitress gave all three of us the same sort of look I'd probably just given the guy myself. I guess she'd already figured she wasn't in for much of a tip from two kids and a bum. She turned away from us and fidgeted with the coffee pot, then started wiping the counter with a rag.

We grabbed a booth. I slid in next to Andy. I didn't really want to face the guy, but it beat sitting next to him. 90

Andy pointed to himself. 'I'm Andy. This is Tommy.'

The man nodded toward Andy, then toward me, but he kept his eyes down and didn't tell us his name. His left hand was shaking. After a minute, he put it on his lap.

The waitress finally came over. 'Ready?' she asked, her pad out and pencil poised. I guess she 95 didn't want to invest too much effort in conversation.

'After you,' Andy said to our guest.

The guy looked at the menu, but didn't speak.

'Get whatever you want,' Andy said. 'It's our treat.'

Our treat? I shot Andy a look. He shrugged, as if he assumed I wouldn't mind. I guess there 100 wasn't anything I could do about it right now. And he'd sprung for a movie last month when I was broke, so it sort of worked out.

The guy glanced up at the waitress, then back at the menu. I thought about the times when someone was treating me and I wasn't sure how much they wanted to spend. I always wrestled with what to get. 105

The waitress cleared her throat, then sighed. I didn't see why she was in such a rush. There weren't any other customers at the moment except for one guy at the counter, eating a donut.

'How about a steak and a salad?' Andy suggested.

The man nodded. In my head, I could hear the ka-ching of the cash register.

'Cokes for us,' Andy added. He glanced at me. 'Split some fries?' 110

I shook my head. 'I'm not hungry.'

The waitress scritched her pencil across the pad, then left.

'Thank you,' the man said.

'Our pleasure,' Andy said. 'Me and Tommy, we've known each other since we were little. I'm a jock. Tommy wants to be, but he's pretty uncoordinated. They let him on some of the teams 115 because they feel sorry for him.' He glanced out the window. 'Nice day, today. Supposed to be sunny the rest of the week. I noticed they're tearing up part of Main Street for the new parking garage.'

Andy kept talking, stopping once in a while to allow the guy to say something if he wanted to, but not asking any questions. I guess Andy talked because that's what people do when they're 120 waiting for their food. And I guess the guy didn't talk because it was hard enough just asking for the food. I wondered how many people had turned him down today. And I wondered how he'd ended up on the street. This close, beneath the whiskers and the dirt, he could pass for one of my uncles. Actually, I had an uncle who looked worse. For that matter, I had an aunt with more whiskers, too. 125

It was starting to sink in that this wasn't any kind of joke. This was just Andy being himself. Of course, if his act of kindness annoyed the waitress, I suspected that was just fine with him, too.

I could smell the steak before it came out of the kitchen. My stomach rumbled, even though I'd stuffed myself on pancakes at breakfast. A whole hour ago. Across the room, the donut eater tossed a couple of coins on the counter and headed up front to pay his bill. 130

A moment later, the waitress came out of the kitchen. She plopped down the thick white plate with a loud clack, then gave us our sodas.

The guy tore into the food, eating so fast at first, I was afraid he'd choke. He finally slowed after half the steak and all of the salad had vanished. No question, he'd been hungry. I sipped my soda and thought about how lucky I was to have a home and a family. Even a family that dragged
135 me to church every Sunday.

Andy kept talking. I talked some, too. The guy didn't talk, but he looked at each of us now as we spoke. I didn't look away when he caught my eye. I tried to imagine who he'd been. Tried to really see him.

Lifting his right hand, he pointed to the pile of French fries on his plate.

140 'Hey, thanks, don't mind if I do,' Andy said. He reached out and grabbed a couple.

He nudged me. I took one and ate it. It didn't kill me. Actually, it tasted pretty good. The three of us sat there and shared the rest of the fries.

The waitress was back the instant the guy swallowed his last bite. I still hadn't finished my soda. 'Pay there,' she said, putting the bill down by Andy's glass and tilting her head toward the
145 register. I gave him all my cash and he went up front.

'Thank you,' the guy said as he stood.

'You're welcome.'

He started to leave, then turned back and held out his hand. We shook. His grip was firmer than I expected. He headed out, stopping by Andy for a moment. They shook hands, too. Andy came
150 back as I slurped the last of my drink. I saw he still had some money. He jammed a dollar in my shirt pocket. 'Can't let my best friend walk around flat broke.' Then he dropped the rest of the money on the table. Three dollars and eighty cents.

'What was that for?' I asked as we left the diner.

'Tip,' he said. 'She works hard. This place is open all night. She's probably been here since four.'

155 'She wasn't very friendly,' I said.

'Would a small tip make her more friendly?' he asked. I guess he had a point.

We walked back through town, reaching the church just as the crowd was coming out the door. I worked my way against the flow, hoping to hook up with my parents before they figured out I hadn't been there during the service.

160 'I'm toast,' I muttered to Andy as I caught sight of Mrs. Skeffington talking to my mom.

When my folks reached me, my dad didn't waste any time. 'I'm very disappointed with you,' he said.

'Sorry.'

'Getting thrown out of a church service. Of all the places to misbehave.' He went on for a while,
165 and I nodded and made the proper noises to show how bad I felt. Out of the corner of my eye, I could see Andy dancing through the same routine with his mom and dad.

Finally, my dad turned to my mom and said, 'Let's go. I'm starving.'

I followed my parents to the car and got inside. Behind us, I saw old Mrs. Wilming hobbling slowly along the sidewalk. Mrs. Skeffington cruised past her, not offering a ride. On the church
170 steps, the Lindens were pulling their little kid by the arms as he dragged his feet and screamed his head off, pleading for a Happy Meal. When they reached level ground, Mrs. Linden gave him a swat on the rear to speed him along.

Through my open window, I heard her say, 'Just wait till I get you home.'

'We're trying to raise you the right way,' my mom said as Dad shot out of the parking lot. 'We
175 want you to have some decent values. Not like that friend of yours.'

**Questions on part 3
(ll. 86–156)**
Complete the following sentences.
1 Andy suggests the man order a steak and salad because the man …
2 Tommy talks about the weather because …
3 The man is polite and generous because …
4 Andy gives the waitress a large tip because …

---

be starving *(infml)* be really hungry
hobble walk weakly and unsurely
swat on the rear smack on the bottom
decent values ['diːsnt] acceptable beliefs about what is right and wrong

tacky *(infml)* showing bad taste

Questions on part 4 (ll. 157–end)

Say whether these statements are true or false:

1 After the service, Mrs Skeffington talks to Tommy's parents about the sermon.
2 The Lindens hit their child to make him walk faster.
3 Tommy's parents tell him off for behaving badly in church.
4 The waitress from the diner gives a beggar money.
5 Tommy loses the dollar bill by accident.

'But he's –'

'Drop it,' Dad warned before I could say anything to defend Andy.

I sighed and settled back in my seat. Dad cursed as he got caught in town by the long red light on Harmony Street. To my right, I saw the waitress from the diner. I guess she was on her way home. A guy in a long overcoat walked up to her, his hand out. She stopped and reached into her pocket. 180

The light changed and we drove off. I looked back, but I didn't get to see what happened. Maybe she gave him something. I'd like to think so.

In the front seats, my parents were playing Invisible Son, talking about me like I wasn't there.

'Tommy needs to show better judgment. That Andy kid is a bad influence,' my dad said. 185

My mom nodded. 'Teaching our son all the wrong things. Running around, getting into trouble. And his mother. Did you see the dress she was wearing? It was so tacky.'

'We'll straighten Tommy out,' my dad said. He floored the gas and tried to beat the next light. It was red by the time he went through it. 'I'm gonna make goddam sure he doesn't skip any more sermons. Somebody's got to teach him right from wrong. I'll tell you something else. Next Sunday, he's sitting up front with us. We'll see he doesn't miss anything.' 190

I reached into my shirt pocket and took out the dollar bill Andy had given me. As my parents continued to discuss the lessons I was going to learn, I held the bill near the window and let the breeze tug at it, then loosened my grip and watched it fly free.

David Lubar. In: Donald R. Gallo (Ed.): Destination Unexpected. Candleweek Press 2003 © David Lubar

TF D Multiple-Choice (p. 73)

1 Reading comprehension: multiple-choice

Choose the correct answer (A, B, C or D) for questions 1–6. Put a cross (✗) in the correct box. The first one (0) has been done for you.

0 The boys are thrown out of church because …
   A   they think Pastor Donald's sermon is too long. ☐
   B   Andy was being rude to Mrs Skeffington. ☐
   C   Andy was making fun of Pastor Donald's sermon. ☒
   D   Tommy was trying to hit Andy. ☐

1 After they are told to leave the church, Tommy is …
   A   worried that he will miss the rest of the sermon. ☐
   B   cross because it is so cold outside. ☐
   C   angry with Andy but relieved to be outside. ☐
   D   only worried about what his parents will say. ☐

2 When Tommy sees the homeless man, he …
   A   is happy that he and his friend can help him. ☐
   B   doesn't want to give him any money. ☐
   C   wants to buy the man a meal. ☐
   D   runs ahead to the diner to avoid him. ☐

3 When Andy offers to buy the homeless man a meal, Tommy …
   A   thinks his friend is testing the man. ☐
   B   offers to help pay for the man's dinner. ☐
   C   is glad that he'll have the chance to talk to a homeless person. ☐
   D   tells the homeless man to leave them alone. ☐

4 While they are waiting in the diner, Tommy realizes that Andy …
  A   is just trying to annoy the waitress. ☐
  B   wants to find out about the homeless man. ☐
  C   thinks the whole situation is just a big joke. ☐
  D   is just acting normally with the homeless man. ☐

5 Andy gives the waitress a large tip because …
  A   she serves them even though she doesn't want a homeless man in the restaurant. ☐
  B   he wants to make her feel bad about the way she treated the homeless man. ☐
  C   he feels bad about bringing a homeless man into the restaurant. ☐
  D   he feels sorry for her because she has to work long hours. ☐

6 Tommy lets go of the dollar bill because …
  A   he realizes that he has let his parents down badly. ☐
  B   he is angry that people don't act the way they talk. ☐
  C   he doesn't want anything more to do with Andy. ☐
  D   the wind is too strong for him to hold on to it. ☐

2 Looking at the characters

a Read the quotes from Pastor Donald's sermon again (ll. 10, 18 –24). What are they about? Summarize Pastor Donald's message in one sentence.

b Give each of the following characters a mark: A ('excellent'), B, C, D or F ('fail') for how well they behave according to the lesson of the sermon:

	A	B	C	D	F
Andy	☐	☐	☐	☐	☐
Tommy's mum	☐	☐	☐	☐	☐
other churchgoers (e.g. Mrs Skeffington)	☐	☐	☐	☐	☐
Tommy	☐	☐	☐	☐	☐
Tommy's dad	☐	☐	☐	☐	☐

Be prepared to explain your marks with quotes from the story.

c Explain your marks to your partner. Try to agree on a mark for each character. Then report your results to the class.

3 Close reading

Read ll. 113–123 again. Describe and comment on the way Andy communicates with the homeless man. Do you think Andy is right to act the way he does in the situation? Why (not)?

4 EXTRA Writing: blog entry

Write a blog entry on this short story. In the posting you should …
  ▪ briefly present what the story is about.
  ▪ discuss how the short story relates to the proverb "Actions speak louder than words".
  ▪ explain why you liked or disliked it.
Write about 150 words.

Hi everybody
I've just finished "Bread on the Water" by David Lubar. …

Language Help

  ▪ Do you really think Andy and Tommy should get the same mark? Andy was …
  ▪ That's true. Let's mark … up/ down.
  ▪ I disagree. Tommy says in line …
  ▪ OK, then we both have … for Tommy.
  ▪ Well, then we'll have to agree to disagree.

LP 37 Agreeing and Disagreeing (p. 29)

SP 43 Writing a Characterization (p. 57)

TT 3 Blog Entry (p. 63)

5 Making small talk

a Describe the cartoon to your partner. What does the caveman do wrong? How do you think the conversation between caveman and cavewoman could develop?

b Work with a partner. Take it in turns to react to the following typical small-talk questions. (Think of a situation in which you might hear them.) Try to keep the conversation going.
1 Excuse me, do you think you could take a photo of me and my friend?
2 Have you been here long?
3 Hey, how's it going?
4 Have you been to this club before?
5 The queues are always long when you're in a hurry, aren't they?
6 Excuse me, those are really cool glasses. Where did you get them?

6 Role play

You have booked a room at a youth hostel in London. When you arrive, the hostel hasn't opened its doors yet and it looks very closed. Another person (your partner) is already waiting.
- Think of a suitable way to start a conversation with your partner.
- Find out some information about your partner.
- Decide what you are going to do while you are waiting.
- Find out if you are interested in seeing the same things in London.
- Suggest some places that you could visit together.

Try to keep the conversation going as long as you can.

CAN-DO STATEMENTS

		Part / Ex	✔
📖	I can understand longer, relatively simple literary texts on themes that are familiar to me (e.g. modern popular literature). (B1/3)	B / Ex 1 B / Ex 2	☐
👀	I can begin, maintain and end a conversation about subjects familiar to me. (B1/1)	B / Ex 5 B / Ex 6	☐
	I can ask and answer questions on familiar themes without preparation. (B1/5)	B / Ex5	☐
	I can take on a role in a simulated everyday or professional situation and also improvise thereby. (B1/9)	B / Ex 6	☐
👄	I can report on subject areas familiar to me, what I have heard, seen, read or experienced and describe my feelings or reactions. (B1/1)	A / Ex 2	☐
	I can describe pictures and tell stories with the help of key words or illustrations. (B1/5)	A / Ex 2	☐
✎	I can write reports or simple articles on events, experiences of a general or a professional nature. These texts may be intended for different media or different personal or professional purposes. (B1/1)	B / Ex 4	☐
	I can describe my personal impression of stories and books, films and plays. (B1/3)	B / Ex 4	☐

Keep going ...
You can do
anything! ☺

UNIT 9 Applying for Volunteer Work

In this unit you will produce a personal statement to apply for a place on a summer project, but it will help you when applying for other things as well: a place at an English-speaking university, for example, or a job in a company where English is the working language.

A Two Job Descriptions Key: 324

Partner A: Look at this page. **Partner B:** Look at the page provided by your teacher.

Overview
Our rural projects in Kenya are located in villages near Lake Nakuru. People there are the poorest in the country, and many villages lack basic facilities and resources.

Our rural projects focus on providing educational facilities, basic sanitation and access to clean water. You may find yourself building a classroom, renovating a school, constructing pit latrines or installing a rainwater harvesting system.

On the project
You'll be met at the airport and introduced to your fellow volunteers before being taken to the village you'll be calling home for the next five weeks.

You'll be amazed by how quickly you feel at home as you settle into village life, and make new friends on the building site and in the classroom!

On the building site you will work with members of the local community and your team to complete the building before you leave. In the classroom you'll be able to bring your enthusiasm and energy to English, maths, music or sports lessons. Our projects are flexible: you can teach, build, or combine the two.

http://www.gapyear.com

---

rural [ˈrʊərəl] in the countryside
facilities *(pl) here: toilets*
educational facilities *(pl)* here: schools
sanitation toilets, showers, washbasins, etc.
pit latrine [ləˈtriːn] hole in the ground used as a toilet
rainwater harvesting system a system for gathering rainwater

---

1 Reading and taking notes

a Read the job advert from an organization that arranges international volunteer work for students. Take notes on what personal qualities and skills they are looking for. (Some things are said directly; others are implied.)

b Compare your notes with your partner. Which qualities/skills are the same? Which are different?

c Discuss the differences between the two texts with your partner. (Think of the style of the text and the information given.) Why are they different?

SP 4 Taking Notes (p. 32)

2 An interview

a Your partner has applied for a place on the Kenyan rural project. Interview him/her to find out if he/she has the qualities needed. Use your notes from **1a** to prepare questions, then do the interview.
Partner A: Have you ever been to a country in the developing world?
Partner B: No, this would be my first time.
Partner A: Would you be prepared to get your hands dirty?
Partner B: Of course, that's not a problem for me.
Partner A: Can you give me an example?
Partner B: ...

b Now it's your partner's turn to interview you. Answer his/her questions. Be prepared to give examples that show you have the qualities needed.

3 Language in Use: multiple-choice

Read the text about gap years. Some words are missing from the text. Choose the correct answer (A, B, C or D) for each gap (1–10) in the text. Put a cross (✘) in the correct box. The first one (0) has been done for you.

TF H Multiple Choice (p. 76)

Many young people like to do a "gap year", which is a year out between school and university or between university and starting work. You can (0) ___ from taking a gap year in many ways. Firstly, it gives you relevant work (1) ___ and may give you some ideas on what you might like to do later as a job. It gives you new skills and (2) ___ and will make your CV look even more impressive. Not least, it will help the local (3) ___ .
You'll learn leadership and problem-solving skills as well as adapting to change and taking risks; you will (4) ___ in confidence and independence. (5) ___ , you'll increase your understanding of the issues facing developing countries and how your contribution can make an (6) ___ . Volunteering can generally be divided into development work or (7) ___ activities to preserve the environment. Examples include building schools in Ghana, working on a (8) ___ project in Brazil or tracking elephants in Namibia.
The first time you can really (9) ___ taking a year out is usually at 17 or 18. But if you don't feel ready then, there are still plenty of opportunities later on in your life. And if you don't want to take a gap year, don't! It's your (10) ___ .

	A	B	C	D
0	☐ succeed	✘ benefit	☐ prosper	☐ advance
1	☐ experiment	☐ trial	☐ experience	☐ test
2	☐ confidence	☐ arrogance	☐ self-consciousness	☐ belief
3	☐ society	☐ company	☐ community	☐ firm
4	☐ rise	☐ gain	☐ add	☐ raise
5	☐ However	☐ Although	☐ Nevertheless	☐ Moreover
6	☐ effort	☐ explosion	☐ effect	☐ impact
7	☐ conservation	☐ destruction	☐ production	☐ distribution
8	☐ illness	☐ disease	☐ health	☐ wellness
9	☐ argue	☐ think	☐ propose	☐ consider
10	☐ selection	☐ choice	☐ option	☐ vote

4 Introducing yourself

a Complete the following sentences with the right form of the verbs. Be careful to use the *simple present* and the *present progressive* correctly.

1 I _____ (like) animals and _____ (go/ride) twice a week. But I _____ (not just ride); I _____ (take) care of my horse regularly. I _____ (plan/be) a vet.
2 I _____ (currently take) a course at a private language school. I _____ (hope/speak) Italian fluently by the end of the year.
3 Although my parents _____ (support) my decision _____ (do) a gap year, I _____ (try/earn) the money myself.
4 I _____ (enjoy/talk) to old people and _____ (help) them whenever I can.
5 I _____ (currently do) a school project that _____ (involve/test) the water quality of a pond near my house twice weekly.
6 I _____ (think) I _____ (be) good with my hands. I _____ (love/build) things and _____ (now work) on a tree house for children at a local adventure playground.

Tip
When you introduce yourself – as in a personal statement – you will mostly need to say:
- who you are, where you live, what sorts of things interest you (you normally use the *simple present* for this),
- what you are currently doing (you normally use the *present progressive* for this),
- what sorts of things you have experienced and done up to now (you normally use the *present perfect* for this).

LP 2 Simple Present and Present Progressive (p. 5)

LP 19 To-Infinitive and Gerund after Verbs (p. 15)

▶▶▶

b Complete the following sentences with the right form of the verbs. Be careful to use the *simple present* and the *present perfect* correctly.

1 I _____ (always be) interested in other cultures. Today I _____ (be) most interested in Africa.

2 I _____ (take) part in the activities of our local fire brigade's youth organization every weekend and _____ (go) to several week-long events throughout the year.

3 For as long as I _____ (can remember), my parents _____ (encourage) me _____ (explore) my interest in nature.

4 Since the third grade I _____ (want/visit) Africa. My interest in the continent _____ (grow) in the last few years.

5 I _____ (often be told) that I _____ (be) very good with children, and I _____ (think) I _____ (want/be) a teacher.

6 I _____ (never be) interested in the things most kids my age _____ (be) interested in. I … (always prefer/read or go/hike).

LP 5 Present Perfect for 'time up until now' (p. 7)

LP 19 To-Infinitive and Gerund after Verbs (p. 15)

SP 12 Working with Pictures (p. 38)

5 Describing qualities and experience

a Look at the photo with a partner and talk about the following:
- What sort of job is the student volunteer doing?
- Does she work through an organization?
- How did they meet?
- …

b Now write a text of 100–150 words about the student volunteer in the photo. (You can choose any form, e.g. a newspaper article, an interview, a diary entry.) Use as many of the phrases from *Language Help* as possible.

Language Help

- improve sb.'s life / quality of life
- give one's (free) time
- use one's special skills
- be dedicated to (doing) sth.
- be eager to help sb./sth.
- be reliable / a reliable person
- feel appreciated/needed
- be a learning experience
- be rewarding

6 Correcting common mistakes

When you get back a homework assignment or test that has been corrected, study the corrections carefully. Use them to start a learning log. It will help you to avoid mistakes. Rewrite the personal statement of Laura Michaelis, making the necessary corrections.

SP 10 Keeping a Learning Log (p. 36)

Personal statement of Laura Michaelis

Since I have been a child, I am fascinated by everything African. My room at home is full of African art, and I even take lessons in Swahili at the local night school since the last two years. Seeing the continent myself is a dream of mine as long as I can remember.

But I'm not just curious about the place and the many cultures there. I'm also interested in helping to improve the lives of some of the poor in Africa.

I am currently attending Friedrich Schiller High School, where we are having a group called Young People Helping. As the name of the group says, we aren't just talking about the problems of the world; we try to solve at least a few of them locally.

For example, I am spending my Saturdays to work in a soup kitchen for homeless people. We are meeting at a church hall at 8.30 a.m. to move tables, clean the kitchen and have the food ready by twelve o'clock. It's hard work, but I feel we are making the lives of the poorest people in our community a little bit better. It's diffcult, of course, to see young children in this situation, but their smiles when they are leaving the hall every week make it all seem worthwhile.

I am seeing a once-in-a-lifetime chance in the Kenyan rural project to combine my love of Africa with my wish to help. I cannot think of a more satisfying way to spend my last summer before I will start my studies in September.

Laura Michaelis

7 Writing: personal statement

a You want to apply for a place on the Kenyan rural project (see **1a** on p. 122). Write your own personal statement. Use the corrected text above as a model.

- Your statement should be about 200–250 words long.
- It should be easy to read – either printed out from a computer or neatly written.
- It should demonstrate that you have the most important qualities you think the organization is looking for in a volunteer.

b Swap personal statements with your partner. Read your partner's statement and make suggestions on how to improve it. Consider what the statement says, the choice of words and grammatical correctness.

c Rewrite your statement if you agree with your partner's suggestions. Then put it in your portfolio.

SP 38 Writing a Personal Statement (p. 55)

SP 32 The Stages of Writing (p. 51)

SP 11 Keeping a Portfolio (p. 36)

CAN-DO STATEMENTS

		Part/Ex	✔
📖	I can get the essential information from simple newspaper and magazine articles that are clearly structured. (B1/1)	A/Ex 1	☐
	I can find information that I need to solve a specific task in various longer texts or text sections. (B1/8)	A/Ex 1	☐
👀	I can give information about myself, my family or my professional life in an interview situation. (B1/7)	A/Ex 2	☐
	I can take on a role in a simulated everyday or professional situation and also improvise thereby. (B1/9)	A/Ex 2	☐
👄	I can describe pictures and tell stories with the help of key words or illustrations. (B1/5)	A/Ex 5	☐
✏️	I can write simple stories, essays and creative texts. (B1/2)	A/Ex 5	☐
	I can introduce myself, e.g. in a letter to a host family, or in a personal statement to a future employer. (B1/ 7)	A/Ex 7	☐

TF L Editing (p. 79)

1 Language in Use: editing ⟁ **Key: 239**

Read this text about Kierra Box, a young British person who became very involved in political activity. In most lines of the text there is a word that should not be there. Write that word in the space provided. Indicate the correct lines with a tick (✔). There are two examples (0, 00) at the beginning.

'Hands up for peace'

Kierra Box		
Kierra Box, who was born in 1985, co-founded the "Hands Up For Peace"	✔	0
campaign in year 2003. This movement was originally set up to protest	*year*	00
against Britain's involvement in the war in the Iraq. The idea behind the	____	1
campaign was very much simple: to collect paper handprints on which	____	2
children wrote their feelings about the war. The handprints were then stuck	____	3
on sticks and be "planted" in front of the Houses of Parliament.	____	4
Kierra Box and her friends collected nearly 3000 hands from young people	____	5
across the world and the idea has not been copied by protest movements	____	6
from Brighton to Australia.	____	7
Since that protest, Kierra Box has had launched a website as a platform for	____	8
anyone under age 24 and has become well-known as a spokesperson for	____	9
young people in Britain on many total different topics, such as protests against	____	10
war or pollution.	____	11
"I don't think of what I've done as amazing. I thought when some things were	____	12
wrong so I tried to do something about them – that's just a logical progression.	____	13
I always find it much more even surprising that people don't get involved in	____	14
anything," she says.	____	15

Alice O'Keeffe: Kierra Box. In: http://www.newstatesman.com, October 17, 2005

TF F Short Answers (p. 74)

2 Reading comprehension: short answers

The following text is part of a speech made by Kierra Box. Read it and answer the questions using a maximum of 4 words. Write your answers in the spaces provided. The first one (0) has been done for you.

Kierra and two friends
_____
_____
_____
_____
_____
_____
_____
_____

0 Who originally set up "Hands Up For Peace"?
1 What was the first idea for a protest that Kierra and her friends had?
2 How are young people at school told to make themselves heard?
3 What question did the organizers ask themselves instead of just saying what they thought?
4 Apart from emails, a website and going to demonstrations, how did they spread their idea?
5 What did they ask people to write on the cut-out hands?
6 How many hands did they hope to get at first?
7 Why have they now changed the name of the organization?
8 What are they asking young people for now?

Basically, "Hands Up For Peace" was an organization set up by three of us when we were 17. We thought about just putting a banner on a bridge over the Thames with the message against war. We were thinking: what would be a young person's message against war. And we were thinking: how are young people told to vote? How do we make our voices heard? And the way we thought that we are generally told to make our voices heard in school is "put your hand up". "Put your hand up if you want to do this." "Put your hand up if you believe in this." "Put your hand up to vote". So we thought: what are we putting our hands up for? How are we going to get ourselves noticed? We're going to put our hands up for peace. And so that was going to be the message on our banner.

And then we began thinking: well, our argument in this is that Blair's going to war, and he's the only one who wants to, and it's undemocratic. How can our protest be democratic? How can we ensure that it's not just us putting up a banner saying "Our hands are up for peace", and not representing all the other young people in the country. We don't know what their hands are up for. We don't know what they're thinking. So we decided to find out. We circulated an email, we started a website, we spread things through word of mouth, we went on the protests and demos at the beginning, and basically, we just told people that if they had a message for peace, they should draw round their hand, they should cut it out on a piece of paper, they should decorate it, and most importantly, they should write their message for peace on their hand, their argument against war. Now these ranged from "I don't like war" to "Peace is best" to a hand filled with an essay about the causes of war, why the war was for oil, and why they felt the war was economically, socially and morally unviable.

And so basically we had a whole range of things. We did put them up in Parliament Square. We aimed for 2000. In the month before war broke out we began collecting them, and we actually had 3000. More kept coming in, even after the war had finished. And the response is so good, we're actually now a different organization. We're called "Hands Up For...". So young people now contact us whenever there's an issue they're upset about. At the moment we're looking at nuclear war and the new arms race, and asking young people to put their hands up for their views on nuclear weapons.

Ministry for Peace speech by Kierra Box

(Tony) Blair (b. 1953) UK Prime Minister 1997–2007
ensure make sure
unviable not successful

3 Listening comprehension: sentence completion (note form)
Listen to the second part of Kierra Box's speech.
While listening, complete the sentences (1–8) using a maximum of 4 words. Write your answers in the spaces provided. The first one (0) has been done for you.

⑫

TF C Short Answers (p. 72)

0	Kierra Box quotes ____ of the introduction to the UN Decade for a Culture of Peace.	*the opening line*
1	She says that for many ____ war is the way forward.	
2	According to her, and most ____ , the way forward is clear.	
3	She says that the message of peace ____ to the people who make decisions in the world.	
4	She points out that Israel, Palastine and her own government used violence to ____ .	
5	She once visited a small graveyard ____ on a school history trip.	
6	The graves in the graveyard were not marked by headstones, but by ____ .	
7	She could not believe that all the names of the dead soldiers in the graveyard were ____ .	
8	She finds it disturbing that this is how ____ have to live and grow up in this century.	

'A greener planet will be a more peaceful and prosperous one too.'

Ban Ki-moon, UN Secretary General

A

Natural Numbers

Example: Divide 5000 buffaloes by fifty hunters = almost nothing left.

1. Divide 200 elephants by seventeen ivory poachers =

2. Divide two rainforests by eight logging companies =

3. Divide one beautiful planet by one greedy species =

Mike Johnson: Natural Numbers. In: Brian Moses/Pie Corbett (Eds.): The Works 2. London: Macmillan Children's Book 2002

B

prosperous rich
ivory poacher hunter who kills elephants illegally for their tusks (ivory)
logging company company that cuts down trees
greedy species ['spi:ʃi:z] a group of animals that eats/ uses more than it needs

**Give water.
Give life.
Give £2
a month.**

WaterAid

C

WaterAid/Caroline Penn

Language Help

- I think what … says is true, but …
- … is so convincing/direct/eye-catching/strange/… that I think …
- I think pictures always interest people, so I'd choose …
- I find …'s argument very convincing, so …
- I can/can't imagine that people will pay attention to …

1 Think – pair – share: different opinions, different aims

a **Think:** Partner A reads texts A–C, Partner B reads texts D–F. Check that you understand them. Then make notes on the message of each text. What might each text have to do with the Topic title and the picture of the planet Earth?

b **Pair:** Describe your three texts to your partner; then compare all six texts. Decide who is most likely to make people think about changing their behaviour: the UN Secretary General (A), the poet (B) or the aid worker (C), the environmentalists (D), the scientist (E) or the activists (F)?

c **Share:** Report to the class and explain your choice.

SP 5 Making Notes (p. 32)

In this topic you will learn about …

- people and the planet   **(WiC)**
- how scientists explain climate change   **(Unit 10)**
- how artists see climate change   **(Unit 11)**
- some solutions to the problem   **(Unit 12)**

D

GREENPEACE *If we don't act against global warming, one out of four living species will become extinct.*

Greenpeace

E

Why conserve?

American scientists have recently estimated that the value [...] of the as yet undiscovered drugs from tropical rainforests is around $150 billion. In other words, the rainforests may be worth more alive, as a source of valuable drugs, than they are dead, when they are used as a source of timber.

University of Bath, U.K.

become extinct die out
plane stupid name of an anti-flying action group (plane as in aeroplane, but also as in plain)
aviation industry industry that makes and flies aeroplanes
bring sb. down to earth *(fig)* make sb. realize that what they are doing is wrong

F

plane stupid
bringing the aviation industry back down to earth!

Anette Schamuhn

2 How we are changing the planet

a In groups of four, do a placemat activity. In your corner of the placemat, write down all the ways you think people are changing the planet (for good or bad).

b Discuss your lists in your group. In the middle of your placemat, write down the two most dangerous and the two best ways we are changing the planet.

c Compare your results with those of other groups. Which was easier: listing changes for the better or listing changes for the worse? Why?

Language Help

- Many things that people do have a positive/negative effect on the planet, e.g. …
- Through genetic engineering scientists are helping us save threatened species / grow more food / …
- Eating imported food / Driving / … is bad for the planet because

SP 2 Brainstorming (p. 30)

24 Increase Your Word Power Online (p. 18)

People and the Planet

The earliest human being were hunters; they moved from one place to another, eating whatever they could find. Sustainability was not an issue for them; the food supply was sustainable: new plants grew and animals were born at the same rate that people consumed them.

Today, of course, most people aren't nomadic, and world population and consumption have increased greatly. We settle in places that were once home to different species of animals or plants, and we dispose of our waste there. As we destroy these habitats, species die out. Overpopulation and the resulting destruction of entire ecosystems are the greatest threats to biodiversity. 5

In recent years, most people in the developed world have become more aware of the damage we are doing to our planet. We try to buy eco-friendly products, i.e. products that will not contribute to the extinction of an endangered species, that don't require too much energy to produce or to transport, and that won't pollute the environment when we throw them away. We prefer things that are made of renewable resources like wood or wool, or at least from materials that can be recycled. 10

15

We have become more and more concerned about climate change in the form of global warming. There can be little doubt that the Earth's temperature is increasing, but until recently, there was little agreement on whether the phenomenon was caused by human activity or had some natural cause. Today, no serious scientist would say that climate change is not influenced by what we do. 20

What can be done about it? It is probably not possible to reverse global warming, but we might be able to slow it down. To do that, we need to reduce emissions of so-called 'greenhouse gases' like carbon dioxide and methane. 25

To help calculate the impact we have on the Earth's climate, environmentalists have developed the concept of the carbon footprint. The larger our footprint, the more we are contributing to the greenhouse effect and global warming. It is hoped that understanding the carbon footprint will help us to reduce it, e.g. by eating locally grown food or driving less. And if we cannot reduce it, we can try to offset our carbon footprint by planting trees or supporting renewable energy projects. 30

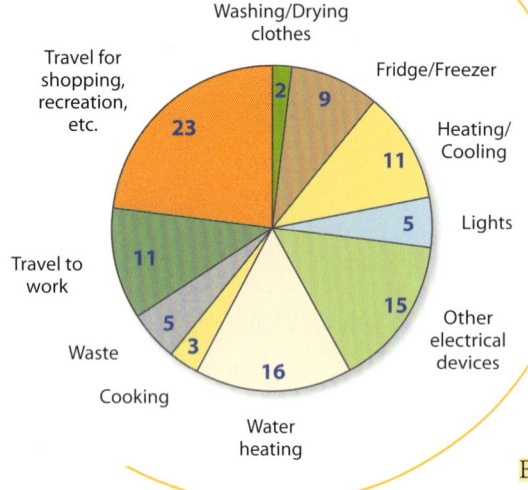

Sources of greenhouse gas for a typical family in %

Washing/Drying clothes — 2
Fridge/Freezer — 9
Heating/Cooling — 11
Lights — 5
Other electrical devices — 15
Water heating — 16
Cooking — 3
Waste — 5
Travel to work — 11
Travel for shopping, recreation, etc. — 23

Language Help

- The pie chart clearly shows that …
- The segment showing … represents / makes up
  - about/roughly/approximately … per cent.
  - the biggest/smallest part.
  - more than … / over half of / three quarters of the whole/total.
- This makes it easier for people to see that …

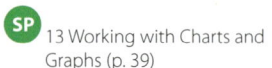
13 Working with Charts and Graphs (p. 39)

1 Sustainable consumption

Look at the text and note down different ways in which consumption affects the environment. Compare your ideas with a partner.

2 Our carbon footprint  Key: 735

a Look at the pie chart. What are the two biggest sources of greenhouse gas for a family? How might a chart like this help people to reduce their carbon footprint?

b EXTRA Go to a website where you can calculate your carbon footprint. How does yours compare with that of your classmates / the Austrian average? How could you reduce or offset your carbon footprint?

3 Language in Use: word formation

TF I Word Formation (p. 77)

Some words are missing from the text. Use the words in brackets to form a word that fits in the gap (1–10). Write your answers in the spaces provided at the end of the text. The first one (0) has been done for you.

Of all the factors that (0) ___ **(threat)** the existence of life on Earth, climate change is perhaps the biggest problem. Some scientists are still hoping for a (1) ___ **(reverse)** of the trend towards a warmer climate, but unfortunately, some of the biggest polluters haven't agreed to a major (2) ___ **(reduce)** of greenhouse gas emissions. Factories need to become more efficient and (3) ___ **(emission)** less carbon dioxide. Thanks to new filtering systems, air (4) ___ **(pollute)** is no longer a problem near modern power stations. The biggest (5) ___ **(contribute)** to greenhouse gases from private households comes from travel. People are (6) ___ **(consume)** oil much faster than the Earth can produce it. Oil is not a sustainable resource. Our activities have also (7) ___ **(influence)** biodiversity on the Earth. It is estimated that three species of plants and animals become (8) ___ **(extinguish)** every hour, often simply because we do not (9) ___ **(disposal)** of our waste properly. If we don't act soon, many habitats will be (10) ___ **(destroy)** for ever.

0 *threaten*
1 _____
2 _____
3 _____
4 _____
5 _____
6 _____
7 _____
8 _____
9 _____
10 _____

4 Interpreting charts and graphs

a Which of the following statements best describes what the graph shows?

1 The graph shows how many tonnes of CO_2 from fossil fuels five different countries or areas emitted from 1990 to 2016.

2 The graph shows how many tonnes of CO_2 from fossil fuels each person in one of five different countries or areas emitted each year from 1990 to 2016.

3 The graph shows the price for a tonne of CO_2 in five different countries or areas between 1990 and 2016.

4 The graph shows the change in the number of tonnes of CO_2 from fossil fuels each person in one of five different countries or areas emitted between 1990 and 2016.

CO_2 EMISSIONS PER CAPITA FROM FOSSIL FUEL USE

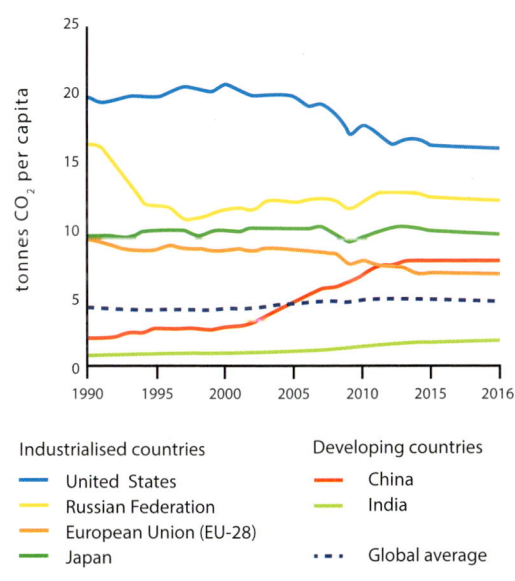

Data from: EDGAR 4.3.2 (1990-2016);
UNPD, 2016

b Complete the description of the graph with the words and phrases from the box.

> covered by ▪ decreased steadily ▪ good progress ▪ highest levels ▪ increased levels ▪ increased ▪ slowly but steadily ▪ increased significantly ▪ reduction ▪ rose ▪ sharp decline ▪ significant increase ▪ similar level ▪ slight rise ▪ unchanged

SP 13 Working with Charts and Graphs (p. 39)

Three of the six countries or areas shown, the United States, the Russian Federation and the EU, reduced their pro capita CO_2 emissions in the time period (1)___ the graph. Two countries, China and India, had (2)___ of CO_2 emissions.

The Russian Federation began with a (3)___ in levels from 1990 to 1994. After 1998 the country's CO_2 emissions went (4)___ upward.

Emissions in the USA (5)___ slightly at first, reaching their (6)___ in 1999. There was a small (7)___ until 2007, after which the figures (8)___ .

The EU has made (9)___ over this period. The figures have (10)___ since 1990.

India's emissions remained almost (11)___ from 1990 to 2004. Since then, there has been a (12)___ in CO_2 emissions.

The most (13)___ in CO_2 emissions per capita has been in China. Since 2002 the emissions have (14)___ and have reached a (15)___ to the EU.

UNIT 10   The Scientist's View

A   What Is Global Warming?

You are going to read two texts on a scientific topic, but written for different audiences.

1   Reading comprehension: multiple matching

The titles and headings of each paragraph of the texts have been removed. Choose the correct title (A or B) and the correct heading for each paragraph (C–H). Write your answers in the spaces provided.

A   The Science of Climate Change

B   Is the Earth Getting Hotter?

C   So it's all good, then? What's the problem?

D   Go on, then – what's the worst that could happen?

E   Human activity and the greenhouse gases

F   By 2 degrees? That doesn't sound so bad.

G   I don't get it.

H   What is the greenhouse effect?

1	2	3	4	5	6	7	8

1 _____

2 _____

Some reflected heat escapes through the atmosphere.

Some reflected heat is trapped by greenhouse gases and further increases the Earth's temperature.

The greenhouse effect

Anette Schamuhn

TF E Multiple Matching (p. 73)

Text 1

Global warming – the planet getting progressively hotter over time – is caused by a process called the 'greenhouse effect'. In simple terms, this happens because the Earth's atmosphere is transparent to sunlight, but not to the heat that comes off the Earth as sunlight heats it up. So the heat is held inside the atmosphere, raising the temperature. This is a bit like the way the glass of a greenhouse lets light in and out but stops heat from escaping, allowing us to grow warm-weather plants in colder countries. Hence the name 'greenhouse effect'. This idea isn't even particularly new. The Irish physicist and mountaineer John Tyndall first described it in 1863 – along with a few other things, like why the sky is blue. He and other scientists also realized that this effect is so important in maintaining global temperatures that there probably wouldn't be life on the planet without it. [...]

3 _____

The problem is that lately this warming effect seems to have been intensifying and speeding up. We think at least part of this might be due to gases spewed out by our cars, planes, factories and power stations, among other things. So most of the arguments about global warming are about whether we should replace or cut down on using these things in order to slow down the pace of the effect. In any case, at the current rate, it looks as if global temperatures will rise by about 2° to 6°C by the year 2100.

4 _____

Maybe not, but even this small rise will have a serious effect on countries all over the world. [...]

5 _____

Well, everything we've said so far is our best guess of what will happen, based on what we know about how the Earth's atmosphere and oceans interact. But things could get more complicated, and (as we often see with simple weather forecasts) predictions about how the atmosphere and oceans will behave can be wrong. It's possible (although unlikely) that the increased heating of the seas could release enough water vapour into the atmosphere to create a 'runaway greenhouse effect', pushing temperatures up so high that trees and crops across the world would die.

⚠ **Trouble Spot**

raise sth. = etwas erhöhen
rise = (an)steigen
affect sb./sth. *(v)* = jdn./etwas beeinflussen
effect (on sth.) *(n)* = Wirkung, Auswirkung (auf etwas)

---

current *(adj)* gegenwärtig, aktuell
currently *(adv)* derzeit, momentan
hence *(fml)* for this reason
maintain sth. keep sth. at a certain level
due to because of
spew sth. out [spjuː] spit or blow out
pace speed
vapour *(BE)* steam
runaway *(adj)* out of control
crop plant grown for food
dilute sth. [daɪˈluːt] mix sth., usually with water, so that it is not so strong or effective
current [BE: ˈkʌrənt, AE: ˈkɜːr-] movement of water in the sea
plunge sth. into sth. else [plʌndʒ] cause sth. to fall suddenly into sth. else

LP 28 Confusables (p. 22)

On the other hand, if enough polar ice melted and diluted the oceans, it could affect the way they circulate (through currents) across the world. One result of this might be stopping or reversing the flow of the Gulf Stream – the current that supplies Europe with warm water – plunging Britain and other countries into long, freezing winters similar to those in the Arctic.

Glenn Murphy: Why Is Snot Green? London: Pan Macmillan 2007

6 _____

7 _____

The term 'greenhouse effect' is used to describe the warming of the Earth's surface and lower atmosphere that is caused by the presence of certain gases which let energy from the sun through to the ground but which also absorb energy as it passes from the ground back through the atmosphere into space. [...]

Text 2

It is important to note that it is not the existence of the greenhouse effect itself that scientists are concerned about. Indeed, the greenhouse effect is a natural phenomenon that has existed since long before human beings began polluting the Earth. And if it weren't for the greenhouse effect, the Earth's climate would be too cold for life as we know it, having an average temperature of -18 °C. What scientists are concerned about is that by increasing the quantities of some of the greenhouse gases in the atmosphere, humans are likely to further increase the temperature of the lower atmosphere and the planet's surface. Some of the gases that play a role in the greenhouse effect are carbon dioxide, methane, nitrous oxide, chlorofluorocarbons, ozone and water vapour. All of these gases except water vapour are currently being emitted into the atmosphere in significant amounts as a result of human activities. The amount that each of the individual greenhouse gases contributes to the overall greenhouse effect varies depending on three things: the extent to which the gas is able to absorb radiation, the amount of the gas existing in the atmosphere, and the period of time that molecules of that gas remain in the atmosphere.

presence ['prezns] being in a particular place
be likely to do sth. probably do sth.
nitrous oxide [ˌnaɪtrəs_'ɒksaɪd] *Distickstoffmonoxid (N2O), Lachgas*
chlorofluorocarbon (CFC) *Fluorchlorkohlenwasserstoff (FCKW)*
emit sth. [i'mɪt] *(fml)* give sth. off
contribute to sth. be a cause of sth.
radiation heat or energy in the form of rays
remain stay
anthropogenic [ˌænθrəpə'dʒenɪk] coming from human
fossil fuels ['fɒsl ˌfjuːəlz] oil, coal and natural gas
deforestation cutting down of forests

8 _____

Of the different greenhouse gases being produced in significant amounts by human activities, carbon dioxide is being emitted in by far the greatest quantities and is the largest contributor to anthropogenic climate change. The primary way that humans are increasing the amount of carbon dioxide in the atmosphere is the burning of fossil fuels for energy and transport purposes. In addition to this, deforestation, and in particular deforestation which involves the burning of forested areas, contributes significant amounts of carbon dioxide to the atmosphere.

Terence Wood: What is the greenhouse effect? In: The Gamma Series of the Royal Socity of New Zealand (Ed.):
The Science of Climate Change, Issue 03/05, June 2005

TF F Short Answers (p. 74)

SP 28 Scanning (p. 50)

2 Reading comprehension: short answers

Now answer the questions on the two texts using a maximum of 4 words. Write your answers in the spaces provided. The first one (0) has been done for you.

0	What process causes global warming?	0	*"the greenhouse effect"*	*Text 1*
1	What does the atmosphere do with the heat from the Earth?	1	_____	
2	Why is the greenhouse effect necessary for life on Earth?	2	_____	
3	What is the problem with the greenhouse effect now?	3	_____	
4	What reason is given for this?	4	_____	
5	What unlikely result of this is mentioned?	5	_____	
6	What other possible result is described?	6	_____	
7	Which greenhouse gas contributes most to climate change?	7	_____	*Text 2*
8	What is the main cause of this greenhouse gas emission?	8	_____	
9	What other cause of this greenhouse gas is mentioned?	9	_____	

3 Understanding the texts

Work with a partner. In what sort of publications might you find these two texts? Why do you think the texts are different? Who do you think the audience is for each one?

4 Working with words

Match the verbs (1–9) to the noun phrases below to make collocations. There is usually more than one correct answer. Use your (online) dictionary to help you.

SP 8 Using a Dictionary (p. 34)

1 absorb	2 burn	3 contribute to
4 create	5 emit	6 maintain
7 produce	8 release	9 reverse

☐ carbon dioxide   ☐ energy   ☐ fossil fuels
☐ the flow of the Gulf Stream   ☐ global temperatures   ☐ radiation
☐ global warming   ☐ greenhouse gases

SP 41 Writing a Summary (p. 56)

5 Writing: summary

Look again at your answers to exercise **2** and the collocations in exercise **4**. Write a short summary of the information about global warming and the greenhouse effect in the two texts. Write about 120 words.

Start like this: *Global warming is caused by the greenhouse effect. This natural phenomenon …*

SP 12 Working with Pictures (p. 38)

TF M Individual Long Turn (p. 80)

6 Speaking: individual long turn

- Describe the diagram on page 88 and explain how the greenhouse effect works.
- Explain some of the possible effects of global warming.
- Suggest some ways in which greenhouse gas emissions could be reduced.

B Species Extinction and Human Activity

The University of Melbourne in Australia broadcasts a regular podcast called "Close Up" in which experts from the university talk about their subjects.

Threatened with extinction?

1 Listening: true/false

13　**a** Listen to the first part of this podcast. Decide whether the statements (1–6) are true (T) or false (F) and put a cross (✘) in the correct box. Write your answers in the boxes provided. The first one (0) has been done for you.

inhabit live in
on death row awaiting death/ execution, like in prison

		T	F
0	The host of the podcast is Professor Nigel Stork.	☐	☒
1	The expert is talking about the disappearance of species around the world.	☐	☐
2	Extinction has only become a major topic since global warming began.	☐	☐
3	Many species around the world are now in danger of disappearing completely.	☐	☐
4	A species that hasn't been seen anywhere for 50 years is officially classified as extinct.	☐	☐
5	Professor Stork thinks that this is a good definition of "extinct".	☐	☐
6	It is easy to determine which species are extinct.	☐	☐

b **EXTRA** Now listen again and correct the false statements. Raise your hand for your teacher to pause the CD when you have heard the information you need.

_____

_____

_____

2 Working with words

Before you listen to the second part of the podcast, find the correct words from the box that match the definitions/synonyms below. Use your (online) dictionary, if necessary.

SP 8 Using a Dictionary (p. 34)

> be prone to • creation • invertebrate • lifespan • marine • organism • outcome • paleontological • predator • preserve • recovery • vertebrate

1　a living thing　　_____
2　keep　　_____
3　to do with the sea　　_____
4　process of improving or becoming stronger again　_____
5　act of making sth. new　_____
6　animal with no backbone　_____
7　animal with a backbone　_____
8　length of time sth. lives or exists　_____
9　result　_____
10　related to the study of fossils　_____
11　likely to suffer from sth.　_____
12　animal that kills and eats other animals　_____

3 Listening comprehension: multiple-choice

14　Now listen to the second part of the podcast. Choose the correct answer (A, B, C or D) for questions 1–5. Put a cross (✘) in the correct box.

TF A Multiple-Choice (p. 71)

1　Why do scientists have no idea of the number of extinct species?
　A　Because there is no catalogue of existing species.　☐
　B　Because there is no catalogue of the species that have gone extinct.　☐
　C　Because they have to wait 50 years for a species to go extinct.　☐
　D　Because some species turn up again after many years.　☐

▶▶▶

2   What does the scientific evidence from the last 300 million years suggest?
  A   That 70–80% of species have gone extinct during this time. ☐
  B   That there have been 7 or 8 periods when mass extinction took place. ☐
  C   That there have been 5 or 6 periods when mass extinction took place. ☐
  D   The species with soft body parts become extinct more quickly. ☐

3   What do scientists believe at this moment in time?
  A   There were more species 300 million years ago than there are now. ☐
  B   There are about the same number of species now as there were 300 million years ago. ☐
  C   There was the highest number of species some time before a period of mass extinction. ☐
  D   There are now more species on Earth than there have ever been. ☐

4   According to Professor Stork species of insects exist on average 10 times longer than …
  A   species of arthropods. ☐
  B   species of invertebrates. ☐
  C   species of vertebrates. ☐
  D   mankind. ☐

5   Which species are most at danger from extinction?
  A   large invertebrates ☐
  B   large vertebrates ☐
  C   elephants in South East Asia ☐
  D   tigers in rain forests ☐

SP 14 Doing Research (p. 40)

SP 15 Doing a Project (p. 41)

4   Research project
Work in small groups and find out on the Internet which species are most in danger of extinction around the world. Choose one species per group and prepare a short presentation. Your presentation should include the following information:
- natural habitat of the species
- current figures/numbers still in existence
- major threats to species
- suggestions for protecting species

TT 1 Informal Email (p. 59)

5   Writing: informal email
You school has decided to raise some money to donate to the World Wildlife Fund. Your donation can be used to "adopt" one endangered species and protect its habitat. Choose one of the species that were presented in exercise **4** and write an email to your English penfriend telling him/her about your school's "Adopt a species" project.
In your email you should …
- explain which species you are going to adopt and why
- describe how you are going to raise some money to donate to the World Wildlife Fund
- suggest ways in which your penfriend's school could also take part
Write about 200 words.

TF N Paired Activity (p. 80)

6   Speaking: paired activity
You and your partner have decided that you have to do something to stop more species becoming extinct and to preserve natural habitats for plants and animals.
Discuss the following activities and evaluate how effective each one might be.
- Raise and donate money to an animal welfare charity.
- Organise a protest against whaling in the Antarctic.
- Help to clean up a local river or wasteland of rubbish.
- Stop eating meat or animal products.
- Protest against building a new shopping centre on fields near your town.
At the end of your discussion, come to an agreement on which three ideas are the most effective.

CAN-DO STATEMENTS

		Part / Ex	✔
👂	I can understand the main points in interviews, reports and presentations. (B1/2)	B / Ex 1 B / Ex 3	☐
	I can understand, fundamentally, native speakers when they speak clearly and directly about subjects familiar to me and use standard language. (B1/4)	B / Ex 1 B / Ex 3	☐
	I can understand the most important elements of radio programmes and sound recordings when they deal with current events or my interests. (B1/5)	B / Ex 1 B / Ex 3	☐
📖	I can understand straightforward factual texts written for a wide audience on subjects related to my field and interest. (B1/2)	A / Ex 1	☐
	I can recognize the essential conclusions in clearly structured argumentative texts. (B1/4)	A / Ex 2	☐
👀	I can begin, maintain and end a conversation about subjects familiar to me. (B1/1)	A / Ex 3	☐
	I can express and give reasons for my opinion in conversations and discussions. Furthermore, I can agree or politely disagree and make other suggestions. (B1/6)	B / Ex 5	☐
👄	I can describe and interpret graphs in simple, connected sentences. (B1/8)	A / Ex 6	☐
✏️	I can write simple, private correspondence, e.g. letters and emails. (B/5)	B / Ex 6	☐
	I can summarize the most important information in a text that deals with a theme I am familiar with. (B1/10)	A / Ex 5	☐

Keep going ... You can do anything! ☺

UNIT 11 Different Points of View

A Countdown for Our Planet

1 Understanding the issues: the poem 'Earth's Clock'

a Summarize the main idea of the poem in one sentence.

b Explain how the poem uses the clock to get its message across.

call come to visit
stooping stance way of standing bent over

Earth's Clock Pat Moon

Imagine that the earth was shaped
Twenty-four hours ago,
Then at 6 a.m. rains fell from the skies
To form the seas below.
At 8 a.m. in these soupy seas
The first signs of life appeared.
The dinosaurs called seventy minutes ago
But at twenty to twelve disappeared.
Man arrived just one minute ago,
Then at thirty seconds to midnight,
Raised himself from his stooping stance
And started walking upright.
In the thirty seconds man's walked the earth,
See what he's managed to do.
Earth's clock continues ticking;
The rest is up to you.

Pat Moon: Earth's Clock. In: Brian Moses/Pie Corbett (Eds.):
The Works 2. London: Macmillan Children's Book 2002

2 Understanding the issues: the song 'River Runs Red'

a Before you listen, make sure you understand the words on the left.

b Look at the song title and speculate on the artist's attitude to the environment.

precious little (infml) very little, almost nothing
Flood (biblical) large amounts of water covering the Earth in the time of Noah
Fall (biblical) when Adam and Eve didn't obey God
drive sb. force sb. to move in a particular direction
black rain radioactive rainfall
conquer take control of a country or city by force
riches (pl) large amounts of money and possessions
commons (pl) the common, not royal or noble, people
strangle kill sb. by squeezing on their throat; *also:* prevent sth. from growing
wrestle sth. battle/fight sth.
pursue sth. follow sth., try to achieve sth.
curse sth. that causes harm or evil
age a particular period of history

River Runs Red Midnight Oil

So you cut all the tall trees down
You poisoned the sky and the sea
You've taken what's good from the ground
But you left precious little for me

Midnight Oil was a popular Australian rock band that sang protest songs – often about the environment. Their lead singer, Peter Garrett, became Australian Minister for the Environment, Heritage and the Arts in 2007.

15

c Listen and make notes on these topics:
- what humans have done to the land
_____
_____

- why they have done this
_____

- what the land looks like now
_____
_____

d Summarize the main idea of the song in one sentence.
_____

3 Talking: comparing the two
Compare the poem and the song with a partner. Look at the last line of each and decide who is more optimistic about the future – the poet or the songwriter? Explain why.

4 EXTRA Making a poster
Do you know other bands / singers / stars who speak out on global issues?

a Work in groups and collect photos, song texts and newspaper articles on one of these bands/singers/stars. Add any other photos that illustrate the issue they are addressing.
Make a poster for the classroom wall.

b Present your poster to the class. Compare some of the photos from your poster. Explain the global issues that your band / singer / star is involved in.

5 Classroom discussion
Discuss the following topic in class: Do you think it makes a difference when stars speak out on global issues?
Give reason for your opinion, using examples from your poster.

Language Help
- I think the … is much more optimistic/pessimistic than the …
- Really? I don't think he sounds as … as the …
- I agree. I think the poem/song is much less optimistic/pessimistic than the …
- For example, in the first line / in line … he says …
- He compares the … to a …

LP 22 Comparison of Adjectives (p. 17)

SP 23 Taking Part in a Classroom Discussion (p. 47)

B Climate Change

'Global Warming' painting by Paul Cumes (2001), mixed media, 183 x 137 cm

SP 12 Working with Pictures (p 38)

1 Interpreting a painting

a Describe the painting – the colours, technique, style. What effects of global warming does it show?

b Write 50–80 words about your reactions to the painting. What message do you think the artist wants to get across? Do you like his painting? Why (not)?

Language Help
- The artist uses … colours and … images.
- The use of curves and circles gives the painting a … style.
- The buildings in the bottom left-hand corner seem … compared to …

Language Help

- The washing on the line shows knickers from …
- At the beginning, …
- As time goes by, …
- This suggests that …

2 Interpreting a poster

a Describe the poster.

b Explain how the washing on the line illustrates the title 'Positive proof of global warming'.

SP 12 Working with Pictures (p. 38)

Positive proof of global warming

18th century   1900   1950   1970   1980   1990   2010

3 EXTRA Talking: comparing the artists' impact

Look again at pp. 20–21. Talk about these questions in small groups:

- Which makes the biggest impression on you: the poem, the song, the painting or the poster?
- Which of the four artists makes their point most convincingly and how?
- Which of the four items do you like best? Is it the one that makes the most impact?

Report your ideas to the class.

4 Talking about the future

If you want to talk about environmental problems or other issues that are in the news, you will not only want to talk about what has happened in the past but also about what consequences our actions could have in the future.

Here you can practise different ways to do that.

LP 7 Talking about the Future (p. 8)

LP 13 Conditional Sentences: Type I (p. 12)

a Complete the following sentences using *will*, *may* or *might*.

1 If I'm not careful about my carbon footprint,
   I'll be helping to destroy the planet / there won't be a planet to save / _____

2 If I don't turn off my computer at night, _____

3 If we don't take better care of the planet now, _____

4 If global warming continues, _____

5 If the ice in the Arctic melts, _____

6 If we don't fly less, _____

7 If we keep buying fruit and vegetables from overseas, _____

8 If we continue to eat so much meat, _____

b Discuss your answers with a partner. Agree on the three consequences you find most threatening.

TF H Multiple Choice (p. 76)

5 Language in Use: multiple-choice

Read the text about climate change on page 23. Some words are missing from the text. Choose the correct answer (A, B, C or D) for each gap (1–12). Put a cross (✘) in the correct box. The first one (0) has been done for you.

Experts are increasingly united in the (0) ___ that the climate change we are experiencing is, at least partly, manmade. The main (1) ___ appears to be the greenhouse gases that we are (2) ___ into the atmosphere, particularly carbon dioxide. Experts (3) ___ global warming, if it is not reduced, will lead to changing weather patterns and an increased frequency of (4) ___ disasters. The polar ice-caps will melt along with and sea levels will rise, causing floods on the one hand, but also drought and more deserts on the other hand. This will lead to the extinction of many animal species and the (5) ___ of their natural habitats.

Many of these events are already occuring and if they (6) ___ as predicted, they will eventually have a strong impact on our (7) ___ of life. Some scientists predict that a new ice age will occur as the flow of the Gulf Stream is reversed. Others think that "runaway global warming" is more likely, with (8) ___ increases in temperature as a result of the greenhouse gases in the atmosphere.

Hollywood has (9) ___ produced several climate disaster movies: *The Day After Tomorrow* (2004) tells the story of a climate disaster that takes place within (10) ___ weeks. Most scientists agree that this could not (11) ___ happen at such a speed, but the film was very successful and helped to increase interest in climate (12) ___ among non-scientists.

	A	B	C	D
0	☐ meaning	☒ opinion	☐ feeling	☐ thinking
1	☐ effect	☐ ground	☐ result	☐ cause
2	☐ releasing	☐ starting	☐ letting	☐ sending
3	☐ mean	☐ believe	☐ advise	☐ tell
4	☐ biological	☐ physical	☐ natural	☐ chemical
5	☐ construction	☐ creation	☐ destruction	☐ conservation
6	☐ pursue	☐ carry out	☐ carry over	☐ continue
7	☐ walk	☐ way	☐ road	☐ path
8	☐ enormous	☐ generous	☐ fabulous	☐ maximum
9	☐ yet	☐ never	☐ ever	☐ already
10	☐ a lot of	☐ a few	☐ many	☐ little
11	☐ possibly	☐ probably	☐ definitely	☐ predictably
12	☐ thoughts	☐ ideas	☐ issues	☐ arguments

6 Creative writing: diary entry

Two possible future results of global warming are "runaway global warming" or a new ice age. Choose one of these scenarios and write a diary entry for the year 2121 that shows its effect on your everyday life.
Write about 150 words.

SP 44 Creative Writing (p. 58)

CAN-DO STATEMENTS

		Part / Ex	✔
👂	I can understand the main points of anecdotes, stories, acted scenes or songs. (B1/3)	A / Ex 2	☐
📖	I can understand a short poem that deals with a theme that is familiar to me.	A / Ex 1	☐
👀	I can express and give reasons for my opinion in conversations and discussions. Furthermore, I can agree or politely disagree and make other suggestions. (B1/6)	A / Ex 3 B / Ex 3	☐
👄	I can report on subject areas familiar to me, what I have heard, seen, read or experienced and describe my feelings or reactions. (B1/1)	A / Ex 5	☐
	I can explain my opinions, plans, intentions and goals clearly and give reasons for them. (B1/4)	A / Ex 5	☐
	I can describe pictures and tell stories with the help of key words or illustrations. (B1/5)	A / Ex 5	☐
✏️	I can write simple stories, essays and creative texts. (B1/2)	B / Ex 6	☐

A Think Globally, Act Locally  Key: 140

1 "Food miles"

a What are "food miles"?

_____

Listen to this explanation of the benefits of buying local food. Note down the five benefits in the left-hand column:

Five benefits of buying local food:

• _____	better/fresher	because	_____
• _____	environment	because	_____
• _____	local economy	because	_____
• _____	health	because	_____
• _____	farming community	because	_____

produce ['– –] (n) food products
genetically-modified seed seed for growing new plants that has been changed genetically

b Now listen again and add one reason/explanation in the right-hand column for each benefit.

2 Comprehension

a How does the kiwi fruit create five times its own weight in greenhouse gases?

b More New Zealand kiwi fruit reach us by boat than by plane. Does that change the argument? Why (not)?

Find out where your lunch has come from

The average kiwi fruit flown in from New Zealand travels 12,000 miles to be part of your lunch.

And, according to the experts, that kiwi fruit creates five times its own weight in greenhouse gases getting there.

Which might lead you to imagine that the little fruit spent the entire trip farting. (As quite a lot of people do on planes. And most of them are oblivious to the fact, because they're wearing huge earphones.)

But in fact it's just because of the fuel employed in getting the fruit here.

Still ... if the image of a farting kiwi fruit makes you think twice about eating stuff flown in out of season, maybe it's a useful one.

Steve Henry: Change the World 9 to 5. 50 Ways to Change the World at Work. London: Faber and Faber 2006

according to experts experts say
fart (taboo, slang) furzen
be oblivious to sth. [əˈblɪvɪəs] not know sth.
employ sth. (fml) here: use sth.

3 Concentrating on style

a The text is written in a light-hearted style. How does the author achieve this?
Think of imagery, humour and sentence length. Find examples of each in the text.

b Write a short, light-hearted text about the journey of some Chilean apples or other fruit to your local supermarket.

4 Mind map: food production

SP 1 Mind Mapping (p. 30)

a Make sure you know the meaning of all the words in the box. Use your (online) dictionary if necessary.

> animal feed ▪ chemicals ▪ distribution ▪ fertilizer ▪ packaging ▪ pesticides ▪ processing ▪
> refrigeration ▪ transport(ation) ▪ water ▪ warehousing

b Think of your favourite food or meal. Make a mind map showing all the different things and activities that are necessary to produce all the ingredients and get them to your home. Add the words in the box above to your mind map and any other items or activities you can think of.

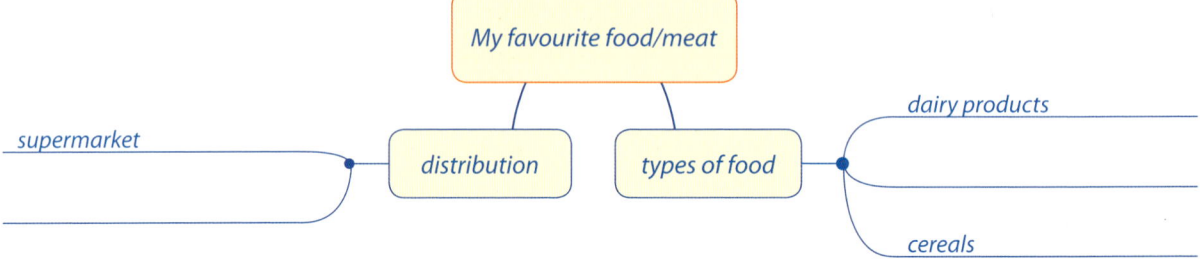

c Compare your mind maps in small groups. Are there any other items you want to add?

5 Doing a project: comparing food sources

SP 13 Working with Charts and
Graphs (p. 39)

SP 14 Doing Research (p. 40)

SP 15 Doing a Project (p. 41)

Split into two groups: one group is going to find out where the fruit and vegetables in your local supermarket come from; the other group is going to find out where the fruit and vegetables at your local farmers' market or organic food shop come from.

▪ Look at the origins of the fruit and vegetables and divide them into groups, as follows:

Local area	Austria	Europe	Rest of world

▪ When you have completed your lists, use a "food miles calculator" on the Internet to work out how far, on average, the food in each group has travelled.
▪ Present your findings to the other group using charts or graphs.

6 Writing: a report

TT 4 Report (p. 64)

You work in the marketing department of an international chain of supermarkets. Your regional marketing director has read about food miles in the press and has asked you for a report on the situation in your supermarkets. Write a report of about 180–200 words, using your findings from exercise **5** above.
In your report you should …

▪ describe the origins of the fruit and vegetables in your supermarkets
▪ compare this with the produce in local farmers' markets
▪ suggest ways in which the company could reduce food miles.

B Greener Travel

When it comes to deciding which means of transport to use for long journeys, the book 50 Ways to Greener Travel *offers this table to help you make the right choices:*

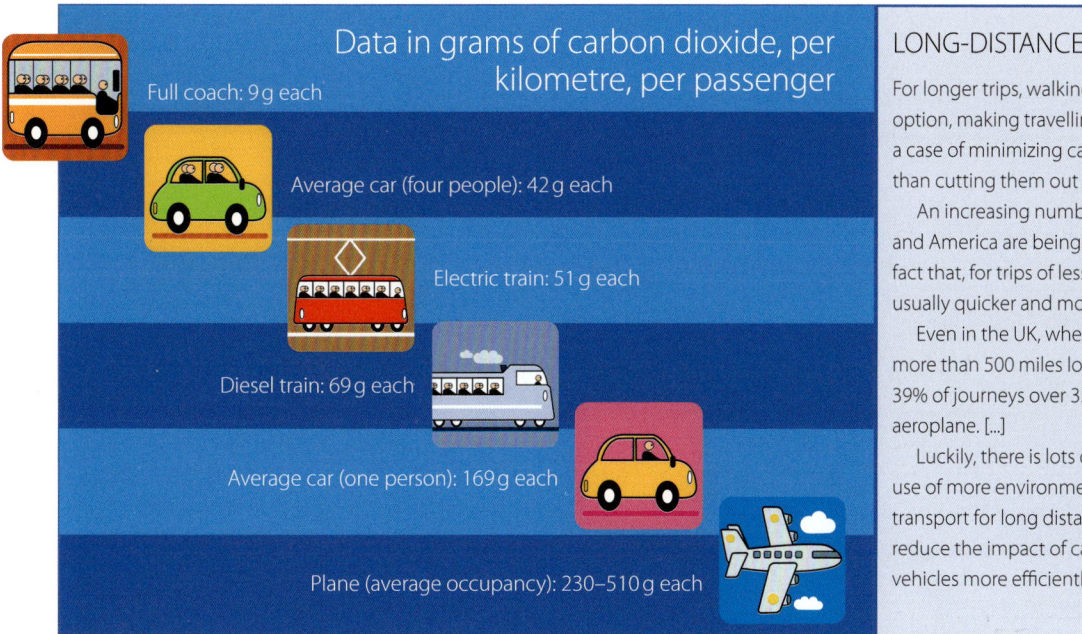

Data in grams of carbon dioxide, per kilometre, per passenger

Full coach: 9 g each

Average car (four people): 42 g each

Electric train: 51 g each

Diesel train: 69 g each

Average car (one person): 169 g each

Plane (average occupancy): 230–510 g each

LONG-DISTANCE TRAVEL

For longer trips, walking and cycling aren't an option, making travelling in greener ways mainly a case of minimizing carbon emissions rather than cutting them out altogether.

An increasing number of long trips in Europe and America are being taken by plane despite the fact that, for trips of less than 500 miles, the train is usually quicker and more convenient.

Even in the UK, where hardly any journeys are more than 500 miles long on our small island, 39% of journeys over 350 miles are now taken by aeroplane. [...]

Luckily, there is lots of scope for increasing our use of more environmentally-friendly modes of transport for long distances, and we can also reduce the impact of car journeys by filling up vehicles more efficiently.

Siân Berry: 50 Ways to Greener Travel. London: Kyle Cathie Limited 2008 © text: Siân Berry, artwork: Aaron Blecha

1 Comprehension

a Summarize the information in the above book extract in one sentence.

b Explain why the carbon emissions per person when travelling by coach are lower than when travelling by car.

 22 Comparison of Adjectives (p. 17)

2 Language in Use: editing

Read this text about travelling by plane. In most lines of the text there is a word that should not be there. Write that word in the space provided. Some lines are correct. Indicate these lines with a tick (✔). There are two examples (0, 00) at the beginning.

TF L Editing (p. 79)

Airplanes and global warming		
Have you ever looked out of the window of a passenger plane from 30,000	✔	0
feet at the vast expanses of empty ocean and on uninhabited land, and	*on*	00
wondered how that people can have any major effect on the Earth? I have.		1
But it is now becoming pretty clear that we are causing a great deal of		2
damage to the natural environment. And the planes which do rush us in		3
comfort to destinations around the globe, contribute in to one of the		4
biggest environmental problems that we are face today – global warming.		5
For those of us lucky enough to have money to spend, and free time to		6
spend it in, there are a huge number of the fascinating places to explore.		7
The cost of air transport has decreased rapidly over the latest years, and		8
for many people, especially in rich countries, it is now possible to fly around		9
the world for little more than a weekly pay packet.		10
Unfortunately, planes produce far many more carbon dioxide (CO_2) than any		11
other form of public transport, and CO_2 is now not known to be a greenhouse		12
gas, a gas which traps under the heat of the sun, causing the temperature		13
of the Earth to rise. Scientists predict that in the near future the climate in		14
Britain will resemble that of the Mediterranean, ironically funny a popular		15
destination for British holidaymakers flying off to seek the sun.		16

Aeroplanes and global warming. In: http://learnenglish.britishcouncil.org

 36 Persuading People (p. 28)

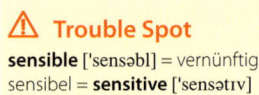
⚠ **Trouble Spot**

sensible ['sensəbl] = vernünftig
sensibel = **sensitive** ['sensətıv]

 27 False Friends (p. 22)

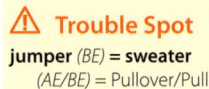
⚠ **Trouble Spot**

jumper (BE) = **sweater**
   (AE/BE) = Pullover/Pulli

3 Convincing people

a Here are ten suggestions on how to live a greener life.
Choose five of these suggestions and try to convince your partner that they are sensible. Take
turns to discuss your explanations.

1   Have a shower, not a bath.
    If you have a shower, you'll use less water than if you have a bath.
    You'll be saving water and you'll be saving your parents' money, too.
2   Walk, don't drive. _____
3   Don't turn up the heat, put on a jumper. _____
4   Put an energy-saving light bulb in your desk lamp. _____
5   Unplug the TV at night. _____
6   Recycle as much as you can. _____
7   Find a holiday job in nature conservation. _____
8   Don't drink bottled water. _____
9   Reuse shopping bags. _____
10 Don't use plastic cups. _____

b Choose the three suggestions you think would be most effective and present them, with your
arguments, to the class.

4 Talking: the best way to travel

Work in groups of three. Each group chooses one of these holiday destinations for an
imaginary family – mother, father and two teenage children:
Lake Garda in Italy, London in the UK or Torremolinos in southern Spain.

a One group member researches the journey from your hometown by air, one by train and one
by car. Think of distances, petrol and ticket prices, time spent travelling, the nearest railway
stations and airports, etc.

b In your group, decide how you want to travel to your destination:
- Each group member presents arguments in favour of his/her means of transport (plane,
  train or car).
- Discuss the three journeys and agree on one way to travel.
- When you have made your decision, consider whether it is the most environmentally-
  friendly way to travel.

c Report back to the class on your discussion.
- Compare and contrast the different means of transport you considered.
- Explain why you chose the one you agreed on.
- Comment on whether it is the most environmentally-friendly way to travel.

C Discussing a Current Affairs Topic

In this part you will prepare and conduct a group discussion on a topic related to 'Our Changing Planet'.

1 Listening to people's opinions

Discussions are not only about talking. You have to listen carefully too.

17

a Look at questions 1–3 below. Then listen to the first part of a classroom discussion on global
warming and take notes.

1   Do you think the discussion leader starts the discussion off well? Why (not)?
2   What does Amy say about the greenhouse effect?
3   What does Max add to her point? What does he do to emphasize his points about the
    effects of global warming?

b Compare notes with a partner. If you can't agree on something, listen again to check.

17

c Look at the questions below and listen to the second part of the discussion.

1 What conclusions does the discussion leader draw? Do you agree with her?

2 Which of the following bad discussion habits can you hear? Who makes them?

Bad habit?	Heard?	Speaker?
Interrupting		
Being rude		
Talking too much		
Not listening to what the previous speaker said		
Not backing up one's statement with facts		

d Which discussion habit do you think is the worst? Explain why.

2 Reporting what you have read or heard

In a discussion, you may want to report something you have read or heard. Or you might want to refer to a point someone else has made.

a Report the following as you would in a classroom discussion. Be careful what tense you use.

1 "Americans use coal to generate 54 % of their electricity, and coal is the single biggest polluter." (newspaper editorial)

   'I read in a newspaper editorial that Americans used coal ..., even though coal was the ...

2 "Steps are being taken to replace older, dirtier factories with more modern, energy-efficient ones." (TV news)

   'They said on the news on TV last night that ...

3 "The 1990s were not a good time for the environment here." (Australian politician)

4 "I have to believe that my party will be able to make a difference on the issue of global warming." (woman at Green Party meeting)

5 "You Europeans cannot expect developing countries like Ecuador to spend money they don't have on cleaner technologies." (Ecuadorian environment minister)

LP 11 Indirect Speech: Statements (p. 11)

LP 29 Verbs of Reporting (p. 23)

b You are having a class discussion. Refer to the following statements made by your classmates earlier in the discussion.

1 "I'm convinced that there's more oil than the oil companies admit." (Jasper)

   'Jasper, you said before that you were convinced there was more ...

2 "The government doesn't care what we think." (Karin)

   'Karin said a while ago that ...

3 "I believed the chancellor when she talked about her climate plans." (Miriam)

4 "I'll be amazed if anybody can prove this new technology will work." (Hassan)

5 "I can't believe that global warming will happen as fast as in the film." (Philip)

Fotolia.com/bluedesign

SP 23 Taking Part in a Classroom Discussion (p. 47)

SP 14 Doing Research (p. 40)

SP 5 Making Notes (p. 32)

Language Help

- The topic that we are going to discuss today is ...
- Let's begin. Who would like to start?
- Please don't interrupt. / Please let ... finish.
- It's ...'s turn next.
- Well, let me summarize: most people in our group think that ... But two people strongly disagree and feel that ...

3 Preparing and conducting a group discussion

Form groups of five to eight students. Each group chooses one of the following topics:
1 No aeroplanes, no problems.
2 Vegetarianism is the answer.
3 Warmer is nicer.
4 Climate change is a myth.

Step 1: Each person collects information on their group's chosen topic. Look through the Topic again, research aspects that interest you in books, on the Internet, in newspapers and magazines, etc. Make notes.

Step 2: Organize your notes. Maybe you want to have material ready to show your group during the discussion: facts and figures, graphs and tables, statistics, cartoons, ...

Step 3: Choose a discussion leader. She/He might find the phrases in **Language Help** useful.

Step 4: Start the discussion. Remember to listen carefully to what other people say. Whenever you can, refer to their points when you speak.

Step 5: At the end of the discussion, your discussion leader summarizes the conclusions you have reached. Listen carefully and correct the summary if necessary.

Step 6: Choose one person to report on the discussion to the class.

CAN-DO STATEMENTS

		Part/Ex	✔
👂	I can understand, fundamentally, native speakers when they speak clearly and directly about subjects familiar to me and use standard language. (B1/4)	C / Ex 1	☐
	I can understand the most important elements of radio programmes and sound recordings when they deal with current events or my interests. (B1/5)	A / Ex 1	☐
📖	I can get the essential information from simple newspaper and magazine articles that are clearly structured. (B1/1)	A / Ex 2	☐
	I can understand straightforward factual texts written for a wide audience on subjects related to my field and interest. (B1/2)	B / Ex 1	☐
👀	I can express and give reasons for my opinion in conversations and discussions. Furthermore, I can agree or politely disagree and make other suggestions. (B1/6)	B / Ex 3 C / Ex 3	☐
	I can take on a role in a simulated everyday or professional situation and also improvise thereby. (B1/9)	B / Ex 4	☐
👄	I can explain my opinions, plans, intentions and goals clearly and give reasons for them. (B1/4)	B / Ex 5	☐
✏️	I can write reports or simple articles on events, experiences of a general or a professional nature. These texts may be intended for different media or different personal or professional purposes. (B1/1)	A / Ex 6	☐

Recent extreme heatwaves 'a result of global warming'

Severe summer heat caused by humans not natural events, says Nasa scientist

Global warming is responsible for the recent series of summer heatwaves, according to James Hansen, the scientist who first alerted the world to the dangers of climate change. Dr Hansen, director of Nasa's Goddard Institute for Space Studies in New York, said that the "climate dice" are now loaded in favour of extreme heatwaves which now affect 10 per cent of the Earth's surface, compared with about 1 per cent in the period between 1951 to 1980.

Dr Hansen said that at least three extreme summers over the past decade, the 2003 heatwave in Europe which killed more than 50,000 people, the 2010 hot summer in Moscow and last year's droughts in Texas and Oklahoma, were almost certainly the result of man-made climate change rather than natural events.

In a study published in the Proceedings of the National Academy of Sciences, Dr Hansen and his colleagues said that rising global temperatures caused by increases in carbon dioxide have significantly increased the probability of such extreme heatwaves.

"This is not a climate model or a prediction but actual observations of weather events and temperatures that have happened," Dr Hansen says in an accompanying article in *The Washington Post*.

Dr Hansen was the first scientist to warn the wider world of the dangers of global warming when in 1988 he gave evidence to the US Senate that the burning of fossil fuels was raising global average temperatures.

Since then, most scientists have been careful not to blame any single weather extreme on climate change. However, in recent years a number of researchers have pointed out that some weather events, such as the 2003 heatwave in Europe, were more extreme than could be expected from natural climate variations.

Dr Hansen said that his study shows that the climate dice have been loaded in such a way as to make unusual hot events more extreme and more frequent.

Slightly adapted from: Steve Connor: Recent extreme heatwaves 'a result of global warming'
In: The Independent, August 7, 2012

dice a small cube made of wood or plastic, with a different number of spots on each side
load (the dice) in favour of sth. *here:* fix (the dice) so that a particular event or number always appears
variation *here:* change in temperature from very high to very low

1 Reading comprehension: multiple-choice

Read the text and choose the correct answer (A, B, C or D) for questions 1–7. Put a cross (✗) in the correct box.

TF D Multiple-Choice (p. 73)

1 Dr Hansen was the first scientist to warn the world about …
 A summer heatwaves. ☐
 B extreme heatwaves. ☐
 C unusual climate events. ☐
 D problems of global warming. ☐

2 Compared to the years 1951 to 1980, extreme summer heatwaves now affect …
 A Europe and America. ☐
 B 1 per cent of the Earth's surface. ☐
 C 10 per cent of the Earth's surface. ☐
 D 50,000 people. ☐

3 Dr Hansen is … that climate change is the cause of the recent number of extremely hot summers.
 A doubtful ☐
 B not quite sure ☐
 C extremely confident ☐
 D 100% certain ☐

▶▶▶

4 According to Dr Hansen and his colleagues, extreme summer heatwaves are … because of global warming.
   A   now slightly more likely ☐
   B   now much more likely ☐
   C   about as likely as before ☐
   D   less likely than before ☐

5 Dr Hansen's claims are based on …
   A   information from weather events in the past. ☐
   B   a computer model of the climate. ☐
   C   a prediction of future weather events. ☐
   D   discussions among climate scientists. ☐

6 According to a number of researchers, the 2003 heatwave in Europe was …
   A   predicted by the computer model. ☐
   B   much hotter than could be expected. ☐
   C   a normal hot summer. ☐
   D   the result of natural causes. ☐

7 Dr Hansen predicts that …
   A   there will be more hot summers. ☐
   B   there will be few summers that are extremely hot. ☐
   C   exceptionally hot summers will take place more regularly. ☐
   D   every summer will get hotter and hotter. ☐

TF C Short Answers (p. 72)

⑱

2 Listening comprehension: sentence completion (note form)
Listen to a podcast about the environment and air travel. While listening complete the sentences (1–9) using a maximum of 4 words. Write your answers in the spaces provided. The first one (0) has been done for you.

0	One person flying in a plane for one hour produces as much CO_2 as one person in Bangladesh does ___ .	*in a whole year*
1	Plane fares may seem to be high, but in reality we ___ for air travel.	
2	Aircraft fuel is not taxed on ___ and planes are not inspected for CO_2 emissions.	
3	The Kyoto agreement does not cover ___ produced by planes.	
4	Aircraft engine manufacturers are trying to make their engines ___ .	
5	___ is being considered as an alternative to aircraft fuel.	
6	The most obvious way for individual travellers to deal with the problem is ___ .	
7	It is hard to persuade people to stay at home because ___ are more popular than ever before.	
8	Environmental groups suggest that business people should use ___ instead of meeting face-to-face.	
9	The Future Forest website will ___ for you to absorb the amount of CO_2 you are responsible for on your flight.	

3 Speaking: individual long turn

TF M Individual Long Turn (p. 79)

- Compare the two photos.
- Explain negative aspects of travelling.
- Suggest some ways in which holiday travellers could reduce their carbon footprint.

4 Writing: informal email

TT 1 Informal Email (p. 59)

Your American penfriend has just written you an email telling you how he and his whole family are flying to Europe in the summer. They plan to visit several countries and fly from one city to the next on their tour.

Write a reply to your friend's email.
- Explain how flying in particular contributes to climate change.
- Describe the dangers of global warming if we don't do anything to stop it.
- Suggest some ways they could see Europe without flying everywhere.

Write about 200 words.

5 Language in Use: open gap-fill

TF K Open Gap-Fill (p. 78)

Read this text about electric cars. Some words are missing from the text. Write the missing words (1–14) in the spaces provided. The first one (0) has been done for you.

Now that car manufacturers are (0) ___ pressure to cut emissions of carbon dioxide (CO_2) and other harmful gases, they (1) ___ started to seriously invest in electric-car technology. This has meant dramatic increases in the range that electric cars (2) ___ travel, huge reductions in charging times and – perhaps most importantly – a big increase in the number (3) ___ public charging points available. Electric cars are becoming (4) ___ popular that the government expects half of all new cars sold in 2027 to (5) ___ battery-powered.

It's now common for an electric car to have a maximum range of well (6) ___ 100 miles (up to 300 miles in some cases) and a charging time of less (7) ___ a couple of hours from a rapid charger. Batteries have also become smaller and lighter in recent years, (8) ___ makes electric vehicles more efficient and easier (9) ___ drive.

Electric vehicles aren't for everyone, (10) ___ . They are still relatively expensive and they don't suit everyone's lifestyle (11) ___ of the fact that you can't just refuel an electric car when you want. This situation is changing slowly and more charging stations (12) ___ emerging all the time. Indeed, the energy company Ecotricity is responsible (13) ___ developing an 'electric highway' from London to Edinburgh, consisting of an extensive network of charging stations (14) ___ the two cities that can give an 80% charge in just 20 minutes.

0	*under*
1	
2	
3	
4	
5	
6	
7	
8	
9	
10	
11	
12	
13	
14	

5 Migrants and Minorities

Alamy/Jonathan Goldberg

migrant ['maɪɡrənt] person who moves from one area or country to another, especially in order to find work

LP 1 Modal Verbs (p. 5)

Language Help

- The most popular country among immigrants from … is …
- They must leave/flee their homeland(s) because …
- There may be war/famine/… in their home country.
- They choose a host country …
- They travel by bus/train/plane/ …

1 Think – pair – share: migration

a Think: What do you know about
- people who immigrate to/emigrate from Europe,
- the countries they come from/go to,
- how they travel?

b Pair: Exchange your ideas with a partner and make notes.

c Share: Discuss your views in class.

In this topic you will learn about …

- people on the move   (WiC)
- what migration means   (Unit 13)
- migrants as minority groups   (Unit 14)
- stereotypes and prejudices   (Unit 15)

Net migration to UK remains at more than 250,000 a year

The Guardian, May 24, 2012

Why Immigrants Are Good for Our Economy

The Atlantic, June 10, 2011

Poland announces amnesty for illegal immigrants

Reuters, December 29, 2011

London, France's sixth biggest city

http://www.bbc.co.uk, May 30, 2012

Local hero Antonio Diaz Chacon says he's an illegal immigrant

New Mexico Independent, August 23, 2011

IRELAND'S RECESSION COULD FORCE 50,000 TO EMIGRATE THIS YEAR

The Guardian, February 20, 2011

migration the movement of large numbers of people
net migration the number of people entering a country minus the number leaving the country
amnesty a period of time in which people can admit to a crime without being punished
recession a difficult time for the economy of a country

2 Looking at headlines

Look at the six headlines above. Choose two that you find interesting or surprising and tell a partner what stories they make you expect.

> ⚠ **Trouble Spot**
>
> **emigrate** = auswandern
> **immigrate** = einwandern

3 What would you do?

a Can you imagine going abroad to work? Which country would you go to? What kind of work could you imagine doing?

b Apart from financially, how else could you profit from this experience? Discuss in class.

LP 14 Conditional Sentences Type II (p. 12)

LP 24 Increase Your Word Power Online (p. 18)

Portlaoise [ˌpɔːt'liːʃə] Irish town

Rotimi Adebari, Mayor of Portlaoise

On the Move ⋆ Key: 213

Although migration is a term used more and more often today, it is not a recent phenomenon, but dates back to the earliest times in history. People have always been on the move in search of better living conditions – at certain times in the past many countries have even relied on migrant workers.

After World War II, Britain welcomed the influx of immigrants when it opened its doors to people from former British colonies who were granted the right to settle and work there. The majority of these immigrants, who are often now in their second and third generations, came from the Indian subcontinent and Afro-Caribbean countries.

At the beginning of the 21st century, the enlargement of the European Union and the UK and Ireland's booming economies tempted Eastern Europeans to make a temporary move across the water. Earning their living in the UK and Ireland, they returned home at the end of the work season. Many immigrants have come to stay, which isn't always looked upon favourably by the native population, who sometimes fear that the immigrants will take away their jobs.

Africans and especially Nigerians have also been known to seek refuge on the shores of the British Isles. Many are seasonal migrants hoping to earn some money, while others are political refugees, fleeing from war or political or religious persecution. Most of them apply for asylum when they arrive. If asylum seekers' applications are rejected, however, they must leave the country or risk being deported.

Some prefer taking that risk to taking the risk of going to prison or worse in their home country. They stay in the host country as illegal immigrants, with severe consequences for the whole family: no home, no job, no schooling. The odd job they do take on is badly paid (if at all) and often dangerous, and they live in constant fear of being deported.

Even legal immigrants do not always find the life that they had imagined, because with the existence of ethnic minorities comes racial conflict – a problem that Britain has been no stranger to in recent years. Nevertheless, the UK and Ireland have been quite successful in accommodating and integrating minority groups into society. If granted residency, the new citizens of foreign origin can vote in elections and even be elected Members of Parliament. In one notable case, an immigrant from Nigeria, Rotimi Adebari, was elected Mayor of Portlaoise.

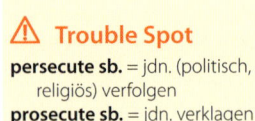

⚠ **Trouble Spot**

persecute sb. = jdn. (politisch, religiös) verfolgen
prosecute sb. = jdn. verklagen

**LP** 28 Confusables (p. 22)

1 Word families

a Add the missing words to the chart below. Some of the words you need are in the text on p. 56. You can find the others in your (online) dictionary.

Abstract noun	Noun: person	Verb/Verbal phrase	Adjective
immigration			————
emigration			————
		deport	————
asylum			————
		persecute	————
	racist	————	
residency			
		seek refuge	fugitive

32 Word Formation: Suffixes (p. 24)

33 Word Stress (p. 26)

8 Using a Dictionary (p. 34)

b Make sentences with five of the words or phrases you have added to the chart, but leave a gap for the words/phrases. Swap papers with a partner. Can he/she complete your sentences?

c Look up the nouns *migration*, *emigration* and *immigration* in your (online) dictionary and make sure you understand the difference between them. Use each of the nouns (or the corresponding verbs) in a sentence that clearly shows each word's meaning.

2 Word power

Collect the words and phrases highlighted in the text on p. 56 in a table or a mind map, using the following categories: *person, action, reasons, problems*, and *general migration terms*. Remember to add new words and phrases as you go through this Topic and words you know from other sources.

25 Collocations (p. 20)

1 Mind Mapping (p. 30)

person	action	reasons	problems	general migration terms

3 Speaking: individual long turn

I You have five minutes to talk about the following.

M Individual Long Turn (p. 80)

- Compare the photos above with the photo of Rotimi Adebari on page 110.
- Speculate on where the people come from and why they have left their home country.
- Reflect on who and what they have left behind and what they miss most.

12 Working with Pictures (p. 38)

UNIT 13   What is Migration?

A   The New Slave Trade?

You are going to hear an interview with Jean-Philippe Chauzy from the International Organization for Migration (IOM) in Geneva.

1   Before you listen

Match the words (1–8) on the left to the definitions/paraphrases (a–h) on the right.

1	clandestine	a	political measure; attitude taken toward a certain issue
2	country of transit	b	secret
3	destination	c	work that sb. is forced to do
4	enforced labour	d	situation in which sb. treats sb. else unfairly, especially to make money from their work
5	estimate	e	a country that sb. passes through without settling there
6	exploitation	f	place to which sb. is going
7	hover	g	a rough calculation
8	policy	h	stay close to

19

2   Listening: true/false

a   Listen to the first part of the interview, then decide whether the statements (1–6) are true (T) or false (F). Put a cross (✗) in the correct box. The first one (0) has been done for you.

	Statements	T	F
0	The International Organization for Migration works with companies and governments to provide jobs for workers.	☐	☒
1	The general definition of "migrant" is someone who leaves their home country to work abroad for a period of time.	☐	☐
2	People who are smuggled across borders can't be classed as migrants.	☐	☐
3	Migration only really started in the 19th century.	☐	☐
4	Every country in the world is affected by migration in one way or another.	☐	☐
5	Countries can be either destination countries or countries of origin, but not both.	☐	☐
6	There are around 135 million migrants in the world at the moment.	☐	☐

b   Listen again and correct the statements that are false.

_____

_____

_____

19

3   Listening and taking notes

a   Before you listen to the second part of the interview, make sure you know the meaning of the words below. Use your (online) dictionary if necessary.

SP 8 Using a Dictionary (p. 34)

staggering ▪ prospect ▪ civil strife ▪ diaspora ▪ facilitate sth. ▪ trafficking

b   Now listen and complete the notes.

> "_____ 1 " = reasons for leaving home country
> - lack of socio-economic _____ 2
> - bad governance (= government)
> - fleeing from conflict and _____ 3
> "_____ 4 " = reasons for choosing new country
> - better-paid _____ 5
> - large diaspora (= immigrant community) to help new arrivals

 ▶▶▶

- highly-organized _____ **6** networks
Smugglers: help people to cross borders _____ **7**
Traffickers: same as smugglers, but keep migrants in exploitative networks

Impact of illegal networks
- for migrants: exploitative; physically _____ **8**
- for host society: impossible for migrants to _____ **9**
- for criminals: _____ **10** of dollars profit

4 EXTRA Doing research

Choose one European country and research the migrant situation there. Think about the following points:
- number of immigrants (where from? work where?)
- number of emigrants (where to? why?)
- effects of migration on society/economy
Present your findings to the class in a suitable visual form.

SP 14 Doing Research (p. 40)
SP 15 Doing a Project (p. 41)
SP 22 Giving a Presentation (p. 46)

B Warsaw on the Thames  Key: 591

Make a list of the English names of the Eastern European member states of the EU. Make sure you know how to pronounce them. The map at the beginning of the book will help you to locate them.

1 Reading and taking notes

Work in groups of three. Read the text below and take notes. Each member of the group should concentrate on one of the following aspects:
- reasons for Polish immigration to the British Isles
- success of Poles in the UK
- changes in everyday life in Britain caused by Polish immigration

SP 30 Reading Non-Fiction (p. 50)
SP 4 Taking Notes (p. 32)

For a footloose generation of Poles, home increasingly means Britain or Ireland. In the three years since Poland joined the EU, millions of Poles have joined a westward exodus, with these two countries as clear favorites. By some reckonings, Ireland now plays host to 200,000 Polish expats – equivalent to 5 percent of the population – while Britain accommodates at least 700,000. By contrast, Spain (population: 40 million), another leading magnet for Poles, has pulled in a mere 150,000. France has been issuing barely 10,000 work permits to Polish citizens. While the mass influx of Eastern Europeans has stirred controversy across Western Europe, it is largely a move of Poles to the British Isles, where they are reshaping culture from politics to schools, media to pub life.

Behind this new Polish connection: Britain and Ireland's warm invitation. When Poland and nine other countries joined the EU in 2004, current members were given the right to delay opening their labor markets to job seekers from the East. Big countries like France and Germany kept their doors shut. But Britain and Ireland threw them wide open, perhaps not quite realizing what they had done. Government experts predicted just 13,000 migrants would come in annually from the new member states.

Some from every country took the bait. Others stayed put. Slovenia's economy was strong. Hungarians have little tradition of emigration. Czechs and Slovaks tended to look for jobs closer to home. But tens of thousands of Latvians and Lithuanians moved across the continent. And Poles responded in record numbers, creating the largest in-migrations in recent British history.

With a population of 39 million, Poland is by far the largest of the new EU members, and it also has a tradition of migration. Facing double-digit unemployment back home, Poles were drawn to Britain and Ireland by strong job prospects in two of Europe's top-performing economies, by the chance to learn English and by budget airlines that slashed the cost of travel. British

exodus *(biblical)* situation in which many people leave a place at the same time
reckoning *(n)* guess, estimate
play host to sb. have sb. as a guest in your house or country
expat *(infml)* person who lives outside his/her home country
equivalent to sth. [ɪˈkwɪvələnt] of the same value as sth.
a mere only
issue sth. give out sth.
stir controversy about sth. [ˈkɒntrəvɜːsi] make people argue about sth.
current up to date
take the bait *here:* to be attracted by sth., like a fish
stay put *(infml)* stay where you are
face sth. be confronted with sth.
double-digit [ˈdɪdʒɪt] two-figure, i.e. 10–99
prospect [ˈprɒspekt] chance, possibility
slash sth. cut sth. drastically

►►►

ponder sth. think about sth. carefully
allure [ə'lʊə] temptation, attraction
raspberry [*BE:* 'rɑːzbəri] *AE:* 'ræzberi]
   a small dark red soft fruit that
   grows on bushes
plant *here:* factory
prompt cards cards with key words
vital ['vaɪtl] very important
restock the ranks of the Roman
   Catholic clergy ['klɜːdʒi] fill the
   posts of Catholic priests
range choice, selection
lager ['lɑːɡə] type of beer
on tap served from a barrel, not in
   bottles or cans
daily *(n)* daily newspaper

forecasters were wrong again when they predicted that most newcomers would stay only long enough to make some money. A survey this summer found that roughly half the new Polish migrants had no intention of leaving.

Now Britain is pondering its new life with a permanent Polish minority. Unlike other migrant groups, the Poles spread out across Britain, often ignoring the allure and expense of the big cities. Polish can be heard in the shipyards of north-eastern England, the raspberry fields of Scotland and the meatpacking plants of western Wales. Some areas of Britain now display road signs in English and Polish. At least one police force gives officers prompt cards with Polish translations of vital phrases. In Ireland, Polish priests have restocked the ranks of the Roman Catholic clergy, and Polish barmen staff the pubs in rural areas. The smartest are already climbing the employment ladder. 'At first people were just grabbing any job they could get,' says Bartek Wasiewski, a London shipping agent who arrived in 2004. Now some who had started out on construction sites have moved into financial jobs or set up their own companies.

With greater affluence comes attention. The largest British supermarket chain, Tesco, now stocks a range of Polish food. The giant Borders bookshop chain offers more than 100 titles in Polish. British pubs sell Polish lager on tap. The Polish-language media include a daily, four weekly magazines and five radio stations. This month a Polish university plans to open a London branch.

William Underhill: Warsaw On The Thames. In: Newsweek Magazine, October 8, 2007

2 Exchanging information
In your group, exchange the information you concentrated on while reading the text. Take notes while the others are speaking.

TF F Short Answers (p. 74)

3 Reading comprehension: short answers
Answer the questions on the text using a maximum of 4 words. Write your answers in the spaces provided. The first one (0) has been done for you.

Britain and Ireland

_____
_____
_____
_____
_____
_____
_____
_____

0 Where did most Polish emigrants go to after Poland joined the European Union?
1 What did some other big European countries do when the eastern European countries joined the EU?
2 Why did fewer Czechs or Slovaks move to Britain and Ireland?
3 Which other nationalities were on the move in large numbers?
4 What made it easy for Poles to travel to Britain and Ireland?
5 Why did Poles spread out across the whole of Britain?
6 What does a survey show about the intentions of the Poles in the future?
7 What did clever Poles start to do after they had found their first job?
8 Which British institutions have started to attract Polish customers?

4 Word power

a In your group, re-read one third of the text each (ll. 1–15; ll. 16–28; ll. 29–50).
Identify and write down new words and expressions to do with migration.
Make sure you include collocations and not just individual words. Look up any item whose
meaning you are unsure of and note down the definition.

Section	Word/expression	Definition
ll. 1–16	footloose (generation), …	
ll. 17–33	stay put, …	
ll. 34–48	permanent (Polish minority), …	

 8 Using a Dictionary (p. 34)

b Exchange lists and add the items to your table/list from *Words in Context* (p. 57, exercise 2).

5 Giving an oral summary

a Look at your notes from exercises **1** and **2** and write down the key facts. Make sure you answer
the following questions:

- When did Polish immigration to the British Isles start?
- What were the reasons for the immigration?
- Where do Polish immigrants work?
- What success have they had in the UK?
- What changes in everyday life in the UK have they caused?

b Compare your answers with a partner. Write the key facts on prompt cards.

c Summarize the text to your partner, using as much of the thematic vocabulary as possible.
Be prepared to present your summary to the class.

> **Language Help**
> - The text deals mainly with / The theme of the text is …
> - This began when …
> - The main reasons were …
> - Other factors include …
> - British and Irish communities have …

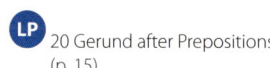 20 Gerund after Prepositions (p. 15)

 30 Reading non fiction (p. 50)

C The Pendulum Effect

Modern-day migration can turn out to be quite short-lived. Before reading this article from a British newspaper, think of reasons why some migrants might want to return home.

Four years after Polish graphic designer Chris Rychter headed to Britain to find work, he and his wife have returned home to Warsaw. Part of a swelling tide of migration back east, they are having a house built in a suburb of the Polish capital.

'It took me just three days to find a job back in Warsaw,' Mr Rychter, 27, said. 'We never saw Britain as home. We went for the adventure and to get some professional experience.'

mauritius images/United Archives

Their return highlights strong economic growth in the new European Union member states and an accelerating slowdown in Britain – and also how quickly a pragmatic, younger European generation has adapted to working in the 21st-century globalized economy.

Mr Rychter's wife, Sabina, has taken her job with a British credit insurance company back to Poland with her.

'You could say I am telecommuting,' she said. 'In today's world, with computers and mobile phones, my presence in head office is not required as before. I can sit here in Warsaw and have the flexibility to do my job.'

Helped by cheap travel as flights between Warsaw and London grew almost tenfold after Poland joined the EU in 2004, the Rychters show how Europe has shrunk and that, contrary to the popular view, migrant flows are not all one-way.

> ⚠ **Trouble Spot**
> **adapt to doing**
> Not: ~~adapt to do~~

pendulum ['pendjələm] a long straight part with a weight at the end that moves regularly from side to side to control the movement of a clock
swelling tide increasing number
accelerate [ək'seləreɪt] get quicker
pragmatic thinking of the practical consequences
credit insurance [ɪn'ʃʊərəns] *Kreditversicherung*
shrink, shrank, shrunk become smaller
turnstile a gate at the entrance to a public building that turns in a circle to let people in
stint *here*: period of time spent working somewhere
plug sth. fill a hole with sth.
gap space or hole in sth.

Getty Images/Gary S. Chapman

▶ ▶ ▶

Economists now talk of a turnstile, or pendulum, effect, with people moving between countries after quite short stints in search of better conditions.

About half the one million people from eastern Europe who moved to Britain after EU enlargement in 2004 have already returned home, according to the Institute for Public Policy Research. And work applications from those eight new states were down 13 per cent in the first quarter of this year, compared with 2007.

For many eastern European migrants, recent currency trends favour a return, and Poland's government wants people back to help plug labour gaps.

Gareth Jones/Kuba Jaworowski: Migration tide turns as east Europeans head back home. In: The Scotsman, June 17, 2008

1 Reading: true/false or not given

Read the text about the Rychters, then decide whether the statements (1–8) are true (T), false (F) or not given (NG) in the text. Put a cross (✗) in the correct box. The first one (0) has been done for you.

	Statements	T	F	NG
0	It took Chris Rychter four years to find a job back home in Warsaw.	☐	✗	☐
1	They wouldn't be able to build a house in Warsaw if they hadn't gone to Britain to work.	☐	☐	☐
2	Young Poles are flexible when it comes to working abroad.	☐	☐	☐
3	Sabina Rychter has also found a new job in Warsaw.	☐	☐	☐
4	The cost of flights between Warsaw and London has sunk a lot since 2004.	☐	☐	☐
5	People from Poland generally go back home because they find it hard to settle in a new country.	☐	☐	☐
6	Half a million people moved from eastern Europe to Britain after European Union enlargement in 2004.	☐	☐	☐
7	More people applied for work permits in Britain in 2007 than in 2008.	☐	☐	☐
8	Poland's government doesn't mind Poles working abroad because the unemployment figures at home are still very high.	☐	☐	☐

2 Talking about the text

a Work with a partner. Why are a lot of Polish workers going back home? Compare the reasons you thought of before reading with the reasons given in the article.

b Talk about the advantages and disadvantages of job migration with your partner. Think about the effects on:
- the country people are leaving
- the people themselves
- the country they are going to.
Be prepared to present your ideas to the class.

3 Writing: blog entry

TT 3 Blog Entry (p. 63)

Hussein, John, Sara and Olga (see p. 117) have just arrived in Austria. Choose one of them and write a blog entry for them:
- describe their situation and lives
- explain what experiences and support they enjoy
- comment on the problems they face
Write about 200 words.

Hussein Salawhari, 19, arrived in Austria after fleeing Afghanistan

John Goodluck, 21, arrived from Ivory Coast to play football for your local Bundesliga team

Sara Cheung, 20, arrived from Hong Kong to study at the local university

Olga Radescu, 18, arrived from Moldova to work as an au pair in a local family

CAN-DO STATEMENTS

		Part / Ex	✔
👂	I can understand the main points in interviews, reports and presentations. (B1/2)	A / Ex 2 A / Ex 3	☐
	I can understand the most important elements of radio programmes and sound recordings when they deal with current events or my interests. (B1/5)	A / Ex 2 A / Ex 3	☐
📖	I can get the essential information from simple newspaper and magazine articles that are clearly structured. (B1/1)	B / Ex 1	☐
	I can understand straightforward factual texts written for a wide audience on subjects related to my field and interest. (B1/2)	C / Ex 1	☐
	I can find information that I need to solve a specific task in various longer texts or text sections. (B1/8)	B / Ex 1	☐
👀	I can begin, maintain and end a conversation about subjects familiar to me. (B1/1)	C / Ex 2	☐
	I can express and give reasons for my opinion in conversations and discussions. Furthermore, I can agree or politely disagree and make other suggestions. (B1/6)	C / Ex 2	☐
👄	I can give a prepared straightforward presentation, which can be followed easily and which I can make interesting for my listeners. (B1/3)	WiC / Ex 4	☐
	I can describe pictures and tell stories with the help of key words or illustrations. (B1/5)	WiC / Ex 4	☐
	I can report the main information in a factual text in a simply way, keeping to the structure of the text. (B1/7)	B / Ex 5	☐
✍	I can write simple stories, essays and creative texts. (B1/2)	C / Ex 3	☐

UNIT 14 Migrants as Minority Groups

A "It's Not All Take, Take, Take" Key: 241

You are going to hear a radio report in which different views on immigration are presented.

1 Looking at both sides

In the first part of the radio report you will hear the views of Andrew Green from Migration Watch, a non-political organization concerned about the scale of migration to the UK, and of Prof. Caroline Whitehead from the London School of Economics.

a Before you listen to the report, make sure you know the meaning and pronunciation of the words and phrases below.

> an issue fraught with tension ■ place strain on sth. ■ community cohesion ■ offset sth. ■ turnover ■ application ■ NHS ■ feeding allowance ■ PhD

b Listen and decide which of the following best describes the topic of the interviews.

20

1 where immigrants come from
2 how many people leave Britain each year
3 who does the low-paid jobs in Britain
4 how many immigrants Britain can cope with

SP 19 Listening for Gist (p. 45)

c Listen again with a partner and take notes. One of you focuses on Andrew Green and listens out for problems regarding the scale of immigration in the UK. The other focuses on Caroline Whitehead and listens out for the types of migrants and migration mentioned.

SP 20 Listening for Detail (p. 45)

d Share your information with your partner. Sum up the general attitude of each expert towards immigration.

Language Help

- … has a positive/negative view of immigration.
- … is in favour of / welcomes / recognizes the benefits of immigration.
- … is clearly against …
- … warns of the problems/ dangers immigration can bring.
- … has no opinion on / is indifferent to the immigration situation.

2 Listening comprehension: multiple-choice **20**

In the second part of the report you will hear the view of Stella Njaka from Brent Women's Advisory Centre, an institution which works with migrants, and of Fatima, one of her clients.

Listen and choose the correct answer (A, B, C or D) for questions 1–5. Put a cross (✘) in the correct box.

picturedesk.com/Andreas Heddergott/SZ-Photo

TF A Multiple-Choice (p. 71)

1 Which of these problems that immigrants face does Stella <u>not</u> mention:
   A living and housing ☐
   B applications for asylum ☐
   C language difficulties ☐
   D caring for young children ☐

2 Why did Fatima come to London?
   A to apply for political asylum ☐
   B to get married ☐
   C to find a job ☐
   D to do a PhD at university ☐

3 What does she want to do now?
   A do a PhD at university ☐
   B return to her home in Morocco ☐
   C get divorced ☐
   D work for her brother ☐

4   According to Stella, who should solve the problem?
    A   the Prime Minister ☐
    B   the local council in Brent ☐
    C   the Secretary of State ☐
    D   the local community ☐

5   How does Stella describe the way Britain treats immigrants?
    A   proper and democratic ☐
    B   insensitive and exploitative ☐
    C   criminal and undemocratic ☐
    D   welcoming and tolerant ☐

3 Comparing the two parts of the interview

Compare the issues mentioned in each part of the report and explain the difference in effect between the two parts.

LP 38 Making Comparisons (p. 29)

4 Language in Use: word formation

Some words are missing from the text. Use the words in brackets to form a word that fits in the gap (1–12). Write your answers in the spaces provided at the end of the text. The first one (0) has been done for you.

TF I Word Formation (p. 77)

LP 32 Word Formation: Suffixes (p. 24)

Immigration is a highly (0) _____ (**controversy**) issue in many countries. On the one hand, there are people who are (1) _____ (**critic**) of immigration. One of these is the spokesman for Immigration Watch, Andrew Green. According to him, unlimited immigration results in enormous population (2) _____ (**grow**). This in turn puts an enormous strain on public services such as (3) _____ (**accommodate**), hospitals and schools. The opponents of unlimited immigration also say that it causes (4) _____ (**tense**) in the local communities. They want (5) _____ (**restrict**) on the number of immigrants because the country can no longer cope with a large influx of (6) _____ (**foreign**).
Other people, such as Professor Whitehead, don't agree with these (7) _____ (**argue**). She points out that there are different types of immigration and that not everyone comes to stay in the country (8) _____ (**permanent**). Not only that, there is also a large number of (9) _____ (**emigrate**) at the same time. She admits that the net number of immigrants is still quite high, but in her opinion many (10) _____ (**serve**) in the city would collapse if there were no immigrants to do them. She also states that many immigrants are more highly (11) _____ (**qualify**) than many people from the native (12) _____ (**populate**). On the whole, she finds that immigration has had a positive impact on society and the economy.

0	*controversial*

1	_____	7	_____
2	_____	8	_____
3	_____	9	_____
4	_____	10	_____
5	_____	11	_____
6	_____	12	_____

5 Writing: blog entry

You have just heard the radio report about Fatima (exercise **2**) and decide to write a post for your own "myviewpoint" blog. In your blog entry you should …

TT 3 Blog Entry (p. 63)

- describe Fatima's situation in London and what she does
- explain why the government doesn't do anything to support her
- comment on the problems illegal immigrants face in their host countries

Write about 200 words.

M Individual Long Turn (p. 80)

23 Taking Part in a Classroom Discussion (p. 47)

6 Speaking: individual long turn ☀ **Key: 898**

The first illegal immigrants …

"I'm sorry, no visa or green card means no admission ..."

- Compare the photo and cartoon.
- Explain what is meant by "illegal" as far as immigrants are concerned.
- Suggest reasons why some migrants might have to cross borders illegally.

7 Group discussion: immigration

Work in groups of four. Each person in the group chooses one role: Andrew Green, Caroline Whitehead, Stella Njaka or the chairperson.

- Spend 5–10 minutes preparing for the discussion by making notes on your character's opinion of immigration. Your notes from exercise **1c** or exercise **2** will help you.
- Discuss this topic in your group: "The government should do more to help immigrants integrate into society." Try to keep the discussion going for 15–20 minutes.

TT 6 Essay (p. 67)

☐ addresses the reader directly
☐ asks a question
☐ expresses the author's opinion
☐ makes a joke
☐ refers to the topic of the essay

- interesting fact(s)
- interesting quotation
- rhetorical question
- the author's opinion
- the thesis of the essay

B Writing an Essay

On p. 121 you can see an example of an essay writing task that you might have to complete in the written Matura exam and a model answer. Read them both and then do the tasks below.

1 Understanding the task and the essay

a Look at the sample essay and identify the following parts: title, introduction, main part, conclusion.

b Read the title and tick (✔) the boxes on the left that best describe what it does.

c Does the writer argue for or against language learning as the key to successful integration? Where does he/she clearly express this opinion?

d Match the three bullet points in the task to paragraphs in the sample essay.

e Which argument does the writer consider to be the most important? Explain your answer.

2 Analysing paragraphs

a Look at the first paragraph (= introduction) of the model essay. Which of the elements on the left does it consist of? (There is one more element than you need.)
Match the sentences in the paragraph to the elements on the left.

b Match the following elements to the sentences of the second paragraph.

concluding/summarizing sentence • example • supporting argument(s) • topic sentence

c Identify the same elements in **b** in the third and fourth paragraphs of the sample essay.

d What does the last paragraph (= conclusion) of the model essay do?

European Language School Association: English Essay Competition
Finding a job, learning the language, making friends, finding a place to live: Can immigrants integrate without learning the local language?
What is your opinion?
Write an essay on the key to successful integration. The writer of the best essay will be awarded a two-week course at a language school of their choice.

You have decided to send in an essay. Argue either for or against language learning as the key to integration. In your essay you should ...

- describe some of the economic problems immigrants face.
- evaluate the importance of language-learning for cultural integration.
- comment on the dangers of a lack of integration.

Give your essay a title. Write about 400 words.

Sample essay: Is language learning the key to integrating immigrants?

David Alaba, the star of the Austrian football team with African and Filipino roots, is a successful footballer and a familiar face in adverts. In fact, he has become the perfect example of successful integration. Alaba was actually born in Austria, but would he have become so popular if he had not grown up speaking the local Viennese dialect? It's doubtful, and I am absolutely convinced that learning the local language is a key part of integration.

First of all, many immigrants are skilled workers or qualified professionals who want to practise their job in their new country and contribute to the economy. However, without any knowledge of the language, they are practically excluded from the employment market. As economic surveys show, the majority of low-paid jobs in developed countries are done by people with an immigrant background. Most of them come hoping to improve their economic situation but their lack of language holds them back.

Another point to consider is the importance of language for cultural integration. Language is necessary in any everday situation, for example buying food or visiting a doctor, where immigrants and people from the host country come into contact. Furthermore, it is absolutely vital to help immigrants understand the things that are important in a society, such as its culture, history and traditions. Immigrants who can't speak the language can't interract socially or culturally with the local community.

The most important point, however, is that it is very dangerous, both for immigrants and for the host country itself, if newcomers only rely on their own immigrant or ethnic group for help. Immigrant groups that remain closed to the outside world and do not make an effort to learn the new language find it difficult to be accepted by the host society. In fact, they may be treated with suspicion and suffer discrimination. As a result, they may become less outgoing, making integration even harder and creating an atmosphere of suspicion that is difficult to break down. Many European states used to help immigrant groups to maintain their own language and customs but now some of them require immigrants to attend language courses and demonstrate that they are willing to integrate.

In conclusion, there are barriers to integration on both sides, but in my opinion the biggest hurdle is the lack of language. Without the ability to understand others, and make oneself understood, immigrants are likely to remain a source of cheap labour cut off from the rest of society and they will not be able to contribute socially or culturally to their new country. (429 words)

3 Structuring an opinion essay
An essay in which you present arguments for or against a thesis, and in which you clearly state your own opinion, is known as an opinion essay.

a Use your answers to exercises **1** and **2** on p.120 to note down what the important parts of an opinion essay are and what each part should include.

b Compare your answers with a partner.

c Read the entry "Writing an essay" in the Companion (see p. 67) and complete any information that is missing in your notes.

4 Linking ideas

a Highlight the linking words/phrases in the sample essay above that guide the reader through the stages of the essay. Where do you usually find these phrases?

b Highlight linking words/phrases that are used to develop arguments or add new aspects to an argument.

c Highlight linking words/phrases that are used to introduce examples.

5 Writing a paragraph

Imagine that you have to write an opinion essay with the following title: "Should German be the only language spoken in Austrian schools?" You decide to argue against the thesis of this essay. You want to use the following three arguments in this order:

- it is necessary to speak and practise different languages in school in order to learn them
- there are ethnic minorities in many countries whose languages are protected
- it is dangerous to dictate what language people speak, as this can lead to oppression

a Put the sentences below for the first argument in the following order:
topic sentence, example, supporting argument, concluding/summarizing sentence.

> **Argument 1**: English, Spanish and French are examples of modern foreign languages. **/** It is not practical to say that only German should be spoken in Austrian schools. **/** Learning languages is part of the daily school life of all school children in Austria. **/** You have to hear and speak languages in order to learn them properly.

b Write a complete paragraph of 60–75 words, linking the ideas with linking words or phrases.

c Use the notes below to write a paragraph developing the second argument.

> **Argument 2**: ethnic minorities in many European countries **/** Hungarians and Slovenians in Austria; German-speaking minority in South Tyrol **/** speaking mother tongue is a basic human right **/** human rights protected by many international agreements

d Make your own notes for the third argument. Present the argument in one paragraph.

 6 Essay (p. 67)

6 Writing an essay

Write a complete essay arguing against the thesis of the essay above, using your three paragraphs as the main part of the essay. Add a title, an introduction and a conclusion.

CAN-DO STATEMENTS

		Part/Ex	✔
👂	I can understand, fundamentally, native speakers when they speak clearly and directly about subjects familiar to me and use standard language. (B1/4)	A / Ex 1 A / Ex 2	☐
	I can understand the most important elements of radio programmes and sound recordings when they deal with current events or my interests. (B1/5)	A / Ex 1 A / Ex 2	☐
	I can get the essential information from simple newspaper and magazine articles that are clearly structured. (B1/1)		☐
📖	I can recognize the essential conclusions in clearly structured argumentative texts. (B1/4)	B / Ex 1	☐
👓	I can express and give reasons for my opinion in conversations and discussions. Furthermore, I can agree or politely disagree and make other suggestions. (B1/6)	A / Ex 7	☐
	I can take on a role in a simulated everyday or professional situation and also improvise thereby. (B1/9)	A / Ex 7	☐
👄	I can give a prepared straightforward presentation, which can be followed easily and which I can make interesting for my listeners. (B1/3)	A / Ex 6	☐
	I can explain my opinions, plans, intentions and goals clearly and give reasons for them. (B1/4)	A / Ex 6	☐
	I can describe pictures and tell stories with the help of key words or illustrations. (B1/5)	A / Ex 6	☐
✏️	I can write reports or simple articles on events, experiences of a general or a professional nature. These texts may be intended for different media or different personal or professional purposes. (B1/1)	A / Ex 5	☐
	I can write simple, private correspondence, e.g. letters and emails. (B1/5)	A / Ex 5	☐

UNIT 15 The Downside of Migration

A Black Hoodie

In the short story 'Black Hoodie', set in modern-day Dublin, three students do a school project on stereotypes. As part of an experiment, 'Ms Nigeria', 'not-Superman's brother' and the narrator steal goods from shops but give them back again so that shop managers will know how best to protect themselves against shoplifters. The fourth person is 'not-Superman', who is in a wheelchair. However, the other three need not-Superman's wheelchair for their shoplifting experiment, so he usually waits somewhere until they return it to him.
Only once do the students keep some stolen sweets. They are arrested shortly after.

hoodie *(BE, infml)* 1. hooded sweatshirt ('Kapuzenjacke'); 2. *(esp. criminal)* young person wearing a hoodie

 29 Reading Fiction (p. 50)

1 Doing a text jigsaw

a Work in groups of six. Your teacher will give each group six different text snippets from the story. Each person in the group chooses <u>one</u> different text snippet (A–F). Read your snippet and make notes in the table.

Snippet	Who?	Where?	When?	What?	Why?

Write down questions that might be answered in the other snippets.

b Tell each other the most important information in your snippet, and ask your questions.

c Together, work out the chronology of the snippets (A–F), based on your understanding of what happens.

1	2	3	4	5	6

d What do you think happens next in the story?
What makes such an ending likely? Exchange ideas and report to the class.

2 Understanding the text

In your groups, talk about the following questions.
1 Why are the young people so worried about the sweets?
2 Why are they so scared when they get to the police station?
3 What makes the narrator feel a bit braver?
4 Why does the detective make the narrator put his hood up?
5 Why does the narrator feel guilty during the interview?
6 Why does the narrator feel proud at the end of the interview?

3 Talking about the characters

a Look again at your text snippet and mark those passages that show you the narrator's feelings either directly (from what you're told) or indirectly (through his behaviour).

b Compare your findings in your group. Which of the adjectives below best describe the narrator? Use your (online) dictionary where necessary.

 8 Using a Dictionary (p. 34)

> angry ▪ anxious ▪ arrogant ▪ brave ▪ calm ▪ cowardly ▪ disciplined ▪ impolite ▪ innocent ▪
> insecure ▪ naive ▪ protective ▪ proud ▪ racist ▪ rude ▪ self-assured ▪ self-conscious ▪
> sensible ▪ silly ▪ strong

c Now decide which adjectives best describe Ms Nigeria and the police detectives involved. Using different colours, mark the relevant passages in your group's snippets. Discuss your decisions in your group.

Language Help

- My part comes before/after your part because …
- But the next part says …
- Shouldn't we learn something about … before …?
- It makes sense / doesn't make sense to describe … before …
- … is probably going to …
- There will be …
- There isn't likely to be … / … isn't likely to …
- I'm sure that …
- In the next few moments …
- I believe that … because …
- I don't agree because if …, then …

4 Discussing the project

a In his interview with the police detective, the narrator explains the school project and how it works. Make sure you understand this by summing up the different steps of the project in class.

> stereotype /ˈsteriətaɪp/ noun
> a fixed idea or image that many people have of a particular type of person or thing, but which is often not true in reality: **cultural/gender/racial stereotypes** ◊ *He doesn't conform to the usual stereotype of the businessman with a dark suit and briefcase.*
> prejudice /ˈpredʒudɪs/ noun
> an unreasonable dislike of or preference for a person, group, custom, etc., especially when it is based on their race, religion, sex, etc.: a victim of racial **prejudice** ◊ *Their decision was based on ignorance and prejudice.* ◊ *There is little prejudice against workers from other EU states.* ◊ *I must admit to a prejudice in favour of British universities.*
>
> *Source: Oxford Advanced Learner's Dictionary 2005*

b Discuss the project in your group. What stereotypes are the young people trying to uncover and change? Give examples from the short story.

c Focus on the character of Ms Nigeria and discuss why such 'obvious' immigrants are so often the target of prejudice. Give examples from the short story.

 5 Article (p. 66)

5 Writing: article

> An article is a short, self-contained piece of writing for a book, (online) magazine or (online) newspaper. The main purpose of an article is to inform or entertain the reader, sometimes to persuade him/her of your own viewpoint.
> An article can be serious or humorous, formal or informal, depending on the type of publication and who the readers are.

> You have been asked to write an article on the theme of "stereotypes" for a youth magazine in the UK called *Teenzine*. In your article you should …
> - describe the project that the students were doing in "Black Hoodie"
> - explain how the project relates to the theme of "stereotypes"
> - comment on how successful you found their project
> Write about 200 words.

M Individual Long Turn (p. 80)

6 Speaking: individual long turn

> Talk about this statement: 'We are all minorities in some way.'
> - List different examples for this saying and explain how it is true.
> - Analyze when you feel like being part of a minority.
> - Assess how we should treat other minorities.

CAN-DO STATEMENTS

		Part / Ex	✔
📖	I can understand longer, relatively simple literary texts on themes that are familiar to me (e.g. modern popular literature). (B1/3)	A / Ex 1	☐
	I can find information that I need to solve a specific task in various longer texts or text sections. (B1/8)	A / Ex 1	☐
👀	I can express and give reasons for my opinion in conversations and discussions. Furthermore, I can agree or politely disagree and make other suggestions. (B1/6)	A / Ex 4	☐
	I can take on a role in a simulated everyday or professional situation and also improvise thereby. (B1/9)	A / Ex 7	☐
✏️	I can write reports or simple articles on events, experiences of a general or a professional nature. These texts may be intended for different media or different personal or professional purposes. (B1/1)	A / Ex 6	☐

1 Reading comprehension: short answers

Read the text below, then answer the questions using a maximum of four words. Write your answers in the spaces provided. The first one (0) has been done for you.

TF F Short Answers (p. 74)

0	What is the reason for building the walls?	*reduce illegal immigration*
1	What is happening to the wall in Naco?	_____
2	Who understands why the immigrants keep coming?	_____
3	Why can't Salvador Rivera be with his American girlfriend?	_____
4	How does Salvador feel about the wall?	_____
5	How did Dan Duley feel about the Berlin Wall?	_____
6	How does he feel about the US border wall?	_____
7	What is the economic solution to the illegal migration problem?	_____
8	Why do the Mexicans keep crossing the border?	_____

Our Wall

At various spots along the dusty, 1,952-mile (3,141 km) U.S.-Mexican border, fences, walls, and vehicle barriers have been constructed since the 1990s to slow illegal immigration. In Arizona, the U.S. state with most illegal crossings, 65 miles (105 km) of walls have been constructed already. There may soon be hundreds more miles of walls.

The 800 or so residents of Naco, Arizona, USA, have been living in the shadow of a fourteen-foot-high (4 m) steel wall for the past decade. Soldiers are helping to extend the barrier 25 miles (40 km) deeper into the desert.

Residents have mixed feelings about the wall. Even those who have let passing illegal immigrants use their phones or given them a ride say the exodus has to stop. And even those who are sick of finding trash in their yards understand why the immigrants keep coming.

"Sometimes I feel sorry for the Mexicans," says Bryan Tomlinson, 45, an engineer for the Bisbee school district. His brother Don adds, "But the wall's a good thing."

At the Hospedaje Santa María on the Mexican side of the border, four people wait for a chance to go over the wall and illegally enter the wealth of the United States. It is a run-down, two-story building, one of many hostels for migrants.

Salvador Rivera, a man in his early 30s, has been here about a year. He worked in Washington State, but, when his mother fell ill, he returned home to Nayarit, Mexico, and is now having trouble getting past the increased security. He left behind an American girlfriend he can no longer reach.

"For so many years, we Mexicans have gone to the U.S. to work. I don't understand why they put up a wall to turn us away. We aren't robbing anybody over there, and they don't pay us very much."

Dan Duley, 50, operates heavy equipment and is a native of Naco on the U.S. side of the border. He was living in Germany after serving in the Air Force when the Berlin Wall came down, and he thought that was a fine thing. But here he thinks something has to be done. "We need help," he says. "We're being invaded. They've taken away our jobs, our security."

But then, as in many conversations on the border, the rhetoric calms down. Duley, along with many other Naco residents, believes the real solution has to be economic, that jobs must be created in Mexico.

Everyone realizes the wall is a police solution to an economic problem. The Mexicans will go over it, under it, or try to tear holes in it. Of the millions of illegal immigrants living in the United States, few would have come if there wasn't a job waiting for them.

Abridged and slightly adapted from: Charles Bowden: Our Wall. In: National Geographic Magazine, May 2007

TF A Multiple-Choice (p. 71)

2 Listening comprehension: multiple-choice

㉑ You are going to listen to a recording about the experience of a hearing person at a deaf convention *(Gehörlosentagung)*. Choose the correct ending (A, B, C or D) for each question (1–6). The first one (0) has been done for you.

0 The speaker thought that South Street Seaport would be empty because …
- A … it is usually a quiet area. ☐
- B … it was late at night. ☐
- C … it was Sunday and the shops were closed. ☐
- D … it was raining. ☒

1 In fact, she found that the area was …
- A … full of people and noisy. ☐
- B … full of people but very quiet. ☐
- C … almost empty of people but very noisy. ☐
- D … almost empty of people and very quiet. ☐

2 When she found out that it was a deaf convention, she felt …
- A … nervous because she didn't know any deaf people. ☐
- B … excited because she was doing a course in sign language. ☐
- C … excited because she admired deaf people. ☐
- D … worried because she didn't know what to expect. ☐

3 Being the only hearing person …
- A … was a big advantage. ☐
- B … was no help at all. ☐
- C … made her realise how fortunate she was. ☐
- D … did not make her feel different to the deaf people around her. ☐

4 She found that she was able to communicate …
- A … easily with the deaf people. ☐
- B … better than the deaf people. ☐
- C … less well than the deaf people. ☐
- D … quickly and efficiently. ☐

5 Her experience made her realise that …
- A … it is really important to learn sign language. ☐
- B … being deaf is not a big problem. ☐
- C … deaf people and hearing people can communicate. ☐
- D … life is difficult for a minority when the majority is intolerant. ☐

6 She thinks that we should help people who do not fit in because …
- A … we are all minorities in some way. ☐
- B … it is the right thing to do. ☐
- C … we will all need help one day. ☒
- D … discrimination is bad. ☐

TT 5 Article (p. 66)

3 Writing: article

> **Immigration – how does it affect you?**
> The media are full of stories about immigration and immigrants, from refugees crossing the Mediterranean to migrant workers from other European countries taking jobs. But how does it really affect you, the young people of Europe. Do you or your friends have an immigrant background? Send your articles to European Youth Magazine. The best entries will will a trip to the European Parliament in Strasbourg.

You decide to write an article for the European Youth Magazine. In your article you should …
- explain why immigration is a controversial topic in many countries
- present some of the main arguments for and against immigration
- describe whether immigration plays a role in your life
- Give your article a title and write about 200 words

4 Language in Use: banked gap-fill

TF J Banked Gap-Fill (p. 78)

Read this text about migration. Some words are missing from the text. For each gap (1–12), choose the correct word (A–O) from the list. There are two extra words that you should not use. Write your answers in the spaces provided. The first one (0) has been done for you.

There are many reasons why people leave their home country to find a better life in a different country. Some are forced to leave because of climatic changes, (0) ___ or starvation; others flee from religious (1) ___ , political oppression or war; a third group of migrants are (2) ___ migrants who are in search of better living conditions.

Some states have (3) ___ encouraged immigration. The United States, for example, recruited (4) ___ mainly from Europe throughout the 19th and 20th centuries while Germany invited guest workers from Turkey, Italy and other southern European states to fuel its booming (5) ___ in the 1950s.

The large (6) ___ of immigrants in some countries can cause racial conflict between immigrant communities and the (7) ___ population, who may fear being swamped by foreigners. In some countries there are policies aimed at giving (8) ___ immigrants the chance to become naturalized (9) ___ , although they often face opposition, (10) ___ in times of economic decline, when immigrants are accused of taking away jobs.

Many immigrants themselves are torn between two (11) ___ and they feel they don't really belong to either. Alienation and uncertainty about their identity are often the result, particularly when they face (12) ___ in societies where they may have lived for two generations.

A actively
B citizens
C cultures
D discrimination
E economy
F economic
G especially
H famine
I illegal
J influx
K native
L persecution
M politicians
N refuge
O settlers

0	1	2	3	4	5	6	7	8	9	10	11	12
H	___	___	___	___	___	___	___	___	___	___	___	___

5 Speaking: paired activity

TF N Paired Activity (p. 80)

Your local council is looking for suggestions on how to overcome prejudice towards immigrant groups and how to integrate them better into the community.

Your school has decided to present students' ideas. Discuss the following suggestions with a partner.

- a weekend camping trip with local and immigrant children
- a joint project to produce a play about an immigrant family's journey to Austria
- a cultural evening where immigrant food and music are presented
- a poster campaign for tolerance towards foreigners
- a sports tournament between local and immigrant teams

Decide which three you would recommend.

Cornelsen Verlag, Berlin: Green/Looking for Alaska

HarperCollins, Publishers, New York, 2009; Oates/After the Wreck, I Picked Myself Up, Spread My Wings, and Flew Away

Cornelsen Verlag, Berlin: Sherman/The Absolutely True Diary of a Part-Time Indian

Random House Children's Books, 2002; Wilson/GIRLS in love

Cornelsen Verlag, Berlin: Hornby/About a Boy

R   *elaxation*
E   *xcitement*
A   *…*
D
I
N
G

1 What is reading?

a With a partner, describe 'reading' – what it is, what it means to you, what it implies ('Reading is …' or 'Reading means …').

b Think of 'READING' as an acronym and find a suitable word for each letter. Discuss the different solutions in class. Agree on the best two.

2 Speculating

a Look at the covers and titles of the seven novels for young-adult readers. Which book do you find most interesting? Why? Take a vote in class.

b Based on the book covers and titles, speculate on what each book might be about. Discuss your ideas with a partner.

In this topic you will learn about …

- the World of Books — (WiC)
- The Curious Incident of the Dog in the Night-Time — (Unit 16)
- The Absolutely True Diary of a Part-Time Indian — (Unit 17)
- Looking for Alaska — (Unit 18)

A

Reasons to read my book:
- You can learn all sorts of secrets about me
- You can have lots of laughs
- You might even cry a bit, too
- PLUS, you get to find out a lot more about BOYS!

B

Will is thirty-six but acts like a teenager. He meets Marcus, the oldest twelve-year-old in the world. Perhaps if Will can teach Marcus how to be a kid, Marcus can help Will grow up.

C

'We went to the moon to have fun, but the moon turned out to completely suck.'
So says Titus, a teenager whose ability to read, write, and even think for himself has been almost completely obliterated by his 'feed', a transmitter implanted directly into his brain.

D

Fifteen-year-old Christopher has a photographic memory. He understands maths. He understands science. What he can't understand are other human beings. When he finds his neighbour's dog lying dead on the lawn, he decides to write a murder mystery about it.

E

Jenna Abbott separates her life into two categories. Before the wreck, she was leading a normal life with her mom in suburban New York. After …

F

Junior is picked on by everyone but his best friend. Determined to get a good education, Junior leaves the rez to attend an all-white school in the neighboring farm town where the only other Indian is the school mascot.

sth. sucks (slang) sth. is very bad
obliterate sth. remove sth., destroy sth.
lawn area of short grass in a garden
pick on sb. tease sb., bully sb.
determined to do sth. [dɪˈtɜːmɪnd] having made a decision to do sth. and not letting anybody or anything stop you
rez (reservation) here: area of land in the USA kept for Native Americans to live in
mascot [ˈmæskət] small figure/toy that is thought to bring good luck, especially for sports teams

Anette Schamuhn

3 Reading blurbs

A "blurb" is the short text on the back of a book designed to attract the reader's interest.

a Read the six extracts from the blurbs and match the texts (A–F) to the covers (1–7). There is one more cover than you need.

b Look at **2a** again. Do you still find the same book the most interesting, or have you changed your mind after reading the blurbs? Why (not)?

c Speculate what the novel without a blurb could be about.

d **EXTRA** Write a short blurb of not more than 50 words for the novel without a blurb, using your ideas from **3c**.
Don't forget that we usually use the present tense when we are talking about the contents of a book, film or play.

 3 Simple Present to Talk about Texts (p. 6)

LP 24 Increase Your Word Power Online (p. 18)

Fotolia.com/Moreen Blackthorne

⚠ **Trouble Spot**

reader = **1.** Leser/in
        2. Lesebuch
        3. Lesegerät

**SP** 1 Mind Mapping (p. 30)

**LP** 25 Collocations (p. 20)

The World of Books

The worldwide success story of the book began in 1439 with the invention of the <mark>printing</mark> press by Johannes Gutenberg, which made books available to a larger <mark>audience</mark>. Our problem today, though, is how to keep up an interest in reading. In 1997, a survey on the <mark>reading habits</mark> of young adults revealed that in Great Britain 35 % of 16- to 25-year-olds read regularly in their free time. By 2001 the figures had risen to almost 40 %. Many parents, teachers, <mark>librarians</mark> and <mark>booksellers</mark> like to think that it was the arrival of the teenage wizard Harry Potter that really inspired kids to <mark>read for pleasure</mark>.

Reading habits change with age, and those teenagers who are not put off by the set books at school quickly move on from <mark>children's literature</mark> to <mark>young-adult fiction</mark> (YA for short) and adult fiction. But regardless of age, it is often the same genres that appeal to readers, namely <mark>science fiction</mark>, <mark>horror</mark>, <mark>love stories</mark>, <mark>murder mysteries</mark>, <mark>biographies</mark>, and of course <mark>fantasy novels</mark> like *Harry Potter*.

When the final <mark>volume</mark> of the *Harry Potter* <mark>series</mark> was <mark>published</mark> in 2007, <mark>booksellers</mark> wondered whether another book could achieve sales similar to these bestsellers. But they needn't have worried: Stephenie Meyer's *Twilight* <mark>saga</mark> about the love between a girl and a vampire has <mark>kept</mark> a large <mark>readership in suspense</mark> despite its dreary <mark>setting</mark> – Forks, Washington, is the rainiest place in the USA. And the film adaptation of *Twilight* (released in 2008) was not only an immediate success, but in turn raised the sales of the book.

At book fairs and festivals, <mark>ebooks</mark> are now one of the main talking points due to their many (and partly future) advantages: they will make it easier for unknown <mark>authors</mark> to get published, they are searchable and better for the environment as no transport costs arise, and the pollution connected, for example, with printing and transporting books is avoided. Moreover, ebook readers can easily contain a small library. Some day they may even be cheaper than printed books because of the paper saved. Still some people fear that ebooks will stop readers from buying printed books. The question remains open – but will <mark>avid readers</mark> really enjoy looking at a screen for hours as much as they previously <mark>enjoyed reading</mark> a book and turning its pages?

1 **Word power: mind map**

Collect the words and phrases highlighted in the text above in a table or a mind map, starting with 'The World of Books' as your topic phrase and the categories *books*, *readers*, *the book trade* as branches. Add more words you already know from other sources. Remember to add new words and phrases as you go through this Topic. Make sure you include collocations.

2 **Activating your vocabulary**

Complete the sentences below using (not only the highlighted) words and expressions from the text above.

1 As a child, he read under the bedcovers, kept _____ by murder mysteries and fantasy _____ alike.
2 Don't let yourselves be _____ by the length of the book – the plot and the characters will make up for it.
3 Victoria is not an _____ reader – the only thing she reads are fashion magazines.
4 Books can be studied, analysed and interpreted, but they can also be read for _____
5 I only read bestsellers; if a book is not an _____ success, I won't touch it.
6 Ebooks are better for the environment as they don't cause as much pollution as _____ books do.
7 When books are made into successful films that usually helps the _____ of the book.
8 People are worried that teenage reading _____ will be changed by Twitter and social networking websites.

3 Evaluating a chart

a Read the following survey of British teenagers' reading top ten likes and dislikes.

 13 Working with Charts and Graphs (p. 39)

Read up	Ranking
Heat magazine	1
Bliss magazine Song lyrics online	2
Computer-game cheats online	3
My own online blog or fan fiction	4
The Harry Potter series	5
Anne Frank's Diary	6
Film scripts	7
Books by Anthony Horowitz	8
The Lion, the Witch and the Wardrobe	9
BBC Online	10
Books by Louise Rennison	10

Fed up	Ranking
Homework	1
Shakespeare	2
Books over 100 pages	3
Reading about skinny celebrities in magazines	4
The books I am made to read by school/my teachers	5
Encyclopedias and dictionaries	6
The Beano	7
The Harry Potter series	8
Maps/Directions	
Facebook	9
Financial Times	10
Anything in another language	10

From: National Literacy Trust: National Year of Reading 2008

read up on sth. read a lot about sth.
be fed up with sb./sth. not like/not want to do sth. any more
Heat British celebrity gossip and news magazine
Bliss British teenage girls' magazine
cheat *(n) here:* a program by which you can go to the next level of a computer game
Anthony Horowitz British screenwriter and author of mystery and adventure stories
The Lion, the Witch and the Wardrobe fantasy novel by C.S. Lewis
Louise Rennison British author of a series for teenage girls
The Beano British children's comic
Financial Times British newspaper containing mostly economic news

b In groups of four, analyse the ranking in the above list: Organize the reading material according to category (e.g. comics). Some may go in more than one category. Which category was most popular in 'Read up', which in 'Fed up'?
Which categories surprised you most? Explain.

c Discuss what the Austrian equivalents of the reading material in the list could be. How would you rank them? Create your own top five list and present your results in class.

d Sum up what you can say about the reading habits of British teenagers based on the two lists and your discussion.

4 Teenage reading habits

a Listen to the interview with five teenagers about their reading habits and fill in the table.

	Andrew	Lorna	Caroline	Merlene	Daniel
What?					
Why ?					
When, where?					

b Answer the questions for yourself. With a partner, compare the teenagers' answers to your own.

5 What makes a good book?

a Write down four or five features which make for a good read.

b Share your ideas with a partner. Agree on the four most important features, then name a book that, for you, fulfils these requirements.

Language Help

- A good book has to be exciting / romantic / scary / realistic / full of suspense / informative / believable /…
- It has to challenge me / grab my attention / make me laugh / cry /…

A Opening Lines

1 First impressions

Sometimes the opening lines of a novel immediately make you want to read on, sometimes you have to force yourself to read on, and sometimes you stop reading altogether.

Read the opening passage of *The Curious Incident of the Dog in the Night-Time* and give it a grade from A–D:

A: I have to read this book! ☐

B: This book sounds interesting. I would have to read more to know if I would like it. ☐

C: I'm not sure whether I would like this book. Perhaps I'll read it in a year or so. ☐

D: I will definitely not read this book. ☐

wound [wuːnd] injury
cancer a serious disease in which growths of cells form in the body and kill normal body cells

2

It was 7 minutes after midnight. The dog was lying on the grass in the middle of the lawn in front of Mrs Shears' house. Its eyes were closed. It looked as if it was running on its side, the way dogs run when they think they are chasing a cat in a dream. But the dog was not running or asleep. The dog was dead. There was a garden fork sticking out of the dog. The points of the fork must have gone all the way through the dog and into the ground because the fork had not fallen over. I decided that the dog was probably killed with the fork because I could not see any other wounds in the dog and I do not think you would stick a garden fork into a dog after it had died for some other reason, like cancer for example, or a road accident.

But I could not be certain about this.

Mark Haddon: The Curious Incident of the Dog in the Night-Time. Berlin: Cornelsen 2008 © Mark Haddon

2 Speculating

a From what you have read, speculate in pairs on who the narrator might be. Consider the following questions and give reasons for your answers.

- Is the narrator male or female?
- Is he or she popular at school?
- Is he or she intelligent?
- Does he or she have a sense of humour?

b Why do you think the first chapter starts with the number 2?

c Look at the book cover and title. Speculate on what the book might be about. What genre could it be?

SP 29 Reading Fiction (p. 50)

B Who Is Telling The Story?  Key: 783

Christopher, the narrator of The Curious Incident of the Dog in the Night-Time, *is reporting a conversation with his teacher Siobhan about the book he is writing.*

Siobhan [ʃə'vɔːn] female Irish first name
approximately [ə'prɒksɪmətli] about
attention the act of listening to, looking at or thinking about sb./ sth. carefully
make the wiggly quotation sign *here:* use the index and middle fingers of both hands to show you are not being serious
The Hound of the Baskervilles a Sherlock Holmes detective story
hound dog that is used for hunting

This is a murder mystery novel.

Siobhan said that I should write something I would want to read myself. Mostly I read books about science and maths. I do not like proper novels. In proper novels people say things like, 'I am veined with iron, with silver and with streaks of common mud. I cannot contract into the firm fist which those clench who do not depend on stimulus.' What does this mean? I do not know. Nor does Father. Nor do Siobhan or Mr Jeavons. I have asked them.

Siobhan has long blonde hair and wears glasses which are made of green plastic. And Mr Jeavons smells of soap and wears brown shoes that have approximately 60 tiny circular holes in each of them.

But I do like murder mystery novels. So I am writing a murder mystery novel.

In a murder mystery novel someone has to work out who the murderer is and then catch them. It is a puzzle. If it is a good puzzle you can sometimes work out the answer before the end of the book.

Siobhan said that the book should begin with something to grab people's attention. That is why I started with the dog. I also started with the dog because it happened to me and I find it hard to imagine things which did not happen to me.

Siobhan read the first page and said that it was different. She put this word into inverted commas by making the wiggly quotation sign with her first and second fingers. She said that it was usually people who were killed in murder mystery novels. I said that two dogs were killed in *The Hound of the Baskervilles*, the hound itself and James Mortimer's spaniel, but Siobhan said that they weren't the victims of the murder, Sir Charles Baskerville was. She said that this was because readers cared more about people than dogs, so if a person was killed in the book readers would want to carry on reading.

I said that I wanted to write about something real and I knew people who had died but I did not know any people who had been killed, except Edward's father from school, Mr Paulson, and that was a murder, and I didn't really know him.

I also said that I cared about dogs because they were faithful and honest, and some dogs were cleverer and more interesting than some people.

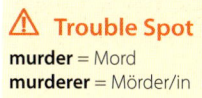

⚠ Trouble Spot
murder = Mord
murderer = Mörder/in

LP 27 False Friends (p. 22)

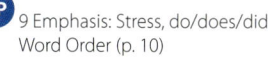
LP 9 Emphasis: Stress, do/does/did, Word Order (p. 10)

Mark Haddon: The Curious Incident of the Dog in the Night-Time. Berlin: Cornelsen 2008 © Mark Haddon

1 Reading: true/false or not given

Read the extract, then decide whether the statements (1–9) are true (T), false (F) or not given (NG) in the text. Put a cross (✘) in the correct box. The first one (0) has been done for you.

	statements	T	F	NG
0	Christopher, the narrator, likes reading proper novels.	☐	☒	☐
1	He reads books about science and maths and he also likes murder mystery novels	☐	☐	☐
2	Mr Jeavons is the headmaster of Christopher's school.	☐	☐	☐
3	Christopher thinks a good murder mystery novel is one that can be solved before you get to the end of the book.	☐	☐	☐
4	Siobhan tells him to write something that other people will want to read.	☐	☐	☐
5	Siobhan tells him to start with something that will grab the reader's attention.	☐	☐	☐
6	Christopher has a lively imagination.	☐	☐	☐
7	Siobhan doesn't believe that Christopher can write a novel.	☐	☐	☐
8	Siobhan thinks that people care more about other people than about dogs.	☐	☐	☐
9	Christopher thinks that most people are more interesting than dogs.	☐	☐	☐

2 Reading between the lines

a What are the characteristics of the types of books that Christopher likes and doesn't like? What does this tell you about his character?

b With a partner, analyse the text for additional information about Christopher.
 1 Look at the things Christopher talks about and describes: What does this tell you about his behaviour?
 2 Does Christopher follow Siobhan's advice? Give examples from the extract to support your statement.
 3 What adjectives would you use to describe Christopher? Naive, mysterious, simple, …

3 Writing a dialogue

Look at the last three paragraphs of the extract. What do Siobhan and Christopher actually say? Rewrite their dialogue using direct speech.

Siobhan: "It is different. It is usually people …"
Christopher: "Two dogs …"

C The Author and the Narrator

You are going to listen to an interview with Mark Haddon, the author of The Curious Incident of the Dog in the Night-Time.

1 Before you listen

Match the words on the left (1–12) with the definitions on the right (a–l).

1	circumscribed	a	referring to mental processes of understanding
2	cognitive	b	understand sb.'s feelings
3	diverse	c	referring to the usual meaning of a word
4	empathize with sb.	d	describe sb. in a particular way, esp. unfairly
5	have a disability	e	have a handicap
6	keep sth. at bay	f	able to think only of one thing
7	incomprehensible	g	form a regular arrangement of sth. on sth. else
8	label sb.	h	stop sth. from having a bad effect
9	literal	i	impossible to understand
10	be obsessed with sth.	j	limited
11	pattern sth.	k	destroy sth.
12	wreck sth.	l	very different from each other

TF A Multiple-Choice (p. 71)

2 Listening comprehension: multiple-choice

㉓ Now listen to the first part of the interview with Mark Haddon. Choose the correct answer (A, B, C or D) for questions 1–4. Put a cross (✘) in the correct box. The first one has been done for you.

0 According to Mark Haddon, what is Christopher's main behavioural problem?
   A   He doesn't like looking people in the face. ☐
   B   He can't empathize with other people. ☒
   C   He doesn't understand what people say to him. ☐
   D   He doesn't like going out on his own. ☐

1 Why doesn't the author use the terms "Asperger's syndrome" and "autism" to describe Christopher?
   A   He doesn't think they are the correct labels for Christopher. ☐
   B   He doesn't want to hurt anybody's feelings. ☐
   C   He thinks his book is about maths rather than autism. ☐
   D   He doesn't think this is the most important thing about Christopher. ☐

2 Which characteristic of Christoper's is <u>not</u> mentioned in the interview?
   A   He doesn't understand jokes. ☐
   B   He never goes out without company. ☐
   C   He only eats green vegetables. ☐
   D   He gets violent if people touch him. ☐

3 How did the author manage to make Christopher's character so real?
A He tried very hard to get him "right". ☐
B He did a lot of research about Asperger's syndrome. ☐
C He tried to make him like a typical person with Asperger's syndrome. ☐
D He imagined all the time what it would be like to be Christopher. ☐

4 According to Mark Haddon, what is the biggest advantage for the author in Christopher's voice?
A Christopher always gets everything wrong. ☐
B Christopher never tells the reader what to think. ☐
C Christopher's voice is very simple to write. ☐
D Christopher can't empathize with other people. ☐

3 The narrator's voice

23

a Now listen to the second part of the interview. Explain why Haddon finds Christopher's voice attractive for a narrator.

b **EXTRA** Haddon describes his narrator as having a 'flat, emotionless' voice. State whether, in your eyes, Haddon has succeeded in achieving this tone of voice. Comment on (the effect of) the extract he reads in the interview.

4 Language in Use: word formation

Some words are missing from the text. Use the words in brackets to form a word that fits in the gap (1–10). Write your answers in the spaces provided at the end of the text. The first one (0) has been done for you.

Autism is a lifelong developmental (0) ___ (**disable**) four times more common in boys than girls. It affects the way a person communicates and relates to people around them. People with autism have (1) ___ (**difficult**) with everyday social interaction, making sense of the world and (2) ___ (**process**) information. However, some telecommunications and IT companies in Denmark have started hiring people with autism due to their high level of (3) ___ (**concentrate**) when working with numbers. Their jobs include administration of databases as well as computer (4) ___ (**program**) and testing.
Asperger syndrome is (5) ___ (**consider**) by experts to be a 'soft' form of autism. People with Asperger syndrome may have problems understanding body language, (6) ___ (**face**) expressions or tone of voice. They might not understand jokes and find other people unpredictable and (7) ___ (**confuse**); as a result they cannot predict what will happen next or understand other people's (8) ___ (**think**), feelings or actions. One common symptom of Asperger syndrome is a series of rules and daily rituals which they insist on adhering to or carrying out. They may also become (9) ___ (**obsess**) with a single object or topic, ignoring everything else. Children with Asperger syndrome often present many facts about their subject of interest, but there will seem to be no point or (10) ___ (**conclude**) in what they say.

5 Creative writing: diary entry

Later in the story, Christopher takes a train to London. (Remember: he never usually goes beyond the end of his street on his own.) Write Christopher's diary entry describing how he gets to the station and buys a train ticket to London. Write about 150 words.

impale sb./sth. on sth. push a sharp pointed object through sb./sth.
forensics connected with scientific tests used by the police when solving a crime
loopy *(infml)* crazy
intuitive going by instinct, not reason
size sb./sth. up form an opinion about sb./sth.
clue a piece of information that helps solve a crime
approach sth. come near to sth.
weep cry *(weinen)*

TF I Word Formation (p. 77)

0 *disability*

1 _____
2 _____
3 _____

4 _____
5 _____
6 _____

7 _____
8 _____

9 _____

10 _____

SP 44 Creative Writing (p. 58)

6 Speaking: individual long turn

TF M Individual Long Turn (p. 80)

- Compare the pictures.
- Give some reasons why many young people don't read books for pleasure.
- Reflect on your own reading habits.

CAN-DO STATEMENTS

		Part / Ex	✔
👂	I can understand the main points in interviews, reports and presentations. (B1/2)	C / Ex 2 C / Ex 3	☐
	I can understand, fundamentally, native speakers when they speak clearly and directly about subjects familiar to me and use standard language. (B1/4)	WiC / Ex 4	☐
📖	I can understand longer, relatively simple literary texts on themes that are familiar to me (e.g. modern popular literature). (B1/3)	A / Ex 1 B / Ex 1	☐
👀	I can express and give reasons for my opinion in conversations and discussions. Furthermore, I can agree or politely disagree and make other suggestions. (B1/6)	B / Ex 2	☐
👄	I can report on subject areas familiar to me, what I have heard, seen, read or experienced and describe my feelings or reactions. (B1/1)	C / Ex 6	☐
✏️	I can write simple stories, essays and creative texts. (B1/2)	C / Ex 5	☐

UNIT 17   The Absolutely True Diary of a Part-Time Indian

A   Opening Lines

1   First impressions

SP 29 Reading Fiction (p. 50)

Read the opening passage of *The Absolutely True Diary of a Part-Time Indian* and give it a grade from A–D:

A: I have to read this book! ☐

B: This book sounds interesting. I would have to read more to know if I would like it. ☐

C: I'm not sure whether I would like this book. Perhaps I'll read it in a year or so. ☐

D: I will definitely not read this book. ☐

The Black-Eye-of-the-Month Club

I was born with water on the brain.

Okay, so that's not exactly true. I was actually born with too much cerebral spinal fluid inside my skull. But cerebral spinal fluid is just the doctors' fancy way of saying brain grease. And brain grease works inside the lobes like car grease works inside an engine. It keeps things running smooth and fast. But weirdo me, I was born with too much grease inside my skull, and it got all thick and muddy and disgusting, and it only mucked up the works. My thinking and breathing and living engine slowed down and flooded.

My brain was drowning in grease.

But that makes the whole thing sound weirdo and funny, like my brain was a giant French fry, so it seems more serious and poetic and accurate to say, 'I was born with water on the brain.'

Sherman Alexie: The Absolutely True Diary of a Part-Time Indian. Berlin: Cornelsen 2009 © Sherman Alexie

a black eye an area of black skin around the eye caused by a blow
cerebral spinal fluid [ˌserəbrəl ˌspaɪnəl ˈfluːɪd] *Hirn- und Rückenmarksflüssigkeit*
skull the hard covering of bone protecting the brain
fancy *(adj)* complicated so it sounds good; intended to impress
grease fluid used to keep parts, e.g. in an engine, running smoothly
lobes *(pl) here:* parts of the brain
weirdo *(infml)* strange
muck up the works *(infml)* prevent sth. from working properly

⚠ **Trouble Spot**

French fries *(AE)* = (potato) chips *(BE)* = Pommes frites
(potato) chips *(AE)* = (potato) crisps *(BE)* = Kartoffelchips

2   Speculating

a From what you have read, speculate in pairs on who the narrator might be. Consider the following questions and give reasons for your answers.
  - Is the narrator male or female?
  - Is he or she popular at school?
  - Is he or she intelligent?
  - Does he or she have a sense of humour?

b What do you think the "Black-Eye-of-the-Month" might be?

c Look at the book cover and title. Speculate on what the book might be about. What genre could it be?

B   'A Very Autobiographical Novel'

You are going to hear part of a panel discussion with Sherman Alexie, the author of The Absolutely True Diary of a Part-Time Indian. *Like the narrator of his book, he is a Native American and grew up on a reservation. He left the reservation school to go to Reardan, a white school outside 'the rez'.*

1   Before you listen

a Speculate on reasons why Alexie, like the hero in his novel, left the reservation school he had gone to in order to go to a white school.

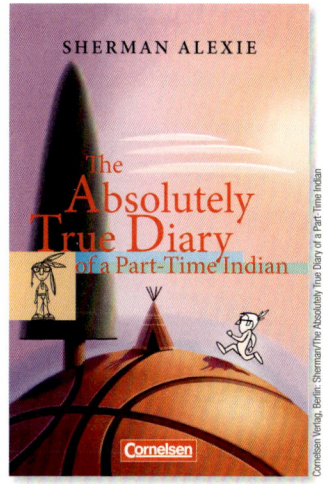

▶▶▶

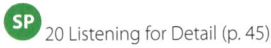

8 Using a Dictionary (p. 34)

b Match the words on the left (1–7) with the definitions on the right (a–g). Use your (online) dictionary for help, if necessary.

1	dork	a	motivation
2	impetus	b	refuse to let sb. be a member of a social group
3	maiden name	c	boring, stupid and unfashionable
4	nerdy	d	a group of people who discuss topics of interest
5	ostracize	e	a nerd (see nerdy)
6	panel	f	a woman's family name before marriage
7	venture	g	a project or activity involving risk or danger

TF C Short Answers (p. 72)

SP 20 Listening for Detail (p. 45)

2 Listening comprehension: short answers

24

Now listen to the extract and answer the questions using a maximum of 4 words. Write your answers in the spaces provided. The first one (0) has been done for you.

0	What did the author have to do to write his book?	*revisit his teenage years*
1	How does he describe his novel?	
2	How does he describe his childhood and the experience of writing about it?	
3	Why did people ostracize him in the reservation?	
4	What did he find in a maths book on the first day of seventh grade?	
5	What terrible tragedy also occured that year?	
6	What was the cause of this tragedy?	
7	What is the good part of writing about a painful childhood?	
8	What thing(s) has he received that really surprised him?	

(Tyler) Perry's (House of Payne)
American TV sitcom that follows three generations of an African-American family; first shown in 2006

3 The author and the narrator

a State the reason Alexie mentions for leaving the reservation school. Why do you think this incident had such an impact on him?

b Does knowing that the novel is autobiographical change your interest in it?

c **EXTRA** Have you ever wanted to write to an author? Make a list of questions you would like to ask Alexie and write an email to him. Write about 150 words.

4 Doing research

In the panel discussion, Alexie mentions the problem of alcohol. Do some research on Native American reservations in the USA.

- Find out some historical facts about the quality of life and the laws on reservations.
- Explain why alcohol and gambling are such a big problem there.
- Make suggestions on how to change the current situation.

Present your findings to the class.

14 Doing Research (p. 40)

15 Doing a Project (p. 41)

22 Giving a Presentation (p. 46)

C Penelope's Dreams

Junior, the narrator of The Absolutely True Diary of a Part-Time Indian, *is now at Reardan, the white school outside the reservation. One day he hears someone being sick in the girls' bathroom. It turns out to be his popular classmate Penelope, who confesses to having bulimia. They become friends although Penelope's racist father Earl doesn't like this.*

bulimia [buˈlɪmiə] medical condition where sb. repeatedly eats lots and then throws it back up again
Penelope [pəˈneləpi]
obvious [ˈɒbviəs] clear
corny *(infml)* not original
defy sb. refuse to obey sb.
smudge sb./sth. make sb./sth. dirty
stud *(infml)* sexually attractive man

1 Reading and taking notes
Read the extract and look for the following information:
- the reasons Junior names for Penelope dating him;
- the effects of their relationship on Junior's status at Reardan.

So I say to Penelope what I always say to Dad when he's drunk and depressed and ready to give up on the world.

'Hey, Penelope,' I say. 'Don't give up.'

Okay, so it's not the wisest advice in the world. It's actually kind of obvious and corny.

But Penelope starts crying, talking about how lonely she is, and how everybody thinks her life is perfect because she's pretty and smart and popular, but that she's scared all the time, but nobody will let her be scared because she's pretty and smart and popular.

You notice that she mentioned her beauty, intelligence, and popularity twice in one sentence?

The girl has an ego.

But that's sexy, too. [...]

Everybody is absolutely shocked that Penelope chose me to be her new friend. I'm not some ugly, mutated beast. But I am an absolute stranger at the school.

And I am an Indian. [...]

Okay, so Penelope and I became the hot topic because we were defying the great and powerful Earl.

And, yeah, you're probably thinking that Penelope was dating me ONLY because I was the worst possible choice for her.

She was probably dating me ONLY because I was an Indian boy.

And, okay, so she was only semi-dating me. We held hands once in a while and we kissed once or twice, but that was it.

That's Penelope!

Totally absolutely gorgeous!

I don't know what I meant to her.

I think she was bored of being the prettiest, smartest, and most popular girl in the world. She wanted to get a little crazy, you know? She wanted to get a little smudged.

And I was the smudge.

But, hey, I was kind of using her, too.

After all, I suddenly became popular.

Because Penelope had publicly declared that I was cute enough to ALMOST date, all of the other girls in school decided that I was cute, too.

Because I got to hold hands with Penelope, and kiss her good-bye when she jumped on the school bus to go home, all of the other boys in school decided that I was a major stud.

▶ ▶ ▶

Even the teachers started paying more attention to me.

I was mysterious.

How did I, the dorky Indian guy, win a tiny piece of Penelope's heart?

What was my secret?

I looked and talked and dreamed and walked differently than everybody else.

I was new.

If you want to get all biological, then you'd have to say that I was an exciting addition to the Reardan gene pool.

So, okay, those are all the obvious reasons why Penelope and I were friends. All the shallow reasons. But what about the bigger and better reasons?

'Arnold,' she said one day after school, 'I hate this little town. It's so small, too small. Everything about it is small. The people here have small ideas. Small dreams. They all want to marry each other and live here forever.'

'What do you want to do?' I asked.

'I want to leave as soon as I can. I think I was born with a suitcase.'

Yeah, she talked like that. All big and goofy and dramatic. I wanted to make fun of her, but she was so earnest.

'Where do you want to go?' I asked.

'Everywhere. I want to walk on the Great Wall of China. I want to walk to the top of pyramids in Egypt. I want to swim in every ocean. I want to climb Mount Everest. I want to go on an African safari. I want to ride a dogsled in Antarctica. I want all of it. Every single piece of everything.'

Sherman Alexie: The Absolutely True Diary of a Part-Time Indian. Berlin: Cornelsen 2009 © Sherman Alexie

dorky *(infml)* clumsy, stupid, boring
gene pool [dʒiːn] all the genes of one species
shallow opposite of deep; only on the surface
goofy [ˈɡuːfi] *(infml)* silly, stupid

Language Help

- I find their relationship totally …
- I can('t) imagine …(-ing) …
- I think it is completely convincing. They are both …
- I don't believe that … would want to …

44 Creative Writing (p. 58)

N Paired Activity (p. 80)

2 Looking at the characters

a What do we find out about Penelope in this extract:
- directly from the narrator (his description of her);
- indirectly from the narrator (how he shows her behaving)?

b Work in small groups. Discuss whether the relationship between Penelope and Junior is convincing and realistic.

3 EXTRA Creative writing: diary entry
Write a diary entry for Penelope in which she describes Junior and her relationship with him.

4 Speaking: paired activity
The European Union is looking for ways to encourage young people to read more books. Your school has decided to send in some suggestions.
Discuss the following ideas with your partner and decide which three suggestions you would recommend:

- free books for all school libraries
- compulsory one hour "reading" per week on all school timetables
- free downloads of ebooks for under-18s
- regular book review competitions with prizes
- author readings every semester in school

5 **Writing: article**

Write a (humorous) article for your school magazine with the title "I learnt more from [name of book] than I did all last year!".

 5 Article (p. 66)

- Describe a book that really made an impression on you.
- Explain how it was relevant to your situation.
- Give reasons why reading fiction is considered so important for young people.

Write about 200 words.

CAN-DO STATEMENTS

		Part/Ex	✔
👂	I can understand the main points in interviews, reports and presentations. (B1/2)	B/Ex 2	☐
📖	I can understand longer, relatively simple literary texts on themes that are familiar to me (e.g. modern popular literature). (B1/3)	A/Ex 1 C/Ex 1	☐
👀	I can express and give reasons for my opinion in conversations and discussions. Furthermore, I can agree or politely disagree and make other suggestions. (B1/6)	C/Ex 4	☐
👄	I can give a prepared straightforward presentation, which can be followed easily and which I can make interesting for my listeners. (B1/3)	B/Ex 4	☐
✒️	I can write simple stories, articles and creative texts. (B1/2)	C/Ex 3 C/Ex 5	☐

UNIT 18 Looking for Alaska

A Opening Lines

1 First impressions

Read the opening passage of *Looking for Alaska* and give it a grade from A–D:

A: I have to read this book! ☐

B: This book sounds interesting. I would have to read more to know if I would like it. ☐

C: I'm not sure whether I would like this book. Perhaps I'll read it in a year or so. ☐

D: I will definitely not read this book. ☐

SP 29 Reading Fiction (p. 50)

underestimate say that sth. is smaller than it really is

ragtag *(infml) here:* not giving a very good impression

geek *(infml)* boring, unfashionable, unpopular person

cavernous like a large cave

persevere continue doing sth, although it is very difficult

awash in sth. *here:* having lots of sth.

delusion a false belief or opinion

dip thick mixture into which pieces of food are dipped before being eaten

festoon decorate

streamer long narrow piece of coloured paper

cavalry ['kævlri] part of an army that fights on horses

one hundred thirty-six days before

The week before I left my family and Florida and the rest of my minor life to go to boarding school in Alabama, my mother insisted on throwing me a going-away party. To say that I had low expectations would be to underestimate the matter dramatically. Although I was more or less forced to invite all my "school friends," i.e. the ragtag bunch of drama people and English geeks I sat with by social necessity in the cavernous cafeteria of my public school, I knew they wouldn't come. Still, my mother persevered, awash in the delusion that I had kept my popularity secret from her all these years. She cooked a small mountain of artichoke dip. She festooned our living room in green and yellow streamers, the colors of my new school. She bought two dozen champagne poppers and placed them around the edge of our coffee table.

And when that final Friday came, when my packing was mostly done, she sat with my dad and me on the living-room couch at 4:56 P.M. and patiently awaited the arrival of the Good-bye to Miles Cavalry.

John Green: Looking for Alaska. Berlin: Cornelsen 2009 © John Green

2 Speculating

a From what you have read, speculate in pairs on who the narrator might be. Consider the following questions and give reasons for your answers.

- Is the narrator male or female?
- Is he or she popular at school?
- Is he or she intelligent?
- Does he or she have a sense of humour?

b What do you think "one hundred thirty-six days before" might refer to?

c Look at the book cover and title. Speculate on what the book might be about. What genre could it be?

B Getting to Know the Narrator

The description of Miles's going away party follows on directly from the opening lines of 'Looking for Alaska'.

Partner B: Look at the page provided by your teacher.

Partner A: Read the following extract describing the going-away party.

And when that final Friday came, when my packing was mostly done, she sat with my dad and me on the living-room couch at 4:56 P.M. and patiently awaited the arrival of the Good-bye to Miles Cavalry. Said cavalry consisted of exactly two people: Marie Lawson, a tiny blonde with rectangular glasses, and her chunky (to put it charitably) boyfriend, Will.

'Hey, Miles,' Marie said as she sat down.

'Hey,' I said.

'How was your summer?' Will asked.

'Okay. Yours?'

'Good. We did Jesus Christ Superstar. I helped with the sets. Marie did lights,' said Will.

'That's cool.' I nodded knowingly, and that about exhausted our conversational topics. I might have asked a question about Jesus Christ Superstar, except that 1. I didn't know what it was, and 2. I didn't care to learn, and 3. I never really excelled at small talk. My mom, however, can talk small for hours, and so she extended the awkwardness by asking them about their rehearsal schedule, and how the show had gone, and whether it was a success.

'I guess it was,' Marie said. 'A lot of people came, I guess.' Marie was the sort of person to guess a lot.

Finally, Will said, 'Well, we just dropped by to say good-bye. I've got to get Marie home by six. Have fun at boarding school, Miles.'

'Thanks,' I answered, relieved. The only thing worse than having a party that no one attends is having a party attended only by two vastly, deeply uninteresting people.

They left, and so I sat with my parents and stared at the blank TV and wanted to turn it on but knew I shouldn't. I could feel them both looking at me, waiting for me to burst into tears or something, as if I hadn't known all along that it would go precisely like this. But I had known. I could feel their pity as they scooped artichoke dip with chips intended for my imaginary friends, but they needed pity more than I did: I wasn't disappointed. My expectations had been met.

John Green: Looking for Alaska. Berlin: Cornelsen 2009 © John Green

chunky heavily built
charitably ['tʃærətəbli] kindly
set the background decoration and furniture on the stage during a play
exhaust sth. [ɪgˈzɔːst] to finish sth. completely
excel at sth. [ɪk ˈsel] be very good at sth.
extend sth. make sth. longer
awkwardness ['ɔːkwədnɪs] *here:* an embarrassing situation
vastly extremely
pity feeling of sympathy and sadness

⚠ **Trouble Spot**

blank = leer, schwarz
blank *(German)* = **shiny**

 LP 27 False Friends (p. 22)

1 Looking at the text

a Answer these questions on the text.
1 Who comes to the party?
2 Describe the atmosphere at the going-away party.
3 Read ll. 10–12 again and state what they tell us about Miles and his attitude towards his classmates and the party.

b Speculate on what happened after the party. Tell your partner. Then ask your partner to tell you what actually happened.

c Swap roles: Listen to your partner's speculations on how the party went. Then tell your partner how it actually went, using the information from your answers to the above questions.

d EXTRA Role-play: You are Miles's mother. You and your partner (Miles's father) are discussing your son's decision to go to boarding school. First, make notes on possible arguments Miles's mother might bring up against boarding school.
Then act out the scene. Try to keep the discussion going for at least two minutes.

Language Help

- The atmosphere is grim/gloomy/ dismal/strained/hostile/icy/…
- Everyone feels awkward / is tense/…

2 Reading between the lines

a With your partner, discuss the 'Great Perhaps' mentioned in Partner B text.

b Based on the information you gathered in **1**, discuss what kind of person Miles is.

c EXTRA Now write a brief characterization of Miles.

Language Help

- When Miles describes/talks about/discusses/…, he reveals that he is …
- Miles's comments on … give us the impression that he is …
- The language Miles uses (e.g. …) shows that …

 SP 43 Writing a Characterization (p. 57)

1 Informal Email (p. 59)

3 Writing: informal email

Hi Miles
I hear you're leaving Florida and this great school and are going to start at a boarding school in Alabama. Wow! That's really amazing!
Do you want to give an interview for the student magazine before you go? It might be interesting to hear what someone who is leaving really thinks of our school.
Maybe you also have some message that you'd like to give to your classmates before you leave?
Let me know if you have time for an interview.
Catch you later
Joey

Write Miles' email reply to the editor of the school magazine. In your email you should …
- explain why you want / don't want to give an interview.
- describe what you like / don't like about the school.
- give your opinion of your classmates.
Write about 250 words.

C Miles and Alaska

One evening Miles meets his fellow student Alaska on a swing on the school campus. Alaska quotes from a historical novel about Simón Bolívar, a South American independence fighter. On his death bed Bolívar is believed to have said, 'Damn it. How will I ever get out of this labyrinth?'

1 Pre-listening

a Do you sometimes listen to audiobooks?
- If so, which ones have you listened to?
- Did you enjoy the experience or not?
List (dis)advantages of audio books compared to printed books.

b Make sure you know the meaning and pronunciation of the words below (mostly parts of the body). Then speculate on the context in which they appear in the novel extract you are going to listen to.

emerald ▪ hot *(infml)* ▪ tank top ▪ flip-flops ▪ calf ▪ hip ▪ arc ▪ waist ▪ arch ▪ butt *(n, infml)*

25
2 Listening to novels

a Listen to the extract from the audio book of *Looking for Alaska*. Exchange your first impressions of Alaska with a partner.

b Were you right about the context of the words (**1b**)? Listen again. One of you notes down what Alaska talks about, the other how Miles describes Alaska.
Compare your results.

c Did you enjoy listening to the extract, or would it have been better to read it? Why?

3 Comparing the narrators

a Work in groups of three. Each person in the groups chooses one of the three narrators: Christopher (Unit 16: *The Curious Incident* …), Junior (Unit 17: *The True Diary* …) or Miles (Unit 18: *Looking for Alaska*).

Collect as much information as you can about "your" narrator from the texts. Think about the following questions:

- Who is he? Where does he live?
- What is his family situation? What does he want to do?
- How does he relate to other people? Who does he like/dislike?
- How does he describe people? What sort of language does he use?

b In your group, make two lists: one with what the narrators Christopher, Junior and Miles have in common, and one with the differences between them. List as many items as possible, then compare your answers with another group.

c Discuss in class …

- which of the three narrators you can identify with more easily and why,
- which of the three narrators you like better as a person and why,
- which of the three narrators you think is more interesting.

 22 Comparison of Adjectives (p. 17)

4 Language in Use: editing

 L Editing (p. 79)

Read this text about ebooks and printed books. In most lines of the text there is a word that should not be there. Write that word in the space provided. Indicate the correct lines with a tick (✔). There are two examples (0, 00) at the beginning.

Ebooks and printed books

An ebook book is a book that is published in digital form, consisting of text,	✔	0
images, or both. Ebooks can have be read on computers, dedicated ebook	have	00
readers or other electronic devices all such as iPads and smartphones.		1
In the early days of computers, the text of a complete book would have had		2
required an enormous amount of memory space, however modern computer		3
chips can record up the contents of a whole library of books on a small hand-held device.		4
This means, of course, that ebooks have some nearly obvious advantages		5
over printed books. Print editions of books are require natural resources, such		6
as paper, and they use up lots valuable energy during printing and transport.		7
Not only that, but they must be stored at great expense to publishers and		8
booksellers as well. An ebook, on the other hand, can be downloaded		9
with one simple mouse click and does not take up any room on your bookshelves.		10
The major disadvantage of ebooks is in that they do not have the physical		11
quality that printed books not have. Many people prefer the feel and smell of a		12
book and find shelves of books in their home attractive and comforting.		13
According to the online bookseller Amazon.com, its sales of it's ebooks		14
outnumbered sales of hardcover books for the first time in July 2010. By		15
January 2011, ebook sales at the Amazon had also overtaken sales of		16
paperback books lately. However, in the overall book market, paperback		17
book sales are still much larger than either from hardcover or ebook sales.		18

5 EXTRA Group discussion: the future of books  **Key: 318**

Work in groups of four. You are going to discuss the following questions: Will ebooks change our reading habits? Will printed books still exist in fifty years' time?

a Two members of the group collect and note down arguments in favour of ebooks; the other two members of the group do the same for printed books.

b Discuss the questions in your group. Try to come to an agreement.

c Choose one member of your group to report your ideas to the class.

 23 Taking Part in a Classroom Discussion (p. 47)

7 Talking about the Future (p. 8)

SP 42 Writing a Review (p. 57)

6 Writing: book review

When you write a book review, you should consider the following points:

- Say what the book is about, giving the title, name of the author, genre and when it was written.
- Give any background information you have on the book and on the author.
- Give a (short) summary of the whole book. Thinking of the five W's (who?, what? when?, where?, why?) may help you. <u>Don't give away the ending!</u>
- You can also present a short extract of the book; your aim should be to make your audience curious and encourage them to read the book for themselves.
- Finish your review with your personal opinion of the book, give reasons for your opinion and say whether you would recommend the work or not.

a Go through the following book review with a partner and discuss whether the different elements mentioned above are dealt with effectively. Highlight any phrases that you could use in a book review.

Book Review: *The Hunger Games* by Suzanne Collins

picturedesk.com/Moviestore/Rex Features

The science-fiction novel 'The Hunger Games', written by Suzanne Collins and published in 2008, is the first part of a trilogy. The third part of the series came out in August 2010. Suzanne Collins has won several awards for the novel and it has also been made into a Hollywood film.

When the book begins, North America has been destroyed and is now divided into 12 districts, ruled by an oppressive government located at the Capitol. Katniss Everdeen, a 16-year-old girl from District 12, takes the place of her younger sister as one of 24 "tributes" selected every year to participate in the Hunger Games at the Capitol. During the Games, which are televised all over the country, children aged 12 to 18 are forced to fight each other like gladiators in a giant arena. At the same time, Katniss has to deal with a romance between herself and Peeta, another tribute from District 12.

This novel has one of the most exciting plots I have ever read and I was dying to find out how the book ended. I was impressed by the description of the futuristic world and the characters are all very strong and develop throughout the book.

While I found this book absolutely gripping, I was surprised it was aimed at an audience of young adults. Some of the scenes are extremely intense and might be disturbing for younger readers. Overall, *The Hunger Games* was an excellent, enthralling read that I highly recommend.

b EXTRA Write a review of an English novel that you have read.

Language Help

- … was written by / is a novel by …
- The novel is set in …
- It tells the story of …
- The main characters are …
- The story is beautifully/awfully written.
- The plot is rather weak/boring/unconvincing.
- I found the book gripping/thrilling/challenging/…

6

"So, in conclusion I would like to say that although I haven't actually read the book, I still found it a fascinating and enriching experience."

Fotolia.com/Kitty

7 Writing: book report

An alternative to a written book review is a presentation of the book in the form of a book report.

- Illustrate the contents of your book briefly and in a structured manner. Choose the most suitable format (e.g. an outline, a text, a diagram, a sketch).
- Introduce the most important characters.
- Present the narrator and the narrative structure (e.g. the time that passes in the book, chapter headings).
- Read a short extract that illustrates an important topic or feature of the book (or bring the audiobook).
- Say something about the time/society that the story takes place in. Choose the most suitable medium (e.g. a poster) and visual aids (e.g. film clips, photos, cartoons).
- Say something about the author, his or her biography and the book's reception, e.g. in (online) reviews.
- To sum up, say why you liked or didn't like the book.

EXTRA Give a book report on an English novel that you have read.

8 EXTRA Group activity

Work in small groups of 3–5 students. Your task is to act out a short scene from an English novel that has made a particular impression on you.

- In your group, decide on a novel and one particular scene in it that you want to act out. (If not everyone in the group has read the book, one person explains the story and the scene to the others.)
- Decide how you want to get across the message of this particular scene. You could act it out as a short play, or you could present it as a series of (TV/radio) interviews with the main characters; your scene might best be portrayed as a court trial, a musical, a quiz show … or whatever you think is best.
- Practise your scene in your group and then present it to the rest of the class.

The whole class should give marks on originality, acting and language.

Language Help

- My favourite character is … because …
- I found … fascinating/funny/ moving/boring/depressing/ scary/exciting/… because …
- I thought the style of writing was …
- I think the setting is important because …
- I think the relationship between … and … is interesting because…
- What I liked (a lot) / didn't like (at all) was …
- I couldn't put it down.
- It was a real page-turner.

 21 Giving a Report on a Book or Film (p. 46)

CAN-DO STATEMENTS

		Part / Ex	✔
👂	I can understand the main points of anecdotes, stories, acted scenes or songs. (B1/3)	C / Ex 2	☐
📖	I can understand longer, relatively simple literary texts on themes that are familiar to me (e.g. modern popular literature). (B1/3)	A / Ex 1 B / Ex 1	☐
👀	I can express and give reasons for my opinion in conversations and discussions. Furthermore, I can agree or politely disagree and make other suggestions. (B1/6)	C / Ex 5	☐
👄	I can describe the plot of a book or film and state my opinion of it. (B1/6)	C / Ex 7	☐
✏️	I can describe my personal impression of stories and books, films and plays. (B1/3)	C / Ex 6	☐
	I can write simple, private correspondence, e.g. letters and emails. (B1/5)	B / Ex 3	☐

C Short Answers (p. 72)

23

1 Listening comprehension: short answers

Listen to the second part of the interview with Mark Haddon (Unit 16, Part C, exercise 3, p. 135) again. Answer the following questions using a maximum of 4 words. Write your answers in the spaces provided. The first one (0) has been done for you.

0	How did Mark Haddon react to the first scene he wrote for the book?	*he found it funny*
1	How does Mark Haddon describe the narrator Christopher's voice?	
2	How did he feel about this voice?	
3	According to Mark Haddon, why does a sad story become sadder if it is told by someone who isn't affected by it at all?	
4	What doesn't Christopher understand about the sad things that are happening around him?	
5	What example, apart from cancer, does Christopher give for a way in which a dog might die?	
6	What does the interviewer describe the way Christopher thinks about the death of the dog?	
7	Why does Mark Haddon find Christopher's voice so funny?	
8	What other aspect of Christopher's voice does Mark Haddon find appealing?	

5 Article (p. 66)

2 Writing: article

The youth magazine "Young Europeans" has asked its readers for articles on the following topic: "Is reading fantasy or science-fiction a complete waste of time?" You decide to send in an article.

In your article you should …
- explain the difference between fantasy/science-fiction and other types of fiction
- comment on the usefulness of both types of fiction
- state your opinion on the title of the article

Write about 200 words.

E Multiple Matching (p. 73)

3 Reading comprehension: multiple matching

Read the text on the opposite page. Parts of the text have been removed. Choose the correct part (A–K) for each gap (1–8). Write your answers in the spaces provided. There are two extra parts that you should not use. The first one (0) has been done for you.

A based on teenagers in 14 developed countries
B whose parents rarely read books with them
C better student reading performance
D whose parents frequently read with them
E where parents and children talk
F make up for social disadvantages
G examined the long-term impact of parental support
H regularly do better in PISA tests
I what they were reading together
J teenage reading skills
K were six months ahead in reading levels

0	1	2	3	4	5	6	7	8
D								

Reading to children has long impact, says OECD study

Parents and children reading together at the start of school makes a long impact, says study.

Children (0) ___ in their first year of school are still showing the benefit when they are 15, says an international study.

An Organisation for Economic Co-operation and Development analysis (1) ___ on literacy.

Discounting social differences, the study found children with early support remained ahead in reading.

It found a strong link between (2) ___ and early parental help.

Talking together

The OECD analysis, (3) ___, found that active parental involvement at the beginning of school was a significant trigger for developing children's reading skills that would carry through until they were teenagers.

On average, teenagers whose parents had helped with reading at the beginning of school (4) ___ at the age of 15.

The report says that parents did not have to be particularly well-educated themselves for this impact to be achieved.

What was important was that parents read books regularly with their children – such as several times a week – and that they talked about (5) ___ .

This parental involvement overrode other social disadvantages and in some countries could represent more than a year's advantage in reading levels at the age of 15 compared with children (6) ___ .

The study, which draws on data from the international Programme for International Student Assessment (PISA) tests, also found a link between teenagers' reading skills and continued engagement with their parents.

Everyday family get-togethers, (7) ___ , could influence school performance, says the research.

"Eating main meals together around the table and spending time just talking with one's children are also associated with significantly (8) ___ in school," says the OECD report.

Reading to children has long impact, says OECD study. In: http://www.bbc.co.uk, November 8, 2011

4 Speaking: individual long turn

TF M Individual Long Turn (p. 80)

- Compare the pictures.
- Explain some of the advantages and disadvantages of ebooks and conventional books.
- Give your opinion: which form of book do you prefer?

Language for Tasks ('Operatoren')

English in Context uses the same special vocabulary ('Operatoren') for tasks that is used in standard tests, including the *Standardisierte kompetenzorientierte Reifeprüfung (SRP)*. Be sure you understand what's required of you when you come across one of the verbs below.

Domäne	Operatoren
Knowledge/Comprehension	*tell, recall, show, explain, define, name, summarize, discuss, demonstrate, list*
Application/Analysis/Synthesis	*compare, analyze, predict, develop, compile, create, formulate, organize, hypothesize*
Evaluation	*interpret, judge, criticize, assess, decide*

Source: Ronald Kemsies, Robert Oszwald: Kompetenzorientiertes Prüfen leicht gemacht. Linz: Veritas Verlag 2011

The instructions say:	What's expected:
analyse *(BE)*, **analyze** *(AE)* ['ænəlaɪz]	Look at something in detail and explain its meaning and/or structure. ('analysieren') *Analyse the main elements of the poster.* ▶ examine
assess [ə'ses]	Show the pros and cons of something in a balanced way, and then give an opinion on it. ('auswerten, beurteilen, bewerten') *Assess the effectiveness of the government's approach to fighting poverty.* ▶ evaluate
characterize *(usu. AE)*, **give/ write a characterization of** ['kærəktəraɪz, ˌkærəktəraɪ'zeɪʃn]	Look closely at the typical features of somebody or something, giving examples and explanations. ('charakterisieren') *Give a characterization of the mother in the story.*
classify *(also:* **put into context***)*	Arrange different things in groups and explain how the things in each group are similar to each other but different from the other groups. ('einordnen, zuordnen') *Identify the different jobs discussed and classify them according to the type of tasks involved.*
comment on ['kɒment]	Express your opinion on something, giving evidence to support your view. ('kommentieren') *Comment on the speaker's belief that …*
compare	Explain similarities and differences between two or more things. ('vergleichen') *Compare how the characters are portrayed in the film and in the novel.*
contrast [kən'trɑːst]	Show the differences between two or more things. ('kontrastieren') *Contrast the rights of African Americans in the 1960s and today.*
define	State the nature and/or meaning of something. ('definieren') *Define the term 'racism' as it is used by the writer.*
describe *(also:* **give/write a description of***)*	State what something or somebody is like, including all the relevant details. ('beschreiben') *Describe the writer's invention and what it is used for.*
discuss	Look carefully at something from all sides before stating your opinion. It should be clear from what has gone before, how and why you arrived at this opinion. ('diskutieren, erörtern') *Discuss how education influences attitudes towards immigration.*
evaluate [ɪ'væljueɪt]	Show the pros and cons of something in a balanced way, and then give an opinion on it. ('einschätzen, bewerten') *Evaluate the author's view of the impact Obama's speech had on his audience.* ▶ assess

The instructions say:	What's expected:
examine [ɪgˈzæmɪn]	Look at something in detail and explain its meaning and/or structure. ('untersuchen, prüfen') *Examine the writer's attitude towards the protagonist.* ▶ analyse
explain	State what something is like and give reasons why it is that way. ('erklären') *Explain the main character's reaction to her mother in the first scene.*
illustrate [ˈɪləstreɪt]	Make something clear by giving examples. ('erläutern, veranschaulichen') *Illustrate the narrator's admiration for the main character.*
interpret [ɪnˈtɜːprɪt]	Analyse the form and content of something and explain its meaning in a wider context, as you see it. Cite examples as evidence to support your interpretation. ('interpretieren') *Interpret the message of the poem.*
justify	Give solid reasons for decisions or conclusions. ('begründen') *Justify your answer.*
outline [ˈ– –]	State the main features and structure of a text. ('umreißen, skizzieren') *Outline the writer's views on …*
point out	Identify something and present it clearly. ('benennen, darlegen') *Point out the keywords in the first paragraph of the text.*
present [prɪˈzent]	(Re)structure something and write it down. ('darstellen') *Present your ideas in a logical order.*
reflect on	Express one's thoughts on something carefully and deeply. ('reflektieren') *Reflect on the situation the main characters are in.*
relate	Identify and explain a connection between two things. ('in Beziehung setzen') *Relate the following short poem to the short story.*
show	Make something clear by giving examples. ('zeigen, darlegen') *Show that you have understood how the cartoonist feels about global warming.* ▶ illustrate
state	Specify something clearly. ('darlegen') *State your opinion on the main character's decision.*
summarize (*also:* **give/write a summary of; sum up**)	Present the main points of something in a short and clear form, leaving out details and examples. ('zusammenfassen') *Summarize the incident in the church in no more than four sentences.*

Check Your Progress – Answer Key

Check Your Progress 1

1 *0A, 1H, 2E, 3I, 4F, 5C, 6D*

2 *0* *did*, *00* ✔, *1* *in*, *2* *really*, *3* *however*, *4* ✔, *5* *the*, *6* *of*, *7* ✔, *8* *which*, *9* *it's*, *10* ✔, *11* *together*, *12* *self*, *13* *too*, *14* ✔, *15* *of*

3 & 4 individuelle Lösungen, siehe Companion TF N Paired Activity (p. 80) und TT 3 Blog Entry (p. 63)

5 *1* *privacy*, *2* *personal*, *3* *user*, *4* *importance*, *5* *anonymity*, *6* *behaviour*, *7* *misunderstood*, *8* *embarrassing*, *9* *posting*, *10* *illegal*, *11* *cyberbullying*, *12* *competition*

Check Your Progress 2

1 *0C, 1C, 2C, 3B, 4A, 5C, 6B*

2 *0* *dangerous, illegal*, *1* *change one's mood*, *2* *change its chemistry*, *3* *highly addictive, mental problems*, *4* *buy drugs, not food*, *5* *health, social effects*, *6* *heroin, cocaine, alcohol*

3 *0* *are*, *00* ✔, *1* *them*, *2* *own*, *3* *the*, *4* ✔, *5* ✔, *6* *yet*, *7* ✔, *8* *which*, *9* *ones*, *10* *to*, *11* ✔, *12* *does*, *13* *the*, *14* ✔, *15* *being*, *16* ✔, *17* *it's*, *18* *on*, *19* ✔, *20* *any*, *21* *of*, *22* ✔

4 & 5 individuelle Lösungen, siehe Companion TF N Paired Activity (p. 80) und TT 4 Report (p. 64)

Check Your Progress 3

1 *1* *the*, *2* *much*, *3* ✔, *4* *be*, *5* ✔, *6* *not*, *7* ✔, *8* *had*, *9* *age*, *10* *total*, *11* ✔, *12* *when*, *13* ✔, *14* *even*, *15* ✔

2 *1* *banner on a bridge*, *2* *put your hand(s) up*, *3* *is our protest democratic*, *4* *through word of mouth*, *5* *a message for/of peace*, *6* *2000*, *7* *the response was good/great*, *8* *views on nuclear war*

3 *1* *(world) leaders*, *2* *of her generation*, *3* *isn't getting through*, *4* *solve their problems / get their point across*, *5* *in France*, *6* *small crosses*, *7* *unknown*, *8* *young people*

Check Your Progress 4

1 *1D, 2C, 3C, 4B, 5A, 6B, 7C*

2 *0* *in a whole year*, *1* *are not paying enough / don't pay enough*, *2* *international flights*, *3* *greenhouse gases / CO2 emissions*, *4* *more efficient*, *5* *hydrogen*, *6* *to not fly / to not use planes*, *7* *exotic destinations*, *8* *teleconferencing / teleconferences*, *9* *plant (enough) trees*

3 & 4 individuelle Lösungen, siehe Companion TF M Individual Long Turn (p. 80) und TT 1 Informal Email (p. 59)

5 *1* *have*, *2* *can*, *3* *of*, *4* *so*, *5* *be*, *6* *over*, *7* *than*, *8* *which*, *9* *to*, *10* *however*, *11* *because*, *12* *are*, *13* *for*, *14* *between*

Check Your Progress 5

1 *0* *reduce illegal immigration*, *1* *getting longer*, *2* *local residents*, *3* *can't cross the border*, *4* *doesn't understand it*, *5* *good it came down*, *6* *necessary to protect USA*, *7* *more jobs in Mexico*, *8* *jobs in USA*

2 *0D, 1B, 2C, 3B, 4C, 5D, 6A*

3 *0D, 1J, 2B, 3N, 4F, 5G, 6A, 7H, 8O, 9C, 10L, 11M, 12K; not used: E, I*

4 individuelle Lösungen, siehe Companion TT 5 Article (p. 66) und TF N Individual Long Turn (p. 80)

Check Your Progress 6

1 *1* *flat, emotionless, toneless*, *2* *he really liked it*, *3* *it doesn't become sentimental*, *4* *why they are sad / that they are sad*, *5* *(in) a road accident*, *6* *strange and/but logical*, *7* *he thinks very strangely*, *8* *he doesn't influence/push reader(s) / people react (very) differently*,

3 *1G, 2J, 3A, 4K, 5I, 6B, 7E, 8C; nicht verwendet F, H*

2 & 4 individuelle Lösungen, siehe Companion TT 5 Article (p. 66) und TF M Individual Long Turn (p. 80)

Content Keys – Übersicht

Student's Book http://english-in-context6.veritas.at

Content Key	Seite, Übung/Unit	Inhalt bzw. Webquest-Titel
343	7	Contents (nach Skills)
722	12, 1/WiC	Ten Commandments
191	16, 1B	An Online Hoax
984	25, 3A	Expressing Yourself Through Poetry
250	33, 2/WiC, 3	UK Crime Statistics
606	36, 4B	Monkey See, Monkey Do, Monkey Hurt
288	42, 5	Crime Prevention
984	45, 5C	The Truth about Drugs
313	64, 7B	Take a Chance (Obama's Speech)
324	78, 9A	Charity Water
239	82, 3/CYP, 1	Nothing's Impossible
735	86, 4/WiC, 2	Carbon Footprint
140	99, 12A	Localwashing is the New Greenwashing
213	110, 5/WiC	On the Move
591	113, 13B	Warsaw on the Thames
241	118, 14A	Rhythm is it
898	120, 14A, 6	Settlers in the US
783	132, 16B	Who is Telling the Story
318	145, 18C, 5	Bookless Library

Companion 5. – 8. http://english-in-context5.veritas.at

Content Key	Seite, Übung	Inhalt bzw. Webquest-Titel
351	5	Answer Key zu Language Practice Übungen (.pdf)
905	18	Visual Dictionary (Link)
580	18	Online Dictionary (Link)
860	26	Word Stress (.mp3; Tracks 2, 3, 4)
316	28, 35	Expressing Opinions (.mp3; Track 5)
256	28, 36	Persuading people (.mp3; Track 6)
502	29, 37	Agreeing and Disagreeing (.mp3; Track 7)
943	29, 38	Making Comparisons (.mp3; Track 8)
670	48	Functional Language: Everyday English
833	50	Reading Fiction: Poetry
385	30	Ergänzungen/Aktualisierungen zu den SRP Text Types (.pdf)
946	53	Answer Key (pdf.) zu 36 Finding Alternatives to Overused Words
354	44	Language for Tasks („Operatoren")
922	66	Ergänzungen/Aktualisierungen zu den SRP Test Formats (.pdf)

CD-Extra – Inhalte

Systemvoraussetzungen

Betriebssystem: Windows XP oder höher, Mac, Linux
Bildschirmauflösung: empfohlen ab 1024 x 768
CD-ROM-Laufwerk und Soundkarte

Inhalt

- ausgewählte Hörübungen (.mp3) aus dem Student's Book, zum Nachhören für daheim
- sämtliche Partner Pages (.mp3) zum Student's Book
- Wordlists (.docx, .pdf), chronological and alphabetical, zum Nachschlagen und individuellen Bearbeiten der Vokabeln

Track-Liste
Laufzeit gesamt: ca. 31 min

Track-Nr.*	Titel	Laufzeit	Unit, Seite, exercise
1	Copyright	00:17	
4	Writing is …	02:22	3A, S. 26, ex. 3
5	Karaoke	02:57	CPY1, S. 28, ex. 1
8	Gangs	02:51	6B, S. 53, ex. 2
9	About Legal and Illegal Drugs	01:49	CPY2, S. 56, ex. 2
10	Take a Chance	03:46	7B, S. 64, ex. 1
12	Kierra Box' Speech	03:02	CPY3, S. 83, ex. 3
16	Food Miles	02:38	12A, S. 99, ex. 1a
18	Airplanes and Global Warming	06:11	CPY4, S. 106, ex. 2
21	At a Deaf Convention	02:09	CPY5, S. 126, ex. 1
23	Interview with Mark Haddon (Part 1, Part 2)	07:22	16C, S. 134, ex. 2+3; CPY6, S. 148, ex. 1

* Auswahl aus Tracks der Class CD

Quellenverzeichnis
Track-Nr.

4   Three Poems - Students from the Santa Fe Indian School will be competing in July at the National Youth Poetry Slam Festival in Washington …". © Santa Fe Indian School

5   Adapted from: Andrew Lam: Communicating Through Karaoke. In: http://www.npr.org, January 25, 2006

8   Adapted from: Gangs are 'alternative to family'. In: http://news.bbc.co.uk, July 8, 2008

9   Adapted from: Drugs and health part 2. In: GCSE Bitesize Science; http://downloads.bbc.co.uk

10   Barack Obama: University of Massachusetts at Boston Commencement Address, June 2, 2006

12   Ministry for Peace speech by Kierra Box

16   Adapted from: Food Miles. In: http://lifecyclesproject.ca

18   Adapted from: Aeroplanes and global warming. In: http://learnenglish.britishcouncil.org

21   Adapted from: http://southpawscopic.tumblr.com

23   Interview with Mark Haddon. Fresh Air / WHYY

Hinweis zur Arbeit mit den Materialien

Sollte beim Einlegen der CD-Extra das Programm nicht automatisch starten, wechseln Sie zum CD-Laufwerk und öffnen Sie das Programm durch Doppelklick auf die Datei index.htm manuell.
Die Menüführung der CD-Extra erleichtert die Suche nach der gewünschten Datei. Jede Datei öffnet sich in einem neuen Fenster.
Die PDF-Dateien können ausgedruckt, aber nicht bearbeitet werden. Zur Anzeige muss der Adobe Reader installiert sein.
Die Microsoft Word-Dateien sind individuell bearbeitbar. Der Seitenumbruch kann je nach Betriebssystem, verwendeten Schriften und Drucker-Einstellungen variieren.
Wenn Sie nur die Audiodateien (.mp3) abspielen wollen, ist das auch in jedem MP3-fähigen CD-Player möglich.